T0319412

STRANDS OF MODERNIZATION

JAPAN AND GLOBAL SOCIETY

Editors: AKIRA IRIYE, *Harvard University*; MASATO KIMURA, *Shibusawa Eiichi Memorial Foundation*; DAVID A. WELCH, *Balsillie School of International Affairs, University of Waterloo*

How has Japan shaped, and been shaped by, globalization – politically, economically, socially, and culturally? How has its identity, and how have its objectives, changed? Japan and Global Society explores Japan's past, present, and future interactions with the Asia Pacific and the world from a wide variety of disciplinary and interdisciplinary perspectives and through diverse paradigmatic lenses. Titles in this series are intended to showcase international scholarship on Japan and its regional neighbours that will appeal to scholars in disciplines both in the humanities and the social sciences.

Japan and Global Society is supported by generous grants from the Shibusawa Eiichi Memorial Foundation and the University of Missouri–St Louis.

Editorial Advisory Board

Frederick R. Dickinson, University of Pennsylvania
Michael Donnelly, University of Toronto
Joel Glassman, University of Missouri–St Louis
Izumi Koide, Shibusawa Eiichi Memorial Foundation
Gil Latz, Ohio State University
Michael A. Schneider, Knox College
Patricia G. Steinhoff, University of Hawaii at Manoa
Patricia Wetzel, Portland State University

For a list of books published in the series, see page 193.

Strands of Modernization

*The Circulation of Technology and Business
Practices in East Asia, 1850–1920*

EDITED BY DAVID B. SICILIA
AND DAVID G. WITTNER

UNIVERSITY OF TORONTO PRESS
Toronto Buffalo London

ISBN 978-1-4875-0908-8 (cloth)
ISBN 978-1-4875-3968-9 (EPUB)
ISBN 978-1-4875-3967-2 (PDF)

Japan and Global Society

Library and Archives Canada Cataloguing in Publication

Title: Strands of modernization : the circulation of technology and business
 practices in East Asia, 1850–1920 / edited by David B. Sicilia and David
 G. Wittner.
Names: Sicilia, David B., editor. | Wittner, David G., editor.
Series: Japan and global society.
Description: Series statement: Japan and global society | Includes bibliographical
 references and index.
Identifiers: Canadiana (print) 20210225742 | Canadiana (ebook) 20210225866 |
 ISBN 9781487509088 (cloth) | ISBN 9781487539689 (EPUB) | ISBN
 9781487539672 (PDF)
Subjects: LCSH: Technology transfer – East Asia – History – 19th century. |
 LCSH: Industrial management – East Asia – History – 19th century. |
 LCSH: Technology transfer – East Asia – History – 20th century. |
 LCSH: Industrial management – East Asia – History – 20th century.
Classification: LCC T174.3 .S77 2021 | DDC 338.9/26095 – dc23

University of Toronto Press acknowledges the financial assistance to its publishing
program of the Canada Council for the Arts and the Ontario Arts Council, an
agency of the Government of Ontario.

Canada Council   Conseil des Arts
for the Arts   du Canada

ONTARIO ARTS COUNCIL
CONSEIL DES ARTS DE L'ONTARIO
an Ontario government agency
un organisme du gouvernement de l'Ontario

Funded by the   Financé par le
Government   gouvernement
of Canada   du Canada

Contents

Foreword

University of Toronto Press, in cooperation with the University of Missouri–St Louis and the Shibusawa Eiichi Memorial Foundation of Tokyo, has launched an ambitious new series, "Japan and Global Society." The volumes in the series explore how Japan has defined its identities and objectives in the larger region of Asia and the Pacific and, at the same time, how the global community has been shaped by Japan and its interactions with other countries.

The dual focus on Japan and on global society reflects the series editors' and publishers' commitment to globalizing national studies. Scholars and readers have become increasingly aware that it makes little sense to treat a country in isolation. All countries are interdependent and shaped by cross-national forces so that mono-national studies, those that examine a country's past and present in isolation, are never satisfactory. Such awareness has grown during the past few decades when global, transnational phenomena and forces have gained prominence. In the age of globalization, no country retains complete autonomy or freedom of action. Yet nations continue to act in pursuit of their respective national interests, which frequently results in international tensions. Financial, social, and educational policies continue to be defined domestically, with national communities as units. But transnational economic, environmental, and cultural forces always infringe upon national entities, transforming them in subtle and sometimes even violent ways. Global society, consisting of billions of individuals and their organizations, evolves and shapes national communities even as the latter contribute to defining the overall human community.

Japan provides a particularly pertinent instance of such interaction, but this series is not limited to studies of that country alone. Indeed, the books published in the series will show that there is little unique about Japan, whose history has been shaped by interactions with China, Korea, the United States, and many other countries. For this reason, forthcoming volumes will deal with countries in the Asia-Pacific region and compare their respective developments and shared destinies. At the same time, some studies in the series will transcend national frameworks and discuss more transnational themes, such as humanitarianism, migration, and diseases, documenting how these phenomena affect Japan and other countries and how, at the same time, they contribute to the making of a more interdependent global society.

Lastly, we hope these studies will help to promote an understanding of non-national entities, such as regions, religions, and civilizations. Modern history continues to be examined in terms of nations as the key units of analysis, and yet these other entities have their own vibrant histories, which do not necessarily coincide with nation-centred narratives. To look at Japan, or for that matter any other country, and to examine its past and present in these alternative frameworks will enrich our understanding of modern world history and of the contemporary global civilization.

Akira Iriye

Acknowledgments

Without the generous support of the Shibusawa Eiichi Memorial Foundation, this project would not have been possible. For many years, the Shibusawa Eiichi Memorial Foundation has supported academic research related to East Asian – especially Japanese – history and East-West relations. This volume is stronger for having evolved through planning sessions, roundtables, conference papers, and panels. We are very grateful to Shibusawa Masahide, Komatsu Jun'etsu, and the Shibusawa Foundation board members and staff for their commitment to this project.

When the editors of this volume asked our fellow chapter authors to send us notes of thanks for the Acknowledgements, they replied in a uniform chorus, their voices joining our own. The situation is a bit unorthodox, for seven out of the eight of us wish to express our heartfelt gratitude to a fellow chapter author. Professor Kimura Masato – along with being a leading authority on the history of Japanese-U.S. relations (see "Contributors") and the author of chapter 8 – for many years until recently was the director of research at the Shibusawa Eiichi Memorial Foundation in Tokyo. A model of care and professionalism, Kimura-san ushered this project to fruition while also overseeing and supporting several others for the foundation.

Several contributors to this volume were privileged to accompany Shibusawa Museum curator Inoue Jun on visits to the Deutsches Museum (Munich); the Museum of American Finance (New York); and the Hagley Museum and Library (Wilmington, Delaware) – visits that benefitted the project intellectually. We are grateful to the curatorial staffs at these fine institutions for orienting us to their artifacts and archival holdings. Jeffer Daykin wishes to thank Jim Carmin of the Multnomah County Library's Special Collections for his support in securing images for chapter 4.

Two anonymous readers for the University of Toronto Press provided insightful critiques of the manuscript and of a revised version, helping us sharpen our arguments and correct some foibles. Acquisitions Editor Daniel Quinlan ushered this project from proposal, to review, to production; and he and "Japan and Global Society" Series Co-Editor David A. Welch were especially helpful as we navigated the revision process. We are also grateful and would like to thank the production staff at University of Toronto Press for their skill and care with the figures that enrich this volume, as well as our copy editor Ian MacKenzie.

We would like to note that we are following the traditional Chinese, Japanese, and Korean practice of listing the family or surname first, followed by the given name. except in cases where individuals regularly use Western name order.

As we acknowledge all this generous assistance, we also humbly recognize our ultimate responsibility for any weaknesses that remain in this book and look forward to learning from them.

David B. Sicilia and David G. Wittner

STRANDS OF MODERNIZATION

Introduction: Capacious Connections with and within East Asia

DAVID G. WITTNER AND DAVID B. SICILIA

Three themes define and animate this collection. First, we depart from the prevailing fashion among historians of East Asian technology transfer, ca. 1850–1920, who privilege the movement of "advanced" technologies from the West to the East. Rather, we see currents moving in multiple directions, with Japan often playing a key role within the region. Second, building on a long-standing scholarly convention to define technology as including much more than physical artifacts, we frame this study with an understanding of "technology and business practices" capacious enough to also include skills, systems of knowledge, tacit knowledge, and the ideologies and other belief systems with which they interact. Indeed, several of the chapters in this volume give greater attention to "soft" embodiments of technology than to physical artifacts. Third, many of the chapters highlight the hybridization that invariably comes with transfer and diffusion of practical knowledge. Stated differently, when technology and business practices cross sociocultural boundaries, there is always adaptation, never pure adoption.

The late nineteenth and early twentieth centuries were a period of extraordinary transfer and diffusion of industry- and transportation-related technology and business methods among and within regions of the world. Most scholars of nineteenth-century technology transfer beyond Europe and North America focus on the West-to-East movement of artifacts, skills, and knowledge. Much of this literature focuses either on the movement of technologies and business methods from Britain to continental Europe or between the so-called developed countries of northwestern Europe and their colonies, dependent states, or countries struggling to modernize in the face of Western imperialist pressure. China, India, Japan, and Mexico are prominent examples of the latter.

This orientation makes sense chiefly because of the disparities in technological and business development and politico-industrial might between West and East during this period. This volume expands directionality from the simple West-to-East paradigm to include East-East translations of technological and business artifacts, know-how, and ideas. In the nineteenth century, Japan tended to be the source of much of that praxis. Japan's influences on China following the Sino-Japanese and Russo-Japanese Wars are well known. For the victorious nation, Japan not only was much closer to China and Korea than Europe or the United States, it also shared cultural similarities and at least some degree of linguistic affinity.[1] More than that, Japan offered proof that a non-Western country could modernize and become a Western-style nation. Whom better to learn from than the country that successfully made the transformation from "backward" to "modern"?

Our primary goal with this collection, therefore, is to expand historical understanding of the myriad ways in which the transfer of technology and business methods unfolded *within East Asia* in the period between approximately 1850 and 1920. A recent edited volume on Latin America shares this orientation in what we hope will be a growing historiographical trend toward seeing regions of the Global South or otherwise outside the West not merely as recipients and importers of "advanced" Western technology but as originators and intra-regional sharers.[2]

Defining technology has been no simple matter, especially in recent decades as scholars have become more deeply engaged in the endeavor. As Eric Schatzberg has chronicled in his perceptive recent intellectual history of the concept, even Lewis Mumford, a pioneering authority on the topic in the early and mid-twentieth century, was imprecise about his definition (and how it differed from one of his key concepts, "technics").[3]

Even so, Mumford did not limit his investigations to technological hardware, an approach that gained momentum in post–Second World War writings. In 1967, the influential Harvard economist and public intellectual John Kenneth Galbraith defined technology as "the systematic application of scientific or other knowledge to practical tasks."[4] By that time a new scholarly community of historians of technology had organized the Society for the History of Technology and launched what remains the field's journal of record, *Technology and Culture*. The title intentionally signaled what has become known as the social construction of technology (SCOT). By the early 1960s, Schatzberg explains, although scholars did not reach a clear consensus about the meaning of technology, the debate settled into stability around three dominant definitions: "the application of science," "industrial arts," and "technique, or instrumental reason."[5] Notably, for our purposes, none privileged artifacts.

Nor has the scholarship since. John Law's 1987 theoretical essay defined technology as "objects, artifacts, and technical practices" and as "a family of methods for associating or channeling other entities and forces, both human and nonhuman.... It is itself nothing other than a set of channeled forces or associated entities."[6] Dennis R. Hershbach, in his 1995 essay on technology and knowledge, argued, "Technology includes important normative, social, political, and ethical aspects, among others."[7] Shortly thereafter, in her history of technology college textbook, Ruth Schwartz Cowan explained (while defining technology), "Even languages and the things that contain languages (such as books, letters, computer software, and student essays) are technologies; they are things that people have created so as to better control and manipulate their social environment."[8] Even economists and economic historians, who tend to prefer the tangible and countable, were offered this definition of technology a major reference work in 2003: "Technology should be regarded as more than the aggregate of manufactured products and the processes that produce them. These artifacts, which are what are often popularly categorized as technology, in practice depend upon broad and deep knowledge bases for their conception and production. Such knowledge bases may be codified into symbols that can be readily circulated, such as printed manuals or lines of software code, but very often are tacit and unexpressed – possibly inexpressible – in any depicted form. Knowledge of this kind cannot be reduced to information, such as often found in economists' treatments of technology."[9]

We are aware that an overly inclusive definition risks becoming no definition at all, and indeed some have leveled that criticism at proponents of SCOT. We stand by the framework, acknowledging that the boundaries between "technology" and "culture" often are hazy. As deployed in this volume, technology includes not only artifacts (e.g., the physical hardware and spaces of industry) but also techniques of production (e.g., formal *and* informal knowledge about machines, their operation, and production processes), management systems (e.g., systems of corporate or industry organization), and ideological interpretations of technologies (e.g., cultural beliefs, intangible uses, and assumptions related to artifacts). In these varied forms, technology is the application of, or capability provided by, knowledge (know-how) in a practical endeavor.

Many of the contributors to this volume pay particular attention to how technology changes when it moves from one society to another. Technology *transfer* has been historically viewed as the movement of technologies from one society to another. The movement of technology *within* a single society, in contrast, is regarded by scholars as *diffusion*.[10] Again, most studies have focused on the movement of what we will term "hard" technologies, i.e., industrial machinery and techniques, rather than "soft" technologies, i.e., ideas related to technological or national economic development or modes of organizing enterprises. The chapters in this collection certainly address the former, but pay equal attention to non-artifact modes of technology transfer. We chronicle how modern banking methods, modes of organizing and governing factories, corporations, and exhibitions, enterprises inspired by a modernizing mission, among others, profoundly reshaped the societies that adopted them during this period. Accordingly, we see this study's sustained attention to "soft" technologies as one of its key contributions.

It is a complicated story of successes, failures, and most importantly, adaptation. As we outline below, Japan seems to have been the exception, the leader as both recipient and exporter of technology at a time when others struggled less successfully to overcome endogenous and exogenous factors ranging from cultural conservatism to pure imperialist desire on the part of Western nations.[11] Japan itself was, of course, developing rapidly economically and technologically during this period. This collection joins a handful of studies that examine the translation of technologies between or among developing countries or – more precisely – among competing developing economies.[12]

For their part, many Japanese saw Southeast Asia in the same light as their European counterparts: a cluster of backward nations possessing an abundance of natural resources. Toward that end, the Meiji government established the Overseas Development Society in 1893, whose purpose was to support Japanese immigration and industrialization in the region. At the same time, nationalists from Burma, Indonesia, Malaysia, the Philippines, Singapore, and Vietnam were looking to Japan for business advice, financial resources, and political backing. That Japanese investors saw Southeast Asia as a potentially lucrative market was no coincidence, and Japanese technologies indeed made their way into the region, at least to the extent that Western colonial governments permitted.[13] The largely untold story is that small businessmen were able to tap into the colonial Southeast Asian market and transfer useful technologies to the general population. For much of Southeast Asia, however, the struggle to modernize would continue until after the Second World War.

Following the Opium War (1839–42), China was torn open by the British, a fact not unnoticed by its neighbors, most importantly Japan. Although this period is not typically viewed as one during which Western industrial technologies were transferred from West to East, it was a time when states began to understand the significance of Western technology, especially military technologies. Even Japan – supposedly closed off from the world, save a small window provided by the Dutch at Deshima, Nagasaki – understood the ability of the Western powers such as Britain, France, and Russia to forcibly pry open once-restricted (or closed) markets. Whether the Japanese government or *daimyō* domains chose to respond in a meaningful way is, however, another story.

In the decades following the Opium War and Treaty of Nanjing (1842), China sought to "self-strengthen," which in its earliest stages meant the adoption of Western military apparatus – firearms, artillery, and warships – and some Western-style industry, although not necessarily the techniques and ideologies that underpinned growing Western military and industrial dominance.[14] The Qing government, in addition to opening Shanghai and Tianjin to Western trade and officials, as per treaty obligations, established a program intended to modernize China's beleaguered army and navy. It built six arsenals and shipyards under the direction of foreign advisers such as Léonce Verny at Ningbo and Prosper

Giquel at Fuzhou, while regional strongmen-cum-leaders such as Zeng Guo-fang and Li Hongzhang directed construction of the Jiangnan Arsenal. Each facility was plagued by its own problems, but inefficiency, corruption, and cultural conflict stand out as common factors that limited the success of China's early attempts to modernize its military along Western lines.

Attempts at industrial reform were similarly unbalanced. The government sponsored the modernization of coal mines and cotton spinning, for example, not to mention building railroads, a telegraph network, and a postal system. As with military self-strengthening, success was mixed, because government officials were not businessmen and thus lacked the requisite practical knowledge and skills to keep industries profitable. The Qing also lacked a modern banking system and a legal structure to support industry, and officials in Beijing refused to deal with foreigners, despite knowing that much Qing modernization was beholden to foreign capital and to the attendant requirements that accompanied borrowing from the Western powers.

At roughly the same time that China struggled to modernize following the proposition of adopting Western technology while strictly maintaining its Confucian identity, the Japanese also sought to advance their position vis-à-vis the West and their Asian neighbors. Quickly realizing that having Western technology and knowing what to do with it were two different things, the Japanese became outstanding students of the West, adopting everything from industrial technologies, organization, and military hardware and strategy, to clothing, food, hairstyles, furniture, and ideologies, to name a few. That the Tokugawa *bakufu*, a semi-feudal, warrior-dominated ruling regime, had collapsed, to be replaced by a more open-minded oligarchy, purportedly ruled by the new Meiji emperor in 1868, certainly played an important role. The point of divergence between China's and Japan's initial responses to Western incursions was the idea that Western technologies could be separated from culture.[15] The Japanese abandoned this proposition even before the fall of the Tokugawa, and it took the Sino-Japanese War (1894–5) to hammer the point home to many (though certainly not all) of China's so-called modernizers.

As a result, the Japanese – relying mostly on domestic capital and foreign advisers – embarked on an unprecedented program of modernization. Leaving no institutional stone unturned, the Meiji oligarchs completely overhauled Japanese society, industry, the economy, and military. Although not without its problems and dissenters, Japan by the mid-1880s was a remade society fashioned from the molds of Britain, France, Germany, and the United States. The government eliminated social class and privilege, sponsored the development of a rail- and telegraph-based infrastructure, and launched dozens of industrial ventures ranging from mining to textiles and printing to cement works. At the same time, the Japanese modernized education and the military to create East Asia's first world-class army and navy modeled on Germany and Britain, respectively. Meiji officials also encouraged the private sector, whether merchants or former samurai, to help build the nation by issuing low- or no-interest long-term loans. For all intents and purposes, Japan had become a Western-style country poised to exert its own influence on East and Southeast Asia.

Korea was a different story altogether. Having maintained an isolationist policy (with the exception of relations with Qing China and some trade missions with Japan), the nation's Joseon government in the 1860s rejected the infiltration of the West, Catholicism in particular. Despite Korea's insularity, French Catholic missionaries sneaked across Korea's northern border with China, intent on saving souls. When a number of Korean converts in government saw opportunities in Russian advances into Korean territory and the accompanying demand for trade, they recommended a pro-French (Catholic) anti-Russian agenda to the government of the newly enthroned child emperor Gojong and his father regent, Lee Ha-ung, the *Deawongun* (prince of the Great Court). Capture and subsequent execution of the errant missionaries ultimately led to Korea's first armed encounter with the West, the 1866 French Campaign against Korea, or *Byeonginyangyo*. Despite apparent victory, the French secured little other than Korea's continued commitment to a policy of isolationism.

In 1871, the United States similarly launched an expedition against Korea following another 1866 incident and subsequent investigations. Regardless, the United States intended to open the last closed East Asian country. In 1866, an American ship, the *General Sherman*, pressed into Korean waters despite local protests. After being engaged by Korean forces, the *General Sherman* was set ablaze and abandoned by its crew. The United States demanded an indemnity and, with none forthcoming, sought an alliance with the French by which to punish Korea with a second expedition. Failing to secure a partner, the U.S. navy attacked Korea in 1871 to exact revenge. Sending a fleet of five gunships, the United States entered Korean waters near present-day Inchon on a stated mission to open the "hermit country" to trade. After the fleet proceeded up the Han River toward the capital, a battle broke out between Korean and American forces that resulted in the destruction of five Korean forts. Yet in spite of the United States' apparent victory, Korea remained closed.[16]

It was not until the Koreans fired on a Japanese ship near Ganghwa in 1875 that they were forced to open to trade and foreigners. Although the political situation within the monarchy had changed, the *Deawongun* had been ousted at the behest of Queen Min, Emperor Gojong's wife, who was far more inclined to enter into intercourse with the West. The Japanese knew they could provoke the Koreans into an attack by exploring coastal waters near Ganghwa Island (the site of the previous incidents with the French and Americans). Japan's gunboat diplomacy not only ended Korean isolationism by opening three ports to Japanese trade, it importantly ended the Joseon dynasty's tributary status with Qing China. Essentially, Korea, a country with little motivation to modernize along Western lines, had just been granted its independence and pulled into Japan's sphere of influence. Much of Korea's early modernization was the result of Japanese imperialist desire and development before and after 1910. Korea's infrastructure, its railroads and telegraph, were the result of Japanese intervention and the need to both modernize and exert colonial authority. Industrial and economic modernization were also driven by Japanese and later Korean investors.

Complementing the historical section of this introduction – which outlined key late nineteenth-century political, social, and military developments in China, Japan, and Korea that shaped their relations with each other and with the West – the next chapter by David Sicilia examines how multinational corporations profoundly shaped the contours of development in each of the three emerging economies. Ever limber and opportunistic, multinationals restlessly searched for new markets, sources of raw materials, and labor supplies. They were one of the leading transnational conduits for the movement of technology. Where and when they chose to expand, Sicilia emphasizes, left a lasting imprint on their host nations. The mix of Western firms – and therefore industries – that took root in China, Japan, and Korea during the period of this study were markedly uneven in their subsequent economic development.

Hon Tze-ki's chapter combines analysis of institutions and culture in its exploration of print and print capitalism in late Qing dynasty China. His is a study of two Shanghai presses that sought different avenues to financial success through the translation of Western print technologies. He demonstrates that the expansion of print capitalism was tied to demands for books that were as varied as the audience. While textbooks were the bread and butter of many presses such as the Commercial Press, others like the Press for the Association for the Preservation of National Learning grew by reprinting ancient texts and artwork. Regardless of what was printed, technologies transferred from the West made it possible to vastly expand production. However, it was important for both publishers that although the "Western" technologies they relied on to serve their readership initially entered China from Britain, they later came from and were improved by Japan, adding a new twist to our understanding of technology transfer, directionality, and knowledge acquisition.

Looking at the mid-nineteenth-century transformation of Japan's textile industries, David Wittner argues that a seemingly unrelated industry, *yōshi*, or Western paper manufacturing, was the missing link for successful and rapid industrialization of two former traditional textile industries. Looking first at silk reeling, Wittner argues that the desire to be "modern" was essential in technological choice. This is seen through the person of Shibusawa Eiichi, who was a low-level, yet influential member of the Meiji government. After Shibusawa left the government, he built Japan's first Western-style paper mill, Shoshi Kaisha, following the same methods and ideas about technology he deployed in silk reeling. Not surprisingly, he encountered several of the same problems. It was at this time that he learned the importance of knowledge over artifact. When he decided to build Japan's first truly modern cotton mill, knowledge (and capital formation) was the first step in creating a modern, Western-style mill.

Jeffer Daykin also examines the translation of a Western technology into Japan but adds several unusual dimensions to the story. First is the technology under examination: the exposition system. Daykin demonstrates that international expositions were themselves technologies. Designed to showcase a nation's industrial prowess and thus level of achieved "modernity," the international expositions were, however, not simply spaces to display technological artifacts. They were an ideological translation and physically transferable technology. Daykin traces the physicality of exposition spaces and argues that their evolution added to their adaptability and thus transferability to non-Western cultures. Even prior to the Meiji Restoration, Japanese visited and participated in international expositions. Understanding their techno-cultural value, the new government was quick to translate the system nationally and locally, all the while actively participating in international events. Daykin notes that China furthered the transferability of this quintessentially Western technology by similarly adopting Western-style expositions from Japan and beyond.

Turning to a quintessentially Japanese technology, the *jinrikisha*, or rickshaw, William Steele chronicles the movement of rickshaws from Japan to China and their subsequent translation into China and Southeast Asia. Steele's story is deceptively complicated. More than being a Japanese invention that was exported to modernizing Asia and later copied in albeit cheaper models, the rickshaw also represents continuities. Beyond contributing to the mobility revolution sweeping the developing world, rickshaws were produced in small shops well into the twentieth century, following the standard mode of production. Whether in Japan, China, or Singapore, there was no mass factory production or state sponsorship of rickshaws, despite their pervasiveness in traditional and colonial society. Rickshaws were not part of Meiji modernization in the sense of government-led industrialization, and so offer a revealing foil to other modes of state and colonial transportation such as the railroads.

The last three chapters in this volume expand our understanding of technology and technology transfer in other directions. Each examines what would be typically considered business practice and relocates it firmly within the realm of ideology, practice, and organization as technology. Chen Yu traces the career of legendary Chinese entrepreneur and businessman Zhang Jian. A Confucian-trained scholar and government official, Zhang left public service following the first Sino-Japanese War to modernize and build China's economy. Establishing nearly two dozen Western-style enterprises and hundreds of Western-style schools, Zhang imported his ideas about business and education from Japan following an extended trip to that country in 1903. As Chen notes, Zhang's visit to the 1903 Osaka Exposition had a profound effect on his thoughts regarding modernization. Seeing Western-style industrialization and education as the two pillars of modernization, Zhang set about creating in his native Jiangsu province a new society inspired by Japan's successful transformation into a Western-style society that maintained its traditional culture.

Much of Meiji Japan's industrialization was the result of government initiative. Many private ventures, however, and especially those that inspired Chinese and Korean modernizers, were the efforts of Shibusawa Eiichi, who established hundreds of businesses in his long career. Shibusawa's version of capitalism is the subject of Kimura Masato's chapter. Shibusawa argued for a moral economy, known as *gappon* capitalism, where banking was the foundation of a thriving, peaceful society. Kimura shows how, as a developing country, Japan imported a Western banking system as a technology and then modified it to suit Confucian sensibilities. Shibusawa's version of Western business and banking management was then exported to East Asia, specifically China and, most importantly, Korea, the subject of the final chapter of this study.

As Korea was opened to foreign penetration by the West and Japan, especially after 1905, it slowly adopted foreign ideas and technologies. One that came from Japan was a modern banking system. Korea's first modern bank was actually Japanese, the Daiichi National Bank established in 1878, following the conclusion of the 1876 Treaty of Ganghwa. It was not until a decade later that Korean officials turned to the idea of establishing their own Western-style banking system. Still another decade would pass before Korean entrepreneurs were able to open the country's first modern banks. Kim Myungsoo's chapter looks at the Hanseong Bank, Korea's first modern bank, and shows the direct ties between it and Shibusawa Eiichi's Daiichi Bank (the successor to the Daiichi National Bank). Hanseong Bank was initially capitalized by Daiichi Bank. As such, its Western methodologies, such as double-entry bookkeeping, and financial regulations, were based on Japanese practices. In an interesting twist, the Hanseong Bank eventually opened a Tokyo branch, completing the circle of banking technology transfer.

Given our claim about the underappreciated importance of intra–East Asian technology transfer, it seems fitting to elaborate on this central theme. Several of the chapters document what Hon calls (in characterizing the spread of print capitalism) the "circuitous, multifarious travel among East Asian cities." And indeed, one of the two presses examined by Hon, the Commercial Press, felt it necessary to partner with the Japanese firm Kinkōdō for a dozen years, beginning in 1903, in order to secure the necessary technical and managerial talent. Steele traces what he calls the "intra-Asia Chinese commercial network" that had previously traded in foodstuffs, handicrafts, and silk before spreading rickshaws through East Asia (and beyond). Indeed, Steele challenges the Westernization paradigm most directly and explicitly. Documenting the thoroughly

East Asian origins and diffusion of the rickshaw, he argues more broadly that "the [Meiji] restoration did not mark the victory of progress (in the form of Westernization) over retrogression." Most notably, the transfer of Western commercial and banking know-how relied on an information and methodological conduit from Japan to China and Korea. Chen and Kim chronicle how Western banking practices reached southeastern China and Korea through Japan, respectively.

This is not to say that there was little Western influence during the period. Several of the chapters deal directly with West-East technology transfer while also highlighting the importance of the East-East nexus. Sicilia recounts the key role of Western multinational corporations in introducing services (such as modern shipping and banking), railroads, utilities, and some consumer products into East Asia. Hon notes China's strong desire for Western learning in the 1890s. Wittner discusses the range of technology transfer from wholesale adoption to selective adaptation. Daykin shows that even when Japan started holding its own exhibitions in the 1870s, it emulated the semi-differentiated format of major exhibitions in Vienna and Philadelphia. And even after Japan quickly became an international exhibition leader, its experts remained "highly attuned" to Western techniques. Moreover, what became standard practice in Japanese, Chinese, and Korean banking originated in the West.

Closely allied with Westernization, and called out in this volume's title, is the theme of modernization. Much of what newly industrializing governments sought to do was driven by the imperative of being "modern." Although it was neither equally understood nor accepted by Japan, China, and Korea, we nonetheless see the desire to be "modern" as a determinant in technology transfer. Again, in the well-worn historiographic tradition, the East modernized by transferring superior Western technologies, institutions, practices, and attitudes. There is, in fact, ample evidence in this volume not only of West-East technology transfer, but of a potent Eastern – especially Japanese – desire to bring Western techniques to its shores and in the process gain international status. As Steele notes, "A fascination with power and speed preoccupied the vision of modernizing societies, and especially their governments."

Chapters here that speak to that issue short-circuit, or at least complicate, the traditional linear story in important ways. Wittner's chapter on the Japanese importation of several Western factory technologies drives a wedge between the importation of the most appropriate and efficient factory system and what he calls "technological choice determined by cultural symbolism." Iron machines, brick buildings, and French filatures did not make the best sense in the Japanese industrial context, but they connected with and projected widely understood optics about cultural modernism. Daykin's chapter on exhibitions, as well as the many accounts of Shibusawa Eiichi's interventions and enterprises, also chronicles a strong Japanese desire to modernize by Westernizing. There were always limits, however. As Kimura explains, government officials and entrepreneurs (such as Shibusawa) were intent on selective importation from the West. As Japan became more "technologically mature," no one expected or desired intact transfer from the originating culture to the receiving one.

The result was hybridization, a concept familiar to historians of technology and technology transfer. What ultimately takes root in the receiving culture melds elements of it with the originating culture. There are several reasons this happens. As a baseline, because technology is socially and culturally constructed – that is, infused with a society's values, politics, institutions, and geography – it is always embedded, never autonomous. Wittner takes hybridization a step further by describing technology transfer as translation, a process through which technologies are recoded in new sociocultural environments. There can be profound practicalities – such as the Chinese preference for lithography from among many Western printing methods because of the pictographic nature of its writing system, as Hon notes. That said, the chapters in this volume repeatedly point to a self-conscious parsing by Japanese, Chinese, and Korean importers of Western technological know-how – all of which suggests a very deliberate and self-conscious process of West-East/East-East hybridization rather than one without agency, inevitable, or unavoidable.

Hon's print capitalists, for starters, sought "to mimic the Western model on the one hand, and to assert an Asian uniqueness on the other." "Asia's mobility revolution (and modernity in general)," Steele observes, "is marked by hybridity." Even the Meiji Restoration "and the new government's commitment to Western 'civilization and enlightenment,'" he continues, "mask important areas of resistance and continuity with the past." Similarly, Chen argues that Zhang Jian stood apart from many reformers in part because he "believed in the value of Western society within a Chinese Confucian context." In his travels to Japan, Zhang had "discovered that Japan was a country that had adopted Western civilization without abandoning its traditional culture."

If hybridization proscribes the unabridged transfer of technology, it follows that local conditions must be receptive in order for technologies to take hold over the long term. Again and again we see that conditions where Western or East Asian technologies became part of the landscape were ripe for reception. Kim notes not only external pressures for financial modernization, but also that "domestic necessity" drove Korea's efforts to modernize its banking system. Kimura illustrates the infusion of Western business practices in Japan with Confucian morality; and Chen underscores Zhang Jian's concern about Chinese power in the wake of the Treaty of Shimonoseki. Steele notes road improvement in urban parts of China as a key precursor to rickshaw importation. In Hon's account, China's abolition of civil service exams and the establishment of a national school system in 1905 primed a vast market for printed textbooks. The same can be said for Japan's and later China's promotion of the exhibition system, as well as both countries' embrace of Western, albeit hybridized, silk-reeling and cotton-spinning technologies and factory organization.

We would be remiss if we did not at least mention the essential role of the state and local entrepreneurs in the process of translating technologies, knowledge, and business practices into new (East Asian) contexts. For its part, Japan's Meiji government is credited with its early industrial modernization almost to the exclusion of entrepreneurial activity. The state played an important role in directly and indirectly stimulating Japanese industrialization. Wittner demonstrates that, for its part, the Meiji government's angst about the declining quality of Japanese raw silk compelled it to intervene repeatedly in the industry and to eventually issue the directive overruling its advisers' recommendations by insisting on a French, rather than a hybrid, reeling system. The Meiji government in Daykin's account exercised a strong hand in the promotion and design of early exhibitions. Even in the chapter by William Steele – who successfully challenges the "state-led" scenario of transportation development – the government inevitably rears its head, such as by prohibiting horse-drawn carts in Edo (later Tokyo) until two years after the Meiji Restoration.

In Akiha Daisuke's remarkable story, Steele notes that rickshaw exports and usage in other parts of Asia surged in the period 1895 to 1915, "precisely the years of the expansion of the Japanese empire." Kim notes that the Pusan branch of Japan's Daiichi Bank in Korea "had close ties to the Meiji government's foreign policy initiatives" and further that "Public Hanseong Bank ... can be thought of as a by-product of the conflict between Russia and Japan over interests in Korea." In China, Zhang Jian's desire to improve the position of entrepreneurs inspired his involvement in Chinese politics and his push for constitutional reform. There, the state was implicated in all varieties of business ventures (government-run, government-supervised, merchant-operated, and government-merchant supervised). Looking at the fate of foreign multinationals in China, Sicilia concludes that "during this period government actors often interfered with foreign actors in ways that severely constrained economic development."

Despite the state's essential role, the agents of technology transfer and diffusion most pivotal in this collection were from the private sector. Most were committed to bringing Western business practices and manufacturing systems to their homelands, either directly or via a neighboring country – adapting foreign hardware and techniques to a particular indigenous cultural vision. These men understood that local and national governments were key stakeholders and were adept at collaboration with the state, sometimes having been key state actors themselves. They were, above all, navigators who strived to unleash the energies and opportunities of the market while tempering its harsh edges; they believed such balance would create the greatest good for their home cultures.

Among these extraordinary men were Akiha Daisuke and his son, who, Steele demonstrates, perceived great need and opportunity for rickshaw transport and built a sprawling distribution network throughout East Asia and beyond. Chen aptly illustrates the entrepreneur-*cum*-nationalist career of Zhang Jian. A member of the local gentry who first served in the Chinese government, Zhang as a private citizen aggressively sought to adopt Western technologies into the Chinese hinterland, while guided by a concept of "people's diplomacy," which was, as Chen explains, "a form of diplomacy promoted by industrialists rather than official governments." Zhang was similarly intrigued by private-versus-state education initiatives.

In this volume, as in many others on Japanese economic development (including some in this same University of Toronto Press series), the indefatigable Shibusawa Eiichi (1840–1931) figures most prominently in this group. A growing body of scholarship, some of it now reaching the West, identifies the First Viscount Shibusawa, who founded approximately 500 enterprises in banking, textile manufacturing, papermaking, brewing, shipping, and other fields, as the "father of modern Japanese capitalism." Helping to build the Meiji government, he served in various capacities from 1869 to 1873. Shibusawa traveled widely, including with a major expedition back and forth across the United States in 1909, when he met with dignitaries (including President Taft) and business leaders and inspected factories and financial institutions. Guided by a philosophy of *gappon* capitalism, Shibusawa also was involved in setting up some 600 educational, charitable, and other social welfare organizations.

Figuring prominently in Wittner's chapter on Westernized technology transfer to Japan, Shibusawa was far from a static figure. Rather, first through silk manufacturing, then papermaking, his thinking evolved toward an "indigenous knowledge first" approach in cotton spinning. We see him in Daykin's chapter as part of the *bakufu* delegation for the *Exposition Universelle* in Paris in 1867, where he became a proponent of national modernization on all fronts and of moral economy. In Kim's chapter, Shibusawa pushed for the modernization of Japanese (and, by extension, Korean) banking through tempered Westernization. In promoting the development of Japanese banking, Kimura's chapter explains, Shibusawa opposed state-managed institutions while at the same time seeing the need to improve the status of banks in late nineteenth-century Japanese society.

We intend for this volume to advance the conversation about a much neglected and profoundly dynamic place and time, where ways of understanding, organizing, and making things circulated – to borrow William Steele's phrasing – like Western and Eastern winds.

NOTES

1 Chinese and Japanese languages are dissimilar grammatically and are parts of different language groups – Chinese being a Sino-Tibetan language, while Japanese is Japonic but related to Korean and the Altaic language family. That said, both share the use of Chinese characters (*hanzi* in Chinese, *kanji* in Japanese), which facilitated the translation and creation of a technological vocabulary from Japanese into Chinese.

2 Eden Media, Ivan Da Costa Marques, and Christina Holmes, eds., *Beyond Imported Magic: Essays on Science, Technology, and Society in Latin America* (Cambridge, MA: MIT Press, 2014).

3 Eric Schatzberg, *Technology: Critical History of a Concept* (Chicago: University of Chicago Press, 2018), 145–51.

4 John Kenneth Galbraith, *The New Industrial State* (Boston: Houghton Mifflin, 1967), 14.

5 Schatzberg, *Technology*, 212–13.

6 John Law, "Technology and Heterogeneous Engineering: The Case of Portuguese Expansion," in *The Social Construction of Technological Systems: New Directions in the Sociology and History of Technology*, ed. Wiebe Bijker, Thomas Parke Hughes, and Trevor Pinch (Cambridge, MA: MIT Press, 1987), 111, 115–16.

7 Dennis R. Herschbach, "Technology as Knowledge: Implications for Instruction," *Journal of Technology in Education* 7, no. 1 (Fall 1995): 32.

8 Ruth Schwartz Cowan, *A Social History of American Technology* (New York: Oxford University Press, 1997), 2.

9 Nick von Tunzelmann, "Technology," in *The Oxford Encyclopedia of Economic History*, ed. Joel Mokyr, 6 vols. (Oxford University Press, 2003), online.

10 John M. Staudenmaier, *Technology's Storytellers: Reweaving the Human Fabric* (Cambridge, MA: MIT Press, 1989), 123.

11 See, for example, David J. Jeremy, ed., *International Technology Transfer: Europe, Japan, and the USA, 1700–1914* (London: Edward Elgar, 1991); David S. Landes, *The Unbound Prometheus: Technological Change and Industrial Development in Western Europe from 1750 to the Present* (Cambridge: Cambridge University Press, 1969); Edward Beatty, "Approaches to Technology Transfer in History and the Case of Nineteenth-Century Mexico," *Comparative Technology Transfer and Society* 1, no. 2 (2003): 167–97; Nathan Rosenberg, "Economic Development and the Transfer of Technology: Some Historical Perspectives," *Technology and Culture* 11 (1970): 550–75; Joel Mokyr, *Lever of Riches: Technological Creativity and Economic Progress* (Oxford: Oxford University Press, 1990).

12 See Debin Ma, "Between Cottage and Factory: The Evolution of Chinese and Japanese Silk-Reeling Industries in the Latter Half of the Nineteenth Century," *Journal of the Asia Pacific Economy* 10, no. 2 (May 2005): 195–213; Lillian M. Li, "Silks by Sea: Trade, Technology, and Enterprise in China and Japan," *Business History Review* 56, no. 2 (Summer 1982): 192–217.

13 See, for example, Eyal Ben-Ari and John Clammer, eds., *Japan in Singapore: Cultural Occurrences and Cultural Flows* (London: Routledge, 2000); and Paul A. Rodell, "Southeast Asian Nationalism and the Russo-Japanese War: Reexamining Assumptions," *Southeast Review of Asian Studies* 29 (2007): 20–40.

14 The Chinese Self-Strengthening Movement occurred between 1861 and 1895 and is typically divided into three stages, 1861–72, 1872–85, and 1885–95. During each stage, the Qing government became more serious about not just technological development but also about modernizing and more thoroughly adopting Western practices.

15 See, for example, Junichi Murata, "Creativity of Technology: An Origin of Modernity?," in *Modernity and Technology*, ed. Thomas J. Misa, Philip Brey, and Andrew Feenberg (Cambridge, MA: MIT Press, 2003), 227–55.

16 See Chay Jongsuk, *Unequal Partners in Peace and War: The Republic of Korea and the United States, 1948–1953* (Westport, CT: Praeger Publishers, 2002), 9–13.

1 Multinationals and Technology Transfer to and within East Asia, 1870–1914

DAVID B. SICILIA

It is difficult to overemphasize the role of multinational enterprises (MNEs) in global economic activity. Today, there are more than 60,000 multinationals operating in the world, and they in turn control more than 800,000 affiliated business firms. Massive streams of capital and know-how course across borders through their arteries. In each wave of economic globalization, MNEs played a key role, whether in their early form as chartered trading companies in the sixteenth and seventeenth centuries (most famously the East India Company); as free-standing companies (enterprises with no home base); or as modern multinational corporations.[1] Business historians have debated the similarities and differences between these three forms of organization, but for the purposes of this chapter, I will emphasize their underlying similarities.[2] All these MNEs were business enterprises that sought profit by exploiting foreign markets, raw materials, or labor, and did so systematically and hierarchically through internal systems of control.

This chapter considers the role played by MNEs in transferring technology and business practices to and among China, Japan, and Korea between 1870 and 1914. As with several of the other chapters in this volume, the directional flow was both West-to-East and East-to-East. Multinational firms sometimes transferred hardware but more commonly acted as conduits for "soft" forms of practical knowledge. My approach is sectoral rather than granular; that is, I am concerned with which industries moved from one nation or region to another via international firm activity, rather than the process through which particular technologies were transferred and adapted. Stated differently, my interest is in the mix of businesses that were planted on Chinese, Japanese, and Korean soil during this period by Western or East Asian firms. Rather than attempting to measure the specific economic impact of each foreign transplanted sector (an exercise made even more complicated by their interactions), I look for broad patterns in connection with what we know about economic development.

This was a crucial period in modern economic development for several reasons. First, it was when the first wave of global integration culminated with levels of international trade, financial integration (aided by an international gold standard that functioned efficiently in much of the developed world), and technology transfer. The Industrial Revolution, which originated in Great Britain, spread during this period to Western Europe and the United States. In doing so, industrialization was changing character; no longer centered in textiles as it had been in England, it was shifting more toward producer goods based on chemical and electrical processes. This shift has inspired many historians to speak of a second Industrial Revolution, with the internal combustion engine and electric light and power at its core. Bound up in European industrialization and economic globalization was imperialism, for the period 1870 to 1914 was also an age when the major European powers (and, to a lesser extent, the United States) aggressively acquired foreign territories throughout Africa, Latin America, and Asia for political and economic control. The key economic motives were to secure sources of raw material and outlets for goods produced by the mother country. As we will see, late imperialism figures prominently in the story of foreign direct investment (FDI) and MNE activity in China, Japan, and Korea during this period.

China garners the most attention in this chapter, Korea the least. The reasons are both historical and interpretative: China experienced the greatest degree of MNE in this period, and the China case serves as a platform for themes carried into the next two cases. The near-absence of MNE activity in Korea between 1870 and the First World War is informative in a different way.

China: A Critical Period of Opening

For China, the period under consideration was pivotal. In the late Qing dynasty, following the establishment of the original five treaty ports in 1842 (by the Treaty of Nanjing), Western economic activity in the coast cities, especially Shanghai, flourished, and by the mid-1890s several major Western powers as well as Russia and Japan were building railroads, mines, and factories in China – along the seaboard but also in Manchuria and some other inland regions. This was the first time the country diversified out of strictly trade in hundreds of years of economic interaction with the West. The China that ended with the Xinhai Revolution in 1911 was in some ways economically very different from the China of a generation earlier. MNEs and FDI played important roles in this story as conduits for the transfer of several modern technologies to China. But the mix of foreign-infused industries and technologies also introduced some important distortions.

Trade, shipping, and banking are vital foundational economic sectors. Following several centuries of rather limited trade with foreigners, China liberalized foreign trade dramatically in the late nineteenth century, step by step. Under the terms of the Treaty of Nanjing, five "treaty ports" were established: Canton, Shanghai, Amoy, Foochow, and Ningpo. The opening of the Suez Canal in 1869 reduced the cost of shipping from London to Singapore by 30 percent.[3] As in much of the world, the British occupied a key position in the shipping that wove together the Southeast China treaty ports with each other and with foreign ports, although Americans launched the first foreign shipping company in China – the Shanghai Steam Navigation Co. – in 1862. In the 1890s, several more U.S. trading firms (Standard Oil Co. [the predecessor of Standard Vacuum Oil Co.], Getz Bros. & Co., Anderson, Meyer & Co., and Connel Brothers & Co.) opened branches in China, and they were joined by several German and French trading houses, encouraged by China's lifting of all trade restrictions in 1898. In 1909, three dozen foreign firms were trading in China. Overall, some three-quarters of Chinese shipping between 1909 and 1913 was foreign-controlled.[4]

International, coastal, and inland shipping also stimulated foreign-owned ship production in China. Much of this was naval stores work to maintain and repair vessels in the treaty port cities, but as foreign manufacturing was legalized with the Treaty of Shimonoseiki in 1895 (which ended the Sino-Japanese War), Japan and other "most favored nations" began to establish shipyards in the port towns. The largest shipyard in China was the Hong Kong and Whampoa Dock Co., owned by the sprawling British shipping and trading firm Jardine, Matheson & Co., which dominated Hong Kong until another British firm (Butterfield and Swire) built the Taikoo Dockyard and Engineering Co. In Shanghai, two other British firms dominated from the 1860s to 1901: Boyd and Co. and S.C. Farnham & Co. By 1913, there were forty-eight treaty ports, although some were semi-restricted "ports of call" where goods but not foreigners could move freely. By that time the Japanese had joined the British as a strong presence in shipping, with Americans and Germans next.[5]

Because trade and shipping worked symbiotically with banking, that service sector expanded in China during the same period, with foreigners taking the lead. Although non-Chinese nations operated local deposit institutions in cities such as Shanghai in the nineteenth century, those banks did not underwrite foreign trade. The British first established a bank in Hong Kong (in 1845) before moving to China three years later by opening the Oriental Banking Corporation in Shanghai. Many others followed, but it was not until 1897 that local Chinese opened the first modern bank. Foreign banking also supported a growing real estate market among foreigners, but it was largely confined to the treaty ports. By 1914, real estate accounted for nearly 10 percent of total foreign investment in China. For its part, the import/export trade accounted for 13.4 percent, ahead of manufacturing (discussed below), which accounted for 10.4 percent of FDI. Before the First World War, then, MNEs and foreign investors were more thoroughly engaged in trading, shipping and shipbuilding, banking, and real estate than in the manufacturing sector.[6]

Their heaviest involvement, however, was in a sector central to nineteenth-century economic development. Nearly a third (31.5 percent of FDI in China at the end of our period) was in railroads.[7] This was in part because railroads were the century's most capital-intensive industry, but also because they were recognized by the world's most advanced economies as an essential precursor to economic development, the most potent element of transportation infrastructure devised up to the time. But the foreigners keen to build a railroad network in China were interested chiefly in their own economic interests, more than in China's. Whether aggressively or not so aggressively imperialist, they saw iron rails as a way of gaining access into the China market, especially its hitherto isolated hinterland. As the political terrain within China shifted during this period, enterprises in Russia, Japan, France, Germany, and Great Britain that were or aspired to be multinational seized opportunities to build railroads in China.

The beginnings were halting and ill-fated. Initially, a British firm proposed in 1863 to build a railroad from Shanghai to Soochow, but the government rejected the proposal. The following year, a toy demonstration railroad constructed in Peking by another British company was promptly destroyed. Getting the message, the powerful British trading company Jardine, Matheson & Co. bought the rights of way for a carriage road between Shanghai and Woosung, concealing their real intention until testing a steam locomotive on a section of track in early 1876. Two months after the line was completed that June, a man was killed by the train. It was too much for already disgruntled government officials, who bought and dismantled the railway and shipped it to Formosa.

During this episode, British engineer John Dixon had cautioned that the railroad would symbolize Western imperialism, and that railroad construction in China would need to await Chinese capital and technical expertise.[8] Chinese authorities opposed the construction of railroads on several grounds, from national security (by giving foreigners easier access to the heartland where the emperor resided), to financial (by draining capital from the country), to competitive (by threatening traditional human-transport jobs). At the heart of the matter was China's determination to resist European colonization. Foreign railroads threatened to undermine that effort. Proving Dixon correct, the first railroad project approved by the Chinese government, in 1878, was proposed by a Chinese mining company (Kaiping Coal Mining Co.). The Tangshan-Hsukochwan Railway would transport coal from one of its mines to Pei Tang.

After that, however, the central government began to approve foreign railroad construction projects. A military defeat by Japan in 1894 (and later, the 1904–5 Russo-Japanese War, fought in Manchuria) underscored the strategic importance of railroads, while at the same time Chinese officials found it impossible to marshal the capital or technical expertise for the projects domestically. So China ushered in its first period of heavy railroad building – much of it foreign-led – between 1895 and 1903. In 1895, France began laying track, nearly all of it along the French-Indochina border. The following year, Russia extended its Trans-Siberian Railway into Manchuria. Then came the Germans. By 1911, four major foreign roads accounted for 41 percent of Chinese railroad mileage: Chinese Eastern Railway (Russian), which was 1073 miles long; the South Manchuria Railway (Japanese), 709 miles; the Yunnan Railway (French), 289 miles; and the Kiaochow-Tsinan Railway (German), 284 miles. The British also operated a 22-mile-long section of the Canton-Kowloon Railway, and the Americans also played a minor role. Nearly all these projects were direct investments rather than loans. And nearly all operated at a loss. Although dependent on foreign technology and capital, Chinese authorities had achieved their political and military ends while continuing to resist imperialism. As purely economic ventures, however, the railroads in this first era were less than successful.[9]

Foreign firms and investors also played key roles in several consumer goods manufacturing businesses in this period, including cotton, silk, cigarettes, tea, and pharmaceuticals. The consumer product with which MNEs penetrated into China the most rapidly and deeply was the cigarette. As a mass-marketed product, the cigarette was young. The American Tobacco Company (ATC) was the first to purchase an automated cigarette-making machine patented by James Bonsack in 1881, and by the end of the decade had so saturated the U.S. market that it began to export heavily, especially to Japan and China. To surmount local competition and jump tariffs, ATC began manufacturing in China. Following its merger with the UK's Imperial Tobacco Company in 1901, the new British-American Tobacco Co. (BAT) modernized its operations and dominated cigarette production in China and many other places. ATC and BAT had introduced mass-produced cigarettes into the China market and profited handsomely, though data on their market share within China are elusive, especially since hundreds of millions of Chinese, especially in rural areas, continued to smoke traditional long pipes or hand-rolled or domestically produced cigarettes.

Thanks to Russian influence, some of the treaty ports featured brick tea manufactories that utilized Russian technology. These produced for export and had very limited impact on the traditional growing and processing techniques employed by the country's vast rural population for millennia. Meanwhile, to serve mainly foreign port town residents, Western entrepreneurs built small-scale manufactories of soap, candles, drugs, and related items. These processes, too, found limited markets and had very little impact on traditional Chinese production methods.

Producer goods manufacturing was conspicuously absent in China during this period, whether capital, plants, and technique flowed in from foreign sources or emerged domestically. Consider the case of the chemical industry, which processed primary products and produced intermediaries that supplied other manufacturers of final products. To the world's leading chemical producers of the early twentieth century, China was chiefly a market and secondarily a source of raw materials, but barely a producer. The Germans (the world leaders in this industry) helped make China the leading user of dyestuffs by the First World War; China was their second-largest customer after the United States.[10]

The German chemical giant BASF began buying raw materials in China in the late nineteenth century, but saw China mainly as a "most promising country" (as managers put it) for dyestuffs sales, thanks to its vast size and the common use of indigo for dying jackets. By this time synthetic indigo was considered superior to the natural product, with sales beginning to grow in the port towns. By the time of the First World War, BASF also was producing some dyestuffs in China. The challenge was reaching the interior. Completion of the Shantung Railroad from Tsingtao improved access to hinterland markets after 1900, but progress was slow, and the outbreak of war halted German dye exports as well as production in China.[11] Compared with many other parts of the pre-war world, China was a limited market for chemicals, with the notable exception of dyestuffs, a limited source of raw materials, and a modest site for manufacturing.

Although China entered the iron age in roughly 600 BCE, it did not produce steel using the Bessemer process or the Siemens-Martin open hearth process (both developed in the middle to late nineteenth century) until long after the period under consideration (although small-scale open-hearth smelting was could be found throughout the countryside). There were no large, high-throughput, continuous-process petroleum refineries, nor any large machine works for electrical equipment, machine tools, sewing machines, or other complicated equipment with interchangeable parts.

Japan: Cautious toward the West, Ambitious in the East

In some key ways, the transfer of technology from Western companies to Japan through trading companies, multinationals, and direct foreign investment was similar to China. But there were important differences as well. During the Meiji period (1868–1912), when Japan took major steps toward economic modernization, it was more welcoming toward Western influences and became a more dominant player in East Asia regional economics than China, while also maintaining considerable independence from outside powers. Meanwhile, Japan looked closer to home for economic connections, often emerging through its own multinational enterprises as a regional economic leader.

As in China, British service companies (shipping, trade, banking) led the way among European interests in Japan. In 1875, half of all imports to Japan came from the United Kingdom, with Britain's Blue Funnel Line alone carrying

70 percent of British-Japanese trade by the 1880s. The British opened five banks in Japan between 1863 and 1866.[12]

But this early foothold belies the fate of most British enterprise in Japan through the Meiji period. As historian Geoffrey Jones observes, Britain's experience in Japan after 1868 followed a pattern of "early success and pioneering followed by decline and insignificance."[13] By 1913, Britain's share of Japanese imports had fallen to 11 percent, while foreigners were by then carrying more than half of Japan's foreign trade. The situation for early British banks in Japan proved equally grim. Two were short lived (Central Bank of Western India and the Commercial Bank Corporation of India and the East operated in Japan only in 1865–6); and two lasted in Japan only two or three decades (Chartered Mercantile Bank of India, London, and China, 1863–86; and Oriental Bank Corporation, 1865–92). Only the Hongkong and Shanghai Banking Corporation (1866) and Chartered Bank of India, Australia, and China (1880) survived the Meiji period. Thus, as two scholars have noted, British merchants, banks, and shipping companies "played a substantial role in the initial development of the external sector of the Meiji economy" but were eclipsed by 1914.[14]

Japanese foreign restrictions are part of the explanation. The Treaty of Shimonoseki (1895) opened China to foreign direct investment, but Japan continued to restrict FDI to treaty ports, and even under the reforms of its 1899 Commercial Law, foreigners were prohibited from investing in key sectors such as transport and banking. Presaging a stance that would persist well into the twentieth century, Japan was resisting foreign control.[15] The Meiji period ushered in many forms of modernization, but not unalloyed openness. As one Japan expert puts it, Japan saw "Western institutions and technologies [as] sources of strength, but the West and Westerners remained a menacing presence."[16]

A second key reason the British and other Westerners did not exercise great economic influence in Meiji Japan was the strength of the nation's own general trading companies. The largest of these *sōgō shōsha*, notes Kazutoshi Maeda, "played a vital role in the transfer of technology to Japan" through the transfer of "materials, machines, manpower, management, and market."[17] Mitsui Bussan, Japan's leading general trading company, began handling trade between Europe and China as early as the 1880s.[18] After reopening its New York branch in 1896, the company traded not only commodities but also textile and other machinery, and railway equipment, and served as the sole agent for the American Locomotive Co. and Carnegie Steel Co.[19]

Japan's trade was focused more intently elsewhere in East Asia rather than toward the West during the Meiji period, another reason Britain's influence diminished. Japanese general trading companies were largely excluded from trade with the West. China was the favored alternative. Most of Mitsui Bussan's more than thirty overseas branches were operating there in 1910. Still, there were limits to Japanese penetration into China in this period.

Following the Treaty of Shimonoseki, Japanese cotton spinners established the Towka Cotton Spinning and Weaving Co. and the Shanghai Cotton Spinning Co., both in Shanghai. But these were short-lived operations, and the parent companies reverted to exporting to China.[20] At this stage, export and foreign investment in China were more manageable than foreign manufacturing for Japanese enterprises.

As for the penetration of foreign manufacturers into Meiji Japan, there were beachheads in some critical infrastructure industries that were motivated in large part by Japan beginning to set its own tariffs under the 1899 Commercial Law. American firms took the lead. Between 1904 and 1910, General Electric moved aggressively into the Japanese electrical industry by forging patent agreements and acquiring controlling interests in Tokyo Electric Company and Shibaura Engineering Works.[21] For its part, Western Electric forged a joint venture with Nihon Electric Company.[22] Railroads came to Japan in the 1870s and 1880s as a state project, although because the nation's capabilities for making locomotives and rails were weak, it relied on foreign imports and expertise.[23] Finally, as in China, American Tobacco set up factories in Japan; by 1901 they were churning out some eight million cigarettes per year.[24]

The British were not shut out of the manufacturing scene completely. They cooperated with Japanese firms to manufacture cordite (1905), steel and armaments (1907), and rubber (1909) in Japan. But British direct foreign investment was focused mainly in the United States and in continental Europe. The Meiji government's protectionism and generous support of Japanese economic development made other arenas more appealing.[25] While building economic and military strength at home, Japan was projecting itself aggressively within the region. "People in Japan were making themselves an integral part of a broad East Asian and global system," historian Andrew Gordon observes.[26] Nowhere was that more true than in Korea, and for that reason Japanese imperialism (economic and otherwise) centrally shaped Korean trade, DFI, and economic development in this period.

Korea: Beginnings of Multinational Technology Transfer

The long-term consequences for Korea when it signed the Treaty of Ganghwa with Japan in 1876 were not immediately or abundantly apparent. But the treaty not only ended Korea's ancient isolation, in particular it opened the door for Japanese penetration and, as one scholar has noted, "brought Korea into the imperialist rivalries of the late nineteenth century."[27] Those rivalries chiefly involved Japan, China, and Russia, and were almost unremittingly tumultuous for the nascent nation. They diverted Korea's focus from economic to political and military matters, discouraged DFI, and disrupted trade.

Initially, Chinese and American influences in Korea appeared promising for economic opening and development. Beginning in 1879, China's relations with Korea were governed by Li Hongzhang, who inveighed on Korea's King Gojong to share China's strategy of "self-strengthening" through the importation of Western technology (especially military technology). Korea established diplomatic ties with the United States in May 1882. Five months later, China issued a regulation that opened parts of Korea to Chinese traders and vice versa. Soon, Korean and the United States were entertaining each other's diplomats.[28]

In truth, China had imposed a variety of formal and informal restrictions on Korea in an effort to keep the smaller nation tightly within its orbit. Both Japan and Russia had been developing closer ties with Korea. The six-month Sino-Japanese War left Japan with a decisive victory in 1895, but was followed by another decade of conflict over Korean control, this time chiefly between Russia and Japan.[29]

These decades of conflict severely hampered externally driven economic modernization in Korea. To be sure, there were a few inroads. Rights to build a railway connecting Seoul with Inchon were pulled from a Japanese company in 1894 and given over (along with gold-mining rights at Usan) to American James Morse. A Russian company was granted timber rights. Railroad construction (financed by both American and Japanese firms) began in 1896, and electric lights began to glimmer in Seoul. But compared with Chinese and Japanese developments, these were meager. Japan began to effectively control Korea at the outbreak of the Russo-Japanese War in 1904, then officially under protectorate status from 1905 to 1910. Japan annexed Korea on 29 August 1910.[30]

Foreign multinationals – and the technologies they channeled – did not penetrate Korea to any meaningful degree until much later. Even textiles remained centered on local use and raw material export rather than manufacturing until after 1919, when the Samil independence movement lifted Japanese Company Law restrictions on modern manufacturing.[31]

Conclusions

The involvement of multinationals in China during the critical period between 1870 and 1914 is a story of mixed outcomes. On the one hand, the Chinese economy opened to outside influences more than ever in its history, and that opening led to significant technological and economic advances. This was especially apparent in the coastal region of the treaty ports, although by the end of the period – in the space of scarcely a decade – an interior network of railroads and telegraphs was beginning to take shape.

In trade and shipping, foreigners and their Chinese associates amplified a centuries-long history of West-East commerce. The British, although in the twilight of their global empire, nevertheless were still the world's premier bankers and shippers, so their central role in Chinese coastal financial services and deep water and coastal shipping was crucial. Modern banking owned and operated by Chinese businessmen followed quickly on the heels of the first Western banks established in the treaty ports. Although finance has fallen into disfavor in the wake of recent national, regional, and global financial crises, the record of economic history is clear: no economy can develop far without a robust financial sector.

In manufacturing, foreign investment and technology transfer also boosted development of several consumer goods industries in China. Cotton manufacturing is a complicated story. Building on hundreds of years of heritage, handicraft manufacturing probably had diffused more broadly in China than anywhere else on earth before foreign manufacturers set up shop, and they continued to operate much as before through most of the country. What changed with the arrival of Western and Japanese firms was the scale and efficiency of output. The foreign mills were larger than their Chinese counterparts, and operated more spindles per worker. This is not surprising, given that they were developed in societies where, unlike China, the substitution of labor with capital was at a premium. Similarly, another ancient Chinese enterprise, tea manufacturing, shifted toward mass production under the influence of foreign investors and managers, in this case from Russia. In both cases, it is doubtful that foreign influences led to an increase in product quality. But as economies of scale for mass markets became increasingly the norm in the global economy in certain industries, the foreign bias toward mass production proved to be a useful influence on the Chinese economy of a century ago.

Foreign influence on infrastructure – transportation, communication, and utility networks – was considerable during this period. And again, theories of economic development are clear that these are indispensable components for advanced economies. After stifling foreign railroad development for antiimperialist reasons, China changed its stance and allowed outside development – again, for diplomatic reasons. For the first time, railroad shipping began to penetrate into the central, especially southern (Manchuria), regions of the mainland. Without foreign capital and technical expertise allowed in for strategic reasons, the Chinese railroad sector would have been delayed by decades.

And yet, as I have suggested, the story was mixed. In addition to looking at what happened, we need to consider what did not happen. Here, the influence of foreign multinational enterprises was constrained in several significant ways. First, in spite of the railroad projects I just discussed, by 1914 China still remained essentially a dual economy. The levels of commerce, investment, banking, and utility development in the treaty ports far exceeded those in nearly all the rest of the country, and much of the foreign-influenced coastal activity was aimed outward rather than domestically. Studies of economic development elsewhere point to the importance of integrating hinterland (or interior or upland) economies with outward-looking maritime trade. In early nineteenth-century United States, for instance, New York City and Philadelphia became dominant port cities in large part because of their upland, interior connections.

Second, during this period, government actors often interfered with foreign actors in ways that severely constrained economic development. They did so purposefully, as part of a larger agenda of resisting European and Japanese imperialist influences. In the age of high imperialism, opening China to more outside economic influences while safeguarding national sovereignty was an extremely difficult course to navigate. But once the government's strategy of assuring national strength and independence became more closely linked to economic development – through the realization that railroads were necessary for national security – it was difficult to quickly cast off deeply rooted bureaucracies and cultures dedicated to protectionism.

Third, it is important to look at the mix of industries affected and not affected by MNE activity. While consumer products can be important in spurring consumption among moderate- and middle-income consumers, they have a relatively limited impact on the structural development of an economy. Consider the case of the consumer goods product transferred to China most rapidly and thoroughly during this period: the mass-produced cigarette. Even though China quickly became a place where cigarettes were made and consumed by the billions after ATC and BAT penetration, China did not become a producer of cigarette-making machinery. Producer industries such as equipment manufacturing are better at encouraging backward and forward linkages. Automobile manufacturing, for example, spurs the production of steel, glass, rubber, petroleum and so on, as well as the development of a large distribution network between manufacturer and final consumer.

This is the central point I wish to make about the impact of multinational enterprise on technology transfer and economic development in China between 1870 and 1914 – the mix of sectors affected by MNEs was key. Viewed from a broad perspective – from a global view of how MNEs were reshaping the global economy before the First World War – China appears to have been largely left out of the story. The leading economies during this period sometimes had robust consumer product sectors such as textiles or food processing, but they always had robust producer goods sectors. Organic and inorganic chemicals, pharmaceuticals, auto manufacturing, electricals, machinery, iron and steel, petroleum – these were the engines of growth in Germany and the United States. Consider a list (published in a survey of MNE history by Geoffrey Jones of Harvard) of leading multinational manufacturing enterprises in 1914, which together operated 111 factories around the world: Singer (sewing machines); J & P Coats (cotton thread); Nestlé (food products); Lever Brothers (soap); Saint-Gobain (glass); Bayer (chemicals); American Radiator (radiators); Siemens (electricals); and L.M. Ericson (telephone equipment). In 1914, none of these firms was based in China, and none operated factories in China.[32] Similarly, the giant U.S.-based McCormick farm equipment company was selling in Africa, New Zealand and Australia, and Russia, but not China, Japan, or Korea.[33]

In the case of Japan, foreign investment, much of it through multinationals, played a key role in establishing a modern foundation of services such as shipping and banking, and infrastructure, and some key manufacturing sectors. Japan was a hungry student of Western economic ways during this period, with military strength and independence key motivators. Yet Japan remained guarded about foreign economic control. At the same time, especially through its powerful general trading companies, Japan transferred key technology to China and Korea.

Korea, much more isolated than China and Japan, began to open to the West and East alike during this period by imperialist intrusions from many directions. Political and military rather than market forces occupied center stage, with very limited advanced technology entering the land before the First World War.

NOTES

1 Geoffrey Jones, *Merchants to Multinationals: British Trading Companies in the Nineteenth and Twentieth Centuries* (Oxford: Oxford University Press, 2000); Mira Wilkins, "Multinational Enterprise to 1930: Discontinuities and Continuities," in *Leviathans: Multinational Corporations and the New Global History*, ed. Alfred D. Chandler Jr. and Bruce Lazlish, 45–79 (Cambridge, MA: Harvard University Press, 2005).

2 Scholars such as Ann Carlos and Stephen Nichols argue for the continuities between trading companies and modern multinationals, while others such as Mira Wilkins are convinced that "there was a wide divide between the modern MNEs and their many precursors." The issue seems secondary in this chapter because the central question concerns the role of foreign private enterprises, of whatever particular configuration, as agents of technology transfer. Ann M. Carlos and Stephen Nicholas, "'Giants of an Earlier Capitalism': The Chartered Trading Companies as Modern Multinationals," *Business History Review* 62, no. 3 (Autumn 1988): 398–419; Wilkins, *Multinational Enterprise to 1930*, 51.

3 Wilkins, *Multinational Enterprise to 1930*, 53–4.

4 Chi-min Hou, *Foreign Investment and Economic Development in China, 1840–1937* (Cambridge, MA: Harvard University Press, 1965), 51, 59–60, 127.

5 Hou, *Foreign Investment and Economic Development in China*, 82.

6 Sikko Visscher, "'Merchants, Empires and Emperors': Global and Local Factors in Elite Composition and Elite Representation of Chinese Businessmen in Colonial

Singapore, 1819–1945," in *Entrepreneurs and Institutions in Europe and Asia, 1500–2000*, ed. Ferry de Goey and Jon Willem Veluwenkamp (Amsterdam: Askant Academic Publishers, 2002), 184; Robert F. Dernberger, "The Role of the Foreigner in China's Economic Development, 1840–1949," in *China's Modern Economy in Historical Perspective*, ed. Dwight H. Perkins (Stanford, CA: Stanford University Press, 1975), 42; Hou, *Foreign Investment and Economic Development in China*, 16, 53.

7 Hou, *Foreign Investment and Economic Development in China*, 16.

8 Marc Linder, *Projecting Capitalism: A History of the Internationalization of the Construction Industry* (Westport, CT: Greenwood, 1994), 64.

9 Hou, *Foreign Investment and Economic Development in China*, 18–19, 24–5, 63–5.

10 L.F. Haber, *The Chemical Industry, 1900–1930: International Growth and Technological Change* (Oxford: Clarendon, 1971), 184–5, 331–3.

11 Werner Abelshauser, Wolfgang von Hippel, Jeffrey Allan Johnson, and Raymond G. Stokes, *German Industry and Global Enterprise – BASF: The History of a Company* (Cambridge: Cambridge University Press, 2004), 83, 88, 96–7, 139–40, 161.

12 R.P.T. Davenport-Hines and Geoffrey Jones, "British Business in Japan since 1868," in *British Business in Asia since 1860*, ed. Davenport-Hines and Jones (Cambridge: Cambridge University Press, 1989), 223.

13 Davenport-Hines and Jones, "British Business in Japan since 1868," 217.

14 Davenport-Hines and Jones, "British Business in Japan since 1868," 217–18, 223–5.

15 Davenport-Hines and Geoffrey Jones, "British Business in Japan since 1868," 219; Thomas K. McCraw, ed., *American versus Japan* (Boston: Harvard Business School Press, 1986), 37.

16 Andrew Gordon, *A Modern History of Japan: From Tokugawa Times to the Present* (New York: Oxford University Press, 2003), 119.

17 Kazutoshi Maeda, "Business Activities of General Trading Companies," in *General Trading Companies: A Comparative and Historical Study*, ed. Shin'ichi Yonekawa (Tokyo: United Nations University Press, 1990), vi–vii.

18 Shin'ichi Yonekawa, "General Trading Companies in a Comparative Context," in *General Trading Companies: A Comparative and Historical Study*, ed. Shin'ichi Yonekawa (Tokyo: United Nations University Press, 1990), 33. By the Second World War, Mitsui Bussan was handling fully a quarter of Japan's foreign trade.

19 Maeda, "Business Activities of General Trading Companies," 35.

20 Tetsuya Kuwahara, "The Business Strategy of Japanese Cotton Spinners: Overseas Operations 1890–1931," in *The Textile Industry and Its Business Climate: Proceedings of the Fuji International Conference on Business History*, ed. Akio Okochi and Shin-ichi Yonekawa, 8:139–66 (Tokyo: University of Tokyo Press, 1982).

21 Mira Wilkins, *The Emergence of Multinational Enterprise: American Business Abroad from the Colonial Era to 1914* (Cambridge, MA: Harvard University Press, 1970), 94.

22 Davenport-Hines and Jones, "British Business in Japan since 1868," 225.
23 Gordon, *A Modern History of Japan*, 99.
24 Wilkins, *Emergence of Multinational Enterprise*, 91.
25 Davenport-Hines and Jones, "British Business in Japan since 1868," 225–6.
26 Gordon, *Modern History of Japan*, 115.
27 Michael J. Seth, *A Concise History of Modern Korea: From the Late Nineteenth Century to the Present* (Lanham, MD: Rowman & Littlefield Publishers, 2010), 13.
28 Seth, *Concise History of Modern Korea*, 14–19.
29 Seth, *Concise History of Modern Korea*, 28–9.
30 Seth, *Concise History of Modern Korea*, 29, 33–5, 37.
31 Jong-Tae Choi, "Business Climate and Industrialization of the Korean Fiber Industry," in *The Textile Industry and Its Business Climate: Proceedings of the Fuji International Conference on Business History,* ed. Akio Okochi and Shin-ichi Yonekawa, 8:249–54 (Tokyo: University of Tokyo Press, 1982).
32 Geoffrey Jones, *Multinationals and Global Capitalism: From the Nineteenth to the Twenty-First Century* (Oxford: Oxford University Press, 2005), 68.
33 Esko Heikkonen, *Reaping the Bounty: McCormick Harvesting Machine Company Turns Abroad, 1878–1902* (Helsinki: Finnish Historical Society, 1995), 138.

2 Print Capitalism and Material Culture: Technology Transfer in Early Twentieth-Century China

TZE-KI HON

For Chinese in the early twentieth century, the West may have been far away and separated by oceans, but it was a concrete reality that they were able to see, hear, feel, taste, and touch. To those who lived in or had visited a metropolis, e.g., Hong Kong and Shanghai, the West was on display in the conveniences of a city: department stores, coffee shops, dance halls, high-rises, horse-racing tracks, movie houses, neon lights, and trams.[1] Those who lived in rural areas were touched by the artifacts of a "Western lifestyle" as the transportation system expanded from the coast to the hinterland.[2] In short, to the Chinese, the West was synonymous with the "age of metal, steam, and chemistry" propelled by technology and machines. It was the "sound, light, heat, and power" that made the West alluring, energizing, and forward-looking.[3]

Among the Western technologies introduced into China, printing was particularly important because of the civil culture of the country. For thousands of years, printing was part of the civil service examination system to select the best and brightest men to serve in the imperial bureaucracy. To prepare for the examinations, the educated elites memorized classical texts and their commentaries. They (or their families) had to have access to copies of classical texts in order to be qualified as members of the literati. Hence, for a long time, there had been a "print market" and a "print culture" in China, where large numbers of skilled workers were employed in the print industry in major urban hubs such as Beijing, Hangzhou, Nanjing, and Kaifeng.[4] But until the nineteenth century, printing in China was done primarily by making impressions on paper with wooden blocks. Also known as xylography, wood-block printing satisfied the needs for printing thousands of Chinese characters at low cost.[5] Furthermore, the economy and flexibility of wood-block printing created a decentralized and unregulated printing industry that suited the loose structure of the Chinese imperial system.[6]

After the Opium War (1839–42), missionaries brought mechanized print technology into China to make copies of the Bible. Western print technology – especially lithography – spread from treaty ports to littoral areas as missionaries settled in the interior. From the 1870s to the 1900s, the "print market" of imperial China was gradually transformed into "print capitalism" as mechanized printing replaced wood-block printing as the preferred means of producing books, journals, and newspapers. As the variety of printed products proliferated, Chinese publishers widely adopted Western print technology, not only because of its speed and efficiency, but also because of the rapid expansion of the reader market that made the cost of importing foreign technology affordable.[7]

Simultaneously, China's transition to "print capitalism" was also a product of East Asian cultural networks. Technology transfer – first lithography and then letterpress – was not a direct transference of technology from Europe (the center) to East Asia (the periphery), but a circuitous, multifarious travel among East Asian cities.[8] This travel – involving dialogues between what was global and what was local – was especially significant during what Douglas Reynolds calls "the golden decade" (1895–1915) of Sino-Japanese relations. The period was "golden" not only because it was in sharp contrast to what happened later when the two countries went to war in the 1930s and 1940s. More importantly, it was "golden" because China and Japan were closely tied in a network of cultural and technological sharing to build an "East Asian modernity." Underlying this cultural and technological network was the belief that East Asia (encompassing China, Japan, and Korea) was a region with a unique culture that could achieve modernity equal to, and yet different from, Europe and the United States.[9] A major characteristic of this network was that it attempted to mimic the Western model on the one hand, and to assert an Asian uniqueness on the other.

To elucidate the complexity of technology transfer in early twentieth-century China, this chapter focuses on two presses in Shanghai: the Commercial Press (*Shangwu yinshuguan*, 1897–present) and the Press for the Association for the Preservation of National Learning (*Guoxue baocunhui yinshua suo*, 1905–11).[10] These presses were chosen partly because of their unique roles in the Shanghai publishing industry, the biggest in the country, and partly because of their different strategies for adopting foreign print technology to serve the Chinese market.

Established in 1897, the Commercial Press became the largest textbook publisher in China by the early twentieth century. In contrast, the Press of the Association for the Preservation of National Learning was a minor press serving a small circle of educated elites interested in ancient books and artwork. Despite their differences in clientele and market share, mechanized print technology allowed the two presses to produce large numbers of books, journals, and texts at lightning speed. Together, they demonstrate the wide range of readers that the modern Chinese printing industry served as Chinese society became increasingly fluid and diverse at the end of the imperial period. More significantly, the two presses show the paramount importance of the East Asian web of knowledge circulation when they relied on Japanese technology to compete in China's expanding print market.

Mechanized Printing

According to Bruce Billings, after European missionaries introduced mechanized printing to China in the early nineteenth century, it took half a century for the new print technology to spread.[11] This temporal gap was due to the process by which print technology was transferred from Europe to China. When the missionaries first introduced mechanized printing to China, they used it primarily to print the Bible and church publications.[12] Although some foreign experts, such as John Fryer, Alexander Wylie, and Young J. Allen, attempted to introduce mechanized printing to Chinese officials, their impact was limited. In contrast, Chinese workers at missionary presses turned out to be more effective in spreading mechanized print technology when they opened their own print shops after learning the skills. After the founding of the national school system in 1905, there were clear market demands for efficient and high-quality printing. Subsequently, Chinese businessmen were willing to invest huge sums of money in modernizing print technology.[13] To gain access to advanced print technology, some businessmen bought defunct missionary presses while others formed partnerships with publishers abroad. As a result, Western technology first gained a foothold in the foreign concessions on China's coast (such as Hong Kong, Macau, and Shanghai), and then gradually spread from the coast to the hinterland.[14]

As Christopher Reed points out, the transfer of print technology to China involved a complex process of matching foreign technology with local needs. According to Reed, three factors were crucial in deciding which type of technology was adopted and how that technology was modified to meet Chinese needs. First was typecasting, i.e., fashioning a mold or a matrix that could create imprints of Chinese characters. Second was media, i.e., whether the print was made on surfaces in relief (letterpress), surfaces that were planographic (lithography), or surfaces that were in intaglio (gravure printing, etching, engraving). Third was the press, i.e., whether the transfer from type to paper was done by pressing two flat surfaces (a typeform and a platon), one flat surface (typeform) and one curved surface (impression cylinder), or two curved surfaces (typeform and impression cylinder).[15]

These three factors were directly linked to the practical needs for printing Chinese characters that were pictorial, based on brush strokes. From the 1870s to the 1910s, Chinese publishers preferred lithography because of its resemblance to traditional wood-block printing and relative low cost. Altogether, seven forms of lithography were introduced to China from the 1840s to the 1930s: stone-based lithography, collotype, stone-based photolithography, stone-based chromolithography, tinplate, offset lithography, and facsimile.[16] All greatly affected the production of printed materials in China.

A major player in adopting lithography was the Commercial Press. Established in Shanghai in 1897 by four former workers in missionary presses, the Commercial Press began as a small company that served the Protestant community by printing fliers and notices.[17] Later, the Commercial Press expanded by incorporating a defunct Japanese press, the Press for Increasing Knowledge (*Guangwen shuguan*). Taking advantage of the increasing demand for Western learning in the late 1890s, the press made its name by printing English dictionaries and English grammar books. It also profited by reprinting popular Chinese classical and historical texts. Equipped with the best printing machines of the time, the press was able to print thousands of copies of a text with stunning clarity on short notice.[18] Like many owners of small presses, the four founders of the Commercial Press were part of a growing number of Chinese skilled laborers who successfully made the transition from "Bible printing" to commercial printing.[19]

In the early 1900s, the Commercial Press was transformed from a small and peripheral press into a giant printing house with deep international connections. From 1903 to 1914, the Commercial Press formed a partnership with Kinkōdō, a major Japanese textbook publisher. During their eleven-year partnership, the Commercial Press benefited from its Japanese partner by adopting its advanced print technology and its modern management techniques.[20] First, the Commercial Press was transformed into a corporation with hundreds of small investors governed by a board of directors. In so doing, it had the financial resources to import the most advanced print technologies from abroad, such as three-color relief media and tinplate planographic media.[21] Second, the press followed in Kinkōdō's footsteps by specializing in publishing textbooks. Through Kinkōdō, the company brought Japanese specialists and craftsmen to Shanghai. For instance, in 1905, the Commercial Press hired Japanese color lithography workers to improve the quality of its photolithographic production.[22] With the help of the Japanese workers, the Commercial Press quickly built a large production unit to publish textbooks.[23]

The company's decision to focus on the textbook market came at the most opportune time. In 1905, just two years after forming its partnership with Kinkōdō, the Qing government abolished the civil service examinations and began building a national school system. With a strong editorial board and an experienced team, the Commercial Press quickly won the lion's share of the textbook market, ensuring a constant flow of income. With its success in printing textbooks, the Commercial Press quickly dominated the Chinese print market.[24] Nevertheless, there was a drawback to its international collaboration. As the Chinese became sensitive to Japanese imperialism in the early 1910s, the Commercial Press had difficulty justifying its partnership with a Japanese

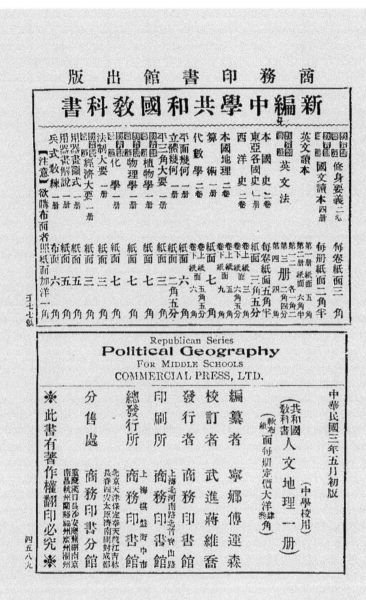

Figure 2.1. 1914 Commercial Press Advertisement Announcing the Publication of a
Series of Secondary School Textbooks for the New Republic of China

company. After several attempts to save the partnership, in 1914, the board of directors of the Commercial Press finally decided to split with Kinkōdō.[25]

In short, the success of the Commercial Press was testimony to the rapid expansion of the Chinese reader market at the turn of the twentieth century. The Commercial Press became a giant printing house when it monopolized the textbook market for the new national school system. The partnership with Kinkōdō certainly gave the press the advanced print technologies and the editing skills to defeat its competitors. But it was the press's decision to enter the textbook market early and its nationwide distribution network that consolidated its dominance.

Mechanized Printing and the New Educated Elite

A smaller but equally important printing company was the Press for the Association for the Preservation of National Essence. Owned by the Association for the Preservation of National Learning (*Guoxue baocunhui*), the press was located on Fourth Avenue (*simalu*) in Shanghai's Anglo-American Concession. In the early twentieth century, Fourth Avenue was known to the locals as "culture street" (*wenhua jie*) because of hundreds of retail outlets, trade associations, stationers, calligraphers, painters, printers, and shops selling the scholar's traditional "four treasures" (brushes, ink, inkstones, and paper). Because of its location, the Press for the Association for the Preservation of National Essence was a hub for writers, artists, calligraphers, painters, and print shop owners. It was part of the public realm of professionals developing in Chinese urban areas.[26]

Formed by workers previously employed at missionary presses, the press provided the main source of income for the Association for the Preservation of National Learning. The press's list of publications was long and included the *Journal of National Essence* (Guocui xuebao), the *Cathay Art Book* (Shenzhou guoguang ji), the *Collected Works of National Essence* (Guocui congshu), the *Collected Works of the Pavilion of Wind and Rain* (Fengyu lou congshu), and history and geography textbooks. From 1905 to 1911, the press altogether published fifteen volumes of the *Cathay Art Book*, hundreds of titles of reprinted writings, and several sets of textbooks for seven provinces.

As the list of publications shows, some of the press's publications were clearly for profit. For example, the *Cathay Art Book* and the *Collected Works of National Essence* were aimed at wealthy and cultured customers who could afford to pay high prices for refined and exotic works.[27] This was particularly true of the *Cathay Art Book*, which contained photo-reproductions of large-size works of art printed with the most advanced collotype printing technology imported from Japan.

A 1909 advertisement in the *Journal of National Essence* stated that the photoreproduction in the *Cathay Art Book* was so "close to real" (*bizhen*) that

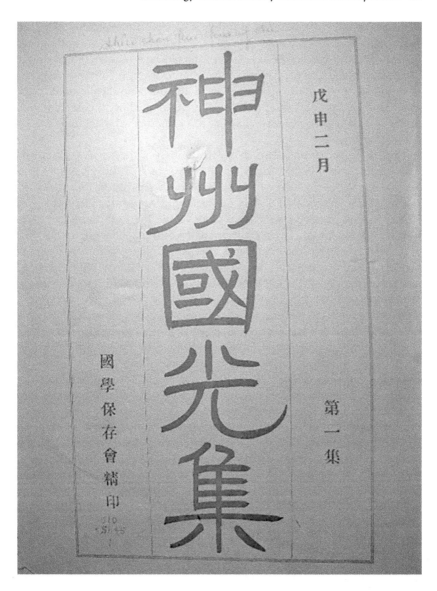

Figure 2.2. Cover Page of the First Issue of the *Cathay Art Book* (Shenzhou guoguang ji 神州國光集). On the Lower Left-hand Corner, the Editors Reminded Their Readers That the Reproduction of Paintings Was Sponsored by the Association for the Preservation of National Learning.

those who bought it would feel as if they possessed the original work of art. Partly selling commercial products and partly preserving ancient works of art, the *Cathay Art Book* catered to genteel customers who wanted to own a piece of art. As for the *Collected Works of National Essence*, it contained reprints of major literary and historical writings of authors from the eleventh to the nineteenth centuries. Most of the reprints were rare editions, banned books, or newly discovered manuscripts, intended to satisfy the bibliophilic interest of the genteel class.

This list of publications also shows that not all of the press's publications were expected to be highly profitable. From 1905 to 1907, the press published textbooks for seven provinces, including subjects such as history, geography, literature, ethics, and classical studies.[28] Considering the fact that there were only eighteen administrative provinces in Qing China, the press essentially published textbooks for more than one-third of the country. More importantly, the press published textbooks immediately after the Manchu government issued its plans for building a national school system in 1904. For a short while, the press was a major player in the textbook market, competing with the Commercial Press in supplying textbooks to the new school system.

The crown jewel of the press was the publication of the *Journal of National Essence* (Guocui xuebao). In six years, from 1905 to 1911, the press used mechanized printing technology to print hundreds of copies of the journal monthly. Combining classical scholarship with art connoisseurship, the *Journal of National Essence* stood out for its high print quality and its clear reproduction of works of art and artifacts. More significantly, the journal aimed to win support of the educated elite who were disillusioned by the abolition of the civil service examinations in 1905. The journal published three genres of writing. First was short essays written in an argumentative style intended to persuade readers to adopt a certain perspective. Usually the theme was the moral responsibility of the learned community to save the Chinese race, to defend the Chinese nation, and to preserve Chinese culture. Occasionally, the writings offered rebuttal to current viewpoints, such as the "uselessness" (*wuyong*) of classical learning and the adoption of Esperanto or *shijie yu* in China. Second was longer, more detailed articles that occasionally had to be serialized for months because of their length. Historically and textually grounded, the long articles offered new accounts of historical events and new interpretations of philosophical writings to support arguments in the short essays. Last was poems and excerpts, which were short but artistic, intended to suit the aesthetic taste of the educated elite. They were often written by established cultural figures. To show that the journal was neutral to academic debates, it included writing by different groups of scholars, such as the Old Script School scholars (such as Zhang Taiyan and Liu Shipei) and the New Script School scholars (such as Liao Ping and Wang Kaiyun).

Figure 2.3. Title Page (*left*) and Back Cover (*right*) of *Guocui xuebao* 11 (1908). On the Back Cover, Readers Were Urged to Subscribe to the Journal.

Every issue of the journal was accompanied by illustrations (paintings, draw-ings, and calligraphy) that were reprinted with the most advanced printing technology from Japan. The visual art in the journal was not just to provide illustrations, it had two important functions. First was to demonstrate that the journal had the full support of academic and art circles. For example, in February 1908, the editors published a series of calligraphies and paintings by established scholars to celebrate the journal's third-year anniversary. The sec-ond reason was to include art in the discourse of the nation so that "national art" (*guohua*) would be an expression of the nation. In the final two years of the journal's existence, from 1909 to 1911, the editors went even further, promoting art and literature. They rearranged sections in the journal so that it included special sections on art and the history of aesthetics.

All in all, the success of the Press for the Society of National Glory demon-strates the close relation between technology transfer and social change. First, by publishing the *Journal of National Essence,* the press targeted educated indi-viduals who were both perplexed and enticed by the founding of the national school system. Replacing the civil service examinations that had defined literati culture for centuries, the national school system provided modern professional training to tens of thousands of young students, and thereby created a huge market for textbooks and supplementary readings.[29] With hundreds of copies circulating every month, the journal directly benefited from the new technology of mechanized printing and sprawling nationwide distribution networks. The journal produced what Joan Judge calls the "middle realm" in modern Chinese society, i.e., journalists, editors, columnists, academicians, and school teachers, who became the new leaders in political discourse.[30] As such, the journal exemplified a momentous change in early twentieth-century Chinese society in which the old literati (who served the imperial dynasty) gave way to a new generation of intellectuals (who competed in the cultural market).[31]

Technology Transfer and Material Culture

As shown in these two examples, the introduction of mechanized printing to China was more than technological advancement or the displacement of traditional and family-based production by modern, industrial, and machine-based production. Instead, technology transfer was facilitated by a creative mixing of foreign and local factors. A case in point was the choice of lithography as the preferred print technology. The decision was not made by government officials or business elites. It was through trial and error that Chinese publishers discovered that lithography was "a culturally sensitive compromise between the limitations of both Chinese xylography and imported typography."[32]

In the same vein, the technology of mechanized printing was disseminated in China not by foreign firms or transnational corporations, but through the local network of knowledge circulation. First introduced into China by missionaries, lithography was modified and reinvented by Chinese publishers to make the printing process more efficient. In streamlining the production line, Chinese publishers such as the Commercial Press not only reduced the cost of production, but also greatly increased the speed and the scale of production.

More significantly, the Chinese adoption of mechanized printing was a result of the expansion of the reader market. As shown in the rapid rise of the Commercial Press, the 1905 decision by the Qing government to replace the civil service examinations with a national school system led directly to the expansion of the reader market. In a short span of time, millions of students became eager customers wanting to buy the most current textbooks and the most advanced supplementary readings. Concurrently, the abolition of the civil service examinations drastically changed the lives of the literati, who had to reinvent themselves in the new social matrix. As shown in the brief success of the Press of the Association for Preserving National Learning, some of the aspiring literati found new jobs in the publishing industry as publishers, editors, and opinion leaders; others reinvented themselves as teachers and textbook writers;

yet others found employment in reproducing ancient texts and selling copied paintings.

Amazingly, all this happened within half a century. Mechanized printing took off in China around 1870 and reached its peak in the 1910s. In these four decades, Chinese publishers and readers enthusiastically accepted mechanized printing as an emblem of the West. They did not care whether the technology came from France, Germany, Great Britain, or the United States. What they cared about was whether the technology worked. As things turned out, of the print technologies that were available at the time, Chinese publishers and readers fell in love with lithography, not only because it was efficient, but because it worked well with traditional xylography and appealed to readers' cultural tastes.

NOTES

1 Leo Ou-fan Lee vividly describes the material presence of the West in China in his portrayal of early twentieth-century Shanghai. See *Shanghai Modern: The Flowering of a New Urban Culture in China, 1930–1945* (Cambridge, MA: Harvard University Press, 1999), 3–42.

2 For a discussion of how the expansion of the transportation system and communication network helped connect coastal cities to the hinterland, see Chen Zhengshu, "*Yanjiang chengshi jiaotong jiegou jindaihua* [The modernization of the structure of transportation in cities along the Yangzi River]," in *Changjiang yuanjiang chengshi yu Zhongguo jindaihua* [Cities along the Yangzhi River and Chinese Modernization], ed. Zhang Zhongli, Xiong Yuezhi, and Shen Zuwei, 272–315 (Shanghai: Shanghai renmin chubanshe, 2002).

3 From the late nineteenth century to the early twentieth century, the Chinese expressed their awe and admiration of Western technology by calling it *shengguang huadian* (sound, light, heat, and power). This expression captured the Chinese fascination with the transformative power of technology that altered their way of life and mode of thinking. For a discussion of the transformative power of technology in relation to Cantonese opera and the cultural matrix of the Pearl River Delta in the early twentieth century, see Rong Shicheng, *Xunmi yueju shengying: Cong hongchuan dao shuiyindeng* [In search of the sound and shape of Cantonese opera: From red boat to movie camera], (Hong Kong: Oxford University Press, 2012), 1–28.

4 The civil service examination system was pivotal to imperial power. It was the vehicle through which imperial power reached to the lowest levels of the empire and created legitimacy of rule. For a discussion of the relation of imperial power, cultural politics, and civil service examinations, see Benjamin Elman, *A Cultural History of Civil Examinations in Late Imperial China* (Berkeley: University of

California Press, 2000), 66–124. For a study of how the examinations helped the expansion of "print culture" and "print market," see Christopher A. Reed, *Gutenberg in Shanghai: Chinese Print Capitalism, 1876–1934* (Honolulu: University of Hawaii Press, 2004), 1–12.

5 Cynthia J. Brokaw, "Introduction: On the History of the Books in China," in *Printing and Book Culture in Late Imperial China*, ed. Cynthia J. Brokaw and Kai-wing Chow, 8–9 (Berkeley: University of California Press, 2005).

6 Brokaw, *Printing and Book Culture*, 9–10. For the rise of a new type of cultural businessman due to the expansion of the print market in late imperial China, see Kai-wing Chow, *Publishing, Culture, and Power in Early Modern China* (Stanford, CA: Stanford University Press 2004), 1–18, 241–51.

7 Reed, *Gutenberg in Shanghai*, 12–22. The introduction of mechanized print technology also helped create a new genre of printed matter – the newspaper. See Barbara Mittler, *A Newspaper for China? Power, Identity, and Changes in Shanghai's News Media, 1872–1912* (Cambridge, MA: Harvard East Asian Monograph 2004).

8 Regarding the transnational travel of knowledge in East Asia, see Lydia H. Liu, *Translingual Practice: Literature, National Culture, and Translated Modernity – China 1900–1937* (Stanford, CA: Stanford University Press, 1995), 1–44.

9 Douglas R. Reynolds, *China, 1898–1912: The Xinzheng Revolution and Japan* (Cambridge, MA: Council on East Studies, Harvard University, 1993), 1–14, 111–26.

10 This chapter is drawn from my research on early twentieth-century Chinese modernity. For a more detailed discussion of the role of print capitalism in shaping the social and cultural landscape of modern China, see Tze-ki Hon, *Revolution as Restoration: Guocui xuebao and China's Path to Modernity, 1905–1911* (Leiden: Brill, 2013), esp. chaps., 1 and 2; and "Technology, Markets, and Social Change: Print Capitalism in Early Twentieth Century," in *Print, Profit, and Perception: Information Production and Knowledge Transmission in Chinese Societies, 1895–1949*, ed. Peiyin Lin and Weipin Tsai, 92–123 (Leiden: Brill, 2014).

11 Bruce H. Billings, *China and the West: Information Technology Transfer from Printing Press to Computer Era* (Taipei: Standard Printing Corporation, 1997), 17–68.

12 For the role of the missionaries in introducing print technology to China, see Reed, *Gutenberg in Shanghai*, 29–32; Billings, *China and the West*, 58. See also Joseph P. McDermott, *The Social History of the Book in China: Books and Literati Culture in Late Imperial China* (Hong Kong: Hong Kong University Press, 2006), 14–15, 24.

13 For more about the spread of printing presses from 1898 to 1911, see Li Renyuan, *Wanching de xinshi chuanbo meiti yu zhishi fenzi: Yi baokan chuban wei zhongxin de taolun* [The modern mass media in late Qing and the intellectuals: A study of the publishing of newspapers] (Taipei: Daoxiang chubenshe, 2005), 5, 1–19, 213–87.

14 See Li Renyuan, *Wanqing de xinshi chuanbo*, 5, 213–87.

15 Reed, *Gutenberg in Shanghai*, 27–52.

16 Reed, *Gutenberg in Shanghai*, 28–9, esp. table 1.1.

17 Li Jiaju, *Shangwu yinshuguan yu jindai zhishi wenhua de chuanbo* [The commercial press and the dissemination of modern knowledge and culture] (Beijing: Commercial, 2005), 27–34.

18 Li Jiaju, *Shangwu yinshuguan yu jindai zhishi wenhua de chuanbo*, 43–4.

19 Dai Ren (Jean-Pierre Drege), *Shanghai Shangwu Yinshuguan 1897–1949* [The Shanghai Commercial Press 1897–1949] (Beijing: Commercial, 2000), 7–26.

20 Tarumoto Teruo, *Shoki Shoimu inshokan kenkyū* [A study of the early Commercial Press] (Shiga-ken, ōtsu-shi: Shimatsu Shōsetsu kenkyū, 2000), 148–201.

21 Li Jiaju, *Shangwu yinshuguan*, 50–60. For the technologies imported from abroad, see Reed, *Gutenberg in Shanghai*, 28–9, table 1.1.

22 Li Jiaju, *Shangwu yinshuguan*, 62.

23 Li Jiaju, *Shangwu yinshuguan*, 38–9, 54–60.

24 Li Jiaju, *Shangwu yinshuguan*, 54–60; Li Renyuan, *Wanqing de xinshi chuanbo*, 5, 281–4; Tarumoto Teruo, *Shoki Shoimu inshokan kenkyū*, 237–72.

25 Li Jiaju, *Shangwu yinshuguan*, 50–1.

26 Reed, *Gutenberg in Shangai*, 16–18, 188–99; Li Renyuan, *Wanching de xinshi chuanbo metiti*, 213–24.

27 For the publication of *Cathay Art Book*, see the advertisements for *Cathay Art Book* in *Guocui xuebao* 41–70 (1908–10). For some of the titles of reprinted texts, see the advertisements for the first volume of *Guocui congshu* in *Guocui xuebao* 27 (1907) and the first volume of *Fengyu lou congshu* in *Guocui xuebao* 69 (1910).

28 For the publication of school textbooks, see the advertisement in *Guocui xuebao* 28 (1907).

29 For a discussion of how the founding of the national school system affected the print market, see the chapters by Peter Zarrow, May-bo Chang, and Tze-ki Hon in *The Politics of Historical Production in Late Qing and Republican China*, ed. Tze-ki Hon and Robert J. Culp (Leiden, Brill, 2007), 21–105.

30 Joan Judge, *Print and Culture: "Shibao" and the Culture of Reform in Late Qing China* (Stanford, CA: Stanford University Press, 1996), 17–31.

31 For a discussion of this change from literati to intellectuals, see Xu Jilin, *20 shiji Zhongguo zhishi fenzi shilun* [A study of the history of the twentieth-century Chinese intellectuals] (Beijing: Xinxing chubanshe, 2005), 1–4.

32 Reed, *Gutenberg in Shanghai*, 27.

3 The Essence of Being Modern: Indigenous Knowledge and Technology Transfer in Meiji Japan

DAVID G. WITTNER

In 1869, Japan's new Meiji government was faced with a dilemma: the quality of Japan's raw silk – its most important and valuable export commodity – had declined, much to the displeasure of the foreign merchant community. To remedy the problem, foreign merchant houses proposed establishing a model filature for the Japanese, an idea promptly rejected by government officials who feared losing further control of the infant internationalizing economy. Faced with mounting complaints and anxious over the potential loss of essential export revenues, however, Vice Minister of Finance Itō Hirobumi convinced his government that it needed to go into the silk reeling business. This is the genesis of Tomioka Silk Mill. Named a UNESCO World Heritage site in 2014, Tomioka more than symbolized the modernizing state; it *was* Japan's icon of industrial modernity, and set the national standard for industrial modernization. What makes the Tomioka story important is that it reveals an understudied aspect of technology transfer– technological choice determined by cultural symbolism. At Tomioka and numerous other early Meiji era industrial sites seeking to exude "modernity," factory design and the selection of industrial machinery often had little to do with studies of economic or technological efficiency. With time and a more developed understanding of how technologies transfer, however, looking "modern" gave way to being "modern."

In what follows, I discuss the transfer of Western industrial silk reeling technologies at Tomioka during the mid-nineteenth century to show that Japanese officials' choices of technologies were often determined by less-than-technical factors. I will then compare some of the patterns for technological choice in the silk reeling industry with parallel experiences in Japan's first venture into the Western-style paper manufacturing industry at Shōshi Kaisha to illustrate how practical experience and embedded beliefs in the cultural value of technological artifacts slowly gave way to more practical considerations for industrial development.

By the 1880s, Japan was well on its way toward becoming a technological nation in every sense of the word. Although foreign machinery continued to flow into Japan, engineers trained at home and abroad rapidly replaced foreign advisers, and local craftsmen continued to develop indigenous technologies well-suited to industrial production. Japan's movement toward the absorption and translation of complete technological systems is seen, in part, through increased government and private efforts to create indigenous sources of technical knowledge.[1] The founding of the Osaka Cotton Spinning Mill will illustrate this point. Rather than simply importing foreign technology and hiring foreign advisers, the mill was an indigenous technological system based on Japanese knowledge and the importation of foreign technological artifacts.

Importing Modernity: Silk Reeling and Tomioka Filature

Throughout the late 1860s, the new Meiji government was faced with a potential financial crisis.[2] The quality of Japan's raw silk had been declining because of increased production and a misguided entrepreneurial spirit that opted for quantity over quality. The foreign merchant community in Yokohama had already started lodging protests with government officials, such as then Vice Minister of Finance Itō Hirobumi, about the poor quality of Japan's raw silk. Some silk exporters went further and offered the government a potential solution to Japan's silk troubles, the creation of a model filature where silk reelers could observe, learn, and adopt Western reeling techniques.

After initially rejecting the foreign proposal, Itō eventually came around to the idea of creating a model filature and persuaded other government officials, including Shibusawa Eiichi, the "father of modern Japanese capitalism," of the importance of such a project. As if laying the groundwork for the dissemination of foreign reeling technologies and placing responsibility with the private sector, the government issued a directive stating that Japan lacked quality reeling machinery and that merchants should adopt and distribute European-style reeling machines.[3] At the same time, however, Itō and Shibusawa began the search for foreign and domestic advisers who could help the government with its filature project.[4] Through a series of personal connections, Itō and Shibusawa were eventually introduced to Paul Brunat, a Frenchman working for the silk wholesaler Hècht, Lilienthal, and Company in Yokohama. The pair eventually hired Brunat, who put together a practical proposal for a filature.

Brunat had practical, technical experience in the silk industry and understood the difficulties associated with technological choice and technology transfer. If he wanted state-of-the-art technology, his choices were limited. The best Western reeling technologies were Italian and French, with the former being less complex and more flexible to the potential demands of a growing industry. Both Italian and French technologies were used for producing high-quality raw silk, but the Italian methods were more adaptable to the Japanese

Figure 3.1. Paul Brunat (*second from right, top row, in white jacket*) and French Workers at Tomioka Filature

Source: Courtesy Tomioka Silk Mill.

situation, as evidenced by earlier *han* (domain) and private initiatives that married Italian reeling technologies to Japanese machinery.

In actuality, Brunat saw state-of-the-art as neither practical nor desirable. He recommended that the new filature blend the best of Western and Japanese technologies – a rather commonsensical approach. Toward that end, he and Odaka Atsutada, the man eventually responsible for day-to-day operations at Tomioka, toured present-day Gunma, Saitama, and Nagano prefectures to observe the state of Japan's silk reeling industry.[5] The pair visited traditional Japanese filatures as well as newer facilities using Western or Western-Japanese hybrid reeling technologies.

In July 1870, Brunat and Odaka arrived at Japan's first Western-style filature in Maebashi run by Hayami Kensō to examine locally manufactured reeling frames that were based on Italian designs.[6] Following what would be the early standard for technology transfer in the silk reeling industry, Hayami sought and found a foreign reeling adviser with whom to collaborate. With his adviser Casper Mueller, Hayami hired local craftsmen to build Japanese-Italian hybrid reeling frames that became the basis of the new improved filature.

Figure 3.2. Hayami Kensō

Source: *Hayami Kensō, Kito kairyo no kaketa shogai: kanei Tomioka seishijocho Hayami Kensō, jiden no nikki no gendai goyaku* [A lifetime of improving silk: Hayami Kensō, director of the government-owned Tomioka silk mill, a modern translation of his autobiography and diary] (Tokyo: Idabashi Papirusu, 2014).

Brunat recommended that the government use machinery that was similar to what was being used at Maebashi, only updated to include the latest technological improvements.[7] With this in mind, Brunat and Odaka conducted tests that helped the pair verify that high-quality silk could be reeled on machines similar to ones made by local artisans for Hayami's Maebashi Filature. Despite Odaka's comments that Maebashi's machines appeared to be insubstantial,[8] the men were impressed with the quality of the silk they produced and commented that a filature like Maebashi was what the government should build. In fact, the men visited Maebashi Filature specifically *because* it was very much what government officials apparently had in mind.

Figure 3.3. Odaka Atsutada

Source: Courtesy Tomioka Silk Mill.

Four months later Brunat submitted his proposal to the Meiji government.[9] Although he recommended building a large facility and using steam
power, he specifically advised against relying on imported reeling machinery.
He believed that the silk reeling industry would be better served by hybrid-
izing Japanese and Western technologies. Making incremental changes to
Japanese methods, he argued, would provide greater benefit to the industry.
Gradual change would also limit financial risk and potential labor problems.[10] In short, the government should follow Maebashi's lead in reeling
frame selection.

Rather than importing machinery from Europe, Brunat stated that the
person responsible for building the machinery should be sent to Europe to

evaluate the pros and cons of Western processes.[11] Only beneficial Western technologies should be hybridized with Japanese reeling machines. With the exception of a steam boiler and steam engine that were beyond Japan's early industrial capabilities, Brunat argued, all the reeling machinery should be manufactured in Japan, under Western supervision, and made from locally available materials.[12]

Meiji officials partially accepted Brunat's recommendations. There were, however, several significant changes. Brunat received government approval to undertake another survey of Japan's silk-producing regions in order to determine the best location for the mill. His plan to substitute steam power for a waterwheel and to hire French women to serve as reeling instructors was also approved. With little or no discussion, however, his recommendation for locally produced, hybrid machinery was summarily rejected. He was ordered to return to France and was told to buy all the machinery necessary for the government's new filature. Despite the fact that most French filatures had abandoned orthodox French reeling technologies in favor of French-Italian hybrids, and that all of Japan's Western-style filatures used machinery based on Italian or Italian-Japanese designs, the Meiji government's filature would strictly rely on French technology. Brunat's recommendations on the size and layout of the mill's physical space were accepted, but the government decided on the materials for its construction – brick – an uncommon commodity in rural Japan that at the time was just making its appearance in Tokyo and Yokohama.

Upon learning of the government's plans, Hayami, the father of Japan's modern silk reeling industry, was dismayed. He not only questioned the government's plans, but also whether Brunat was actually qualified.[13] And Brunat was not the only person with whom Hayami would disagree. Under orders from then Commissioner of Revenue Matsukata Masayoshi, Hayami and Shibusawa Eiichi were sent to visit several filatures and formulate a joint report with recommendations on how to improve Japan's raw silk industry. Hayami was a proponent of locally produced hybrid machinery, of limiting the role of foreign advisers, and of industrial self-reliance.[14] Shibusawa's world perspective and vision for industry was greater. Small scale and using machines that Odaka called *gatagata* (rickety) was not what he had in mind.[15] The government's filature and machinery needed to be more "modern." And the two men failed to agree. Although Hayami's views were ultimately presented in the report to Matsukata, Shibusawa's vision built Tomioka.

The question then is why Japanese officials chose to ignore at least two men (Brunat and Hayami) who had significant technical experience in the silk reeling industry, opting to build a filature using potentially impractical and controversial technologies. Other than to demonstrate that the government was in control of its technological future, and that it actually had options in accepting foreign advice, why ignore evidence that supported a more appropriate techno-logical choice?

There are several theoretically practical reasons why government officials opted for French technologies. First and simplest, Brunat was French. His expe-rience was in the French reeling industry and his Lyons-based employer, Hècht, Lilienthal, and Company, was the firm through which the Meiji government had contracted to import all its reeling equipment. The Japanese government also had significantly greater political and economic ties to France than Italy. One could argue that the new government was simply being politic with its decisions.

It may have been more "diplomatically correct" for the government to send Brunat to France with instructions to purchase and import a turnkey French filature. Relying on orthodox French reeling technologies, however, was more problematic. French reelers had largely abandoned orthodox French tech-nologies in favor of hybridized French-Italian methods. By the 1870s, Italian reeling methods had been adopted throughout Europe and were considered to be decidedly superior.[16] The primary technological difference between the Italian and French methods that applied to choice of technologies in Japan was *croisure*. Invented in the late eighteenth century, this is the process by which the reeled threads were crossed over one another to remove water from the thread and strengthen it. The French method, *chambon*, and the Italian method, *tavelle* or *tavelette*, spread rapidly throughout the silk producing regions of Europe during the first half of the nineteenth century until the shortcomings of the *chambon* method became widely known.[17] Beyond being more technically complex, *chambon* also limited the number of threads that could be reeled per machine.[18] At the time Tomioka was being designed and built, the typical European filature – and all others in Japan employing West-ern technology – relied on the *tavelle* or *tavelette* method of *croisure*.[19] Brunat, Hayami, and men associated with the Japanese government with knowledge of silk reeling all knew this, yet some government officials insisted on utiliz-ing strictly French methods.

Given that government officials knew that there were better technologies available for their model filature, it appears that neither technological ratio-nality nor economics was a determinant for choice of technique. In fact, alternative factors typically less identified with technological choice guided the government's decisions. Choice of technique and the subsequent transfer of industrial technologies were based on an understanding of the cultural values embodied within technological artifacts. Following this belief, tech-nologies were selected so that the government's filature would demonstrate "progress," "civilization," and "modernity." Technological artifacts would set Japan apart from its Asian neighbors and eventually "lesser" European countries.

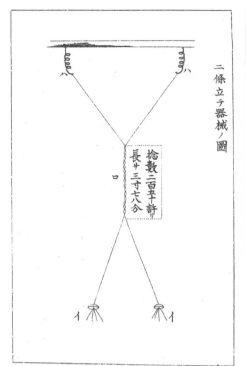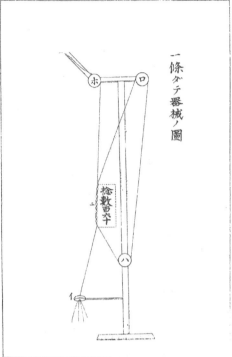

Figure 3.4. *Chambon* (*left*) and *Tavelle* (*right*) Methods of *Croisure*

Source: Itō Moemon, *Chūgai sanji yōroku* [Digest of domestic and foreign silkworms] (Tokyo: Itō Moemon, 1886), 547, 549.

As far as Tomioka's designers were concerned, all European (reeling) technologies were not created equal. Their judgment, however, was not based on technical assessment, it was a cultural or symbolic evaluation. Following observations on trips to Europe from 1866 through 1867 and the ongoing Iwakura Mission (1871–3), European countries – just like the non-European world – were not considered equal. Shibusawa and Itō, among others, identified an obvious hierarchy of European nations, with countries such as Great Britain and France at the top, Italy, Belgium, Switzerland, Holland, and Spain falling further down the ladder.

What separated the "modern" and "civilized" from "traditional" and "uncivilized" or "savage" was industry, material wealth, and one's predilection for technological development. Industrial nations *were* "modern" nations. Beginning with the Industrial Revolution, Western Europeans (and later Americans) began to differentiate themselves from the rest of the world on the basis of scientific and technological achievement. Rather than being fields of study, science and technology in the nineteenth century became the basis for cultural comparison.[20] Criteria such as miles of railroad track and degree of industrialization objectivized the standard by which Europeans judged their superiority.[21] By the time Japan re-entered the world scene in 1854, the belief that science and technology determined a country's "level of civilization" was long accepted. A corollary to technological achievement – material wealth – further demonstrated the "progress" of European countries over the non-West.[22] If ever the phrase "He who dies with the most toys wins" had global cultural significance, it was during the Victorian era. This was a fact of which the Japanese became rapidly aware.

Beginning with his 1866–7 trip to France – and as noted in Kimura Masato's contribution to this volume – Shibusawa learned the importance of technological artifacts in determining a country's "level of civilization." He and Sugiura Yuzuru traveled extensively and were able to observe Europe's technological hierarchy of nations firsthand.[23] In France, the men traveled by train – a fully modern mode of transportation. In Italy, they commented that their mode of transportation had been reduced to a less-than-modern horse-drawn carriage.[24] They spoke of France and French industry in glowing terms. The Swiss silk industry was quaint, i.e., traditional, and Italy's silk industry was altogether excluded from their travel diary in favor of uncomplimentary remarks about ongoing political problems related to unification. Comments on Italian industry in general paled in comparison to discussions of the French.[25]

Above all, Shibusawa and Sugiura were most impressed at the Fifth International Exhibition in Paris. As Jeffer Daykin notes in his chapter, it was an event that only served to reinforce the (technological) hierarchy of nations. If for no other reason, Shibusawa was in awe at the sheer size and volume of France's contributions to the exhibition, fully one-half. Other countries such as Italy, Holland, and Switzerland contributed a mere thirty-second combined![26] Shibusawa's observations were not limited to the exhibition space and France's industrial achievements. Its high-quality products, city streets, and use of paper money fully impressed the traveler,[27] and these were all things Japan needed if it too was to be a "modern" nation.

Shibusawa returned from his trip to Europe to find a new Japan in the making. The Tokugawa government collapsed in May 1868, and despite his best efforts to remain out of the fray, he accepted a position as chief of the new government's Taxation Bureau. Shibusawa initially intended to remain in the private sector, but his overseas experience, disdain for Japan's "feudal" past, and efforts to develop a modern Japanese economy illustrate his intrinsic nationalism and desire to reformulate Japan into a "modern" nation. For him, it was essential that the government's filature rise above anything established by domain authorities or the private sector.[28] In a world where "modern" technologies made "modern" nations, Tomioka Filature could not be simply another factory. Tomioka had to demonstrate Japan's "level of civilization" and the legitimacy of the new Meiji government.

Hayami's Maebashi Filature was a fully functional filature capable of producing high-quality silk. It relied on European hybrid machinery, served as a model factory and training ground for reelers from other parts of Japan, and had technologies that were widely copied and disseminated. Eventually the mill was internationally recognized for high-quality silk. Maebashi Filature, however, was not "modern." The initial mill was small, even after the factory was expanded.[29] The mill building was a traditional-style Japanese structure made of wood. The only difference between the Maebashi Filature and a traditional *zaguri* mill was the machinery – which was based on improved traditional designs.

The problem with following Hayami's and Brunat's advice on building hybrid machines was that they were unimpressive. Made of wood and appearing flimsy, they were too traditional and failed to embody the Victorian values of strength and permanence found in iron machinery. If the government was going to build a model factory, men like Shibusawa and Itō would not allow it to demonstrate anything that reeked of tradition. It was essential that the government's model factory be "modern," and this determined which technologies would be adopted at Tomioka. Regardless of practicality, Tomioka would be built from brick and its machines iron.

It is in some ways ironic that the government's filature, which was theoretically designed to facilitate the dissemination of superior reeling technologies, was the only filature in Japan to use French methods. Despite frequent claims to the contrary, all other Western-style filatures in Japan relied on Italian-based technologies. Traditional Japanese filatures, or those using so-called improved methods, were housed in wooden buildings, used wooden machinery, the *tavelette* method of *croisure*, and either hand or water power to turn the machines.[30] By the 1880s, many reelers adopted the use of steam to heat the water used in the reeling process, but few made the jump to steam power until the turn of the century or beyond. Simply put, Tomioka's technologies were beyond the financial and technological capabilities of the majority of Japan's entrepreneurs.

Tomioka's greatest value to Japan is not found in the transfer of appropriate technologies that could be disseminated to the private sector. Nor was it a model of economic efficiency. Rather, the cultural symbolism associated with Tomioka's technological artifacts proved to be its greatest asset. The amalgamation of iron, brick, and steam-powered artifacts into Japan's technological landscape made the government's filature an exemplar of "modernity," "progress," and "civilization." Its very existence allowed Japan to become for many European or American observers the premier Asian nation.[31] Through its adoption of Western technologies and exhibition culture, Japan was seen as following the West's lead by enthusiastically embracing its science and technology.

Following the 1873 International Exhibition in Vienna, Tomioka became the centerpiece of Japanese modernization. Japanese silk won fourteen medals, and the government was presented with a Medal of Honor for its efforts to improve silk production.[32] It did not matter that silk reeled at Maebashi and the government's other filature in Akasaka were included in the medal count. Tomioka was the object of official praise because it alone demonstrated a level of "modernity" and "civilization" not embodied in the other filatures. Silk reelers from all over Japan flocked to Tomioka to study the mill. The empress and empress dowager, not to mention a variety of other government officials, also visited the filature. With each visit the aura of Japan's "modern" silk mill grew. Tomioka's technologies were an ideal – they were artifacts that could be embraced but not attained by the private sector. In fact, Tomioka's aura was really all that many private sector reelers wanted to embrace. Their silk mills, whether traditional or Japanese-Italian hybrid, were capable of producing high-quality raw silk. It was their reputations that could benefit from an infusion of Tomioka's "modernity."

The importance of being "modern" did not end with Tomioka. It guided industrial policy, public works projects, and some private business initiatives until the end of the century. The government's other industrial ventures – its ironworks, mines, factories, mills, and shipyards, not to mention railroads – all relied on the most "modern" technologies, or technologies that were believed to be the most "modern." Arguably practical in some instances, some projects such as the railroads were built specifically because they would demonstrate the state's authority and were the hallmarks of "civilization and enlightenment" and a "modern" nation.[33]

Behind the scenes, Tomoika was not without its problems. In its desire to be "modern," the government failed to see the big picture of industrialization. No one considered who would actually work at the mill, from whence raw materials would be procured, and what type of factory organization system was appropriate for rural Japan. The only thing the mill could count on was a government revenue stream, and that depended on someone in power defending its purpose, which was often ill-defined. By and large, Tomioka failed as a model of economic efficiency, taking nearly two decades before it was self-reliant and profitable. During its time as a government-owned filature, one thing that Shibusawa and Itō began to understand, however, was the value of acquired technological knowledge.

Figure 3.5. Tomioka Filature ca. 1876, Hasegawa Chikuyo Print

Source: http://archive.wul.waseda.ac.jp/kosho/chi05/chi05_04104/chi05_04104_p0001.jpg.

Of Paper and Pulp, Transforming Technology Transfer

At the same time that the government was building Tomioka, Shibusawa was setting his sights on another strategic industry, *yōshi* or Western-style paper manufacturing. Shibusawa believed that the West's successful "cultural and scientific development" was tied to higher education. It followed that if Japan was to develop into a "modern" nation it needed a printing industry for books and newspapers, and that required paper.[34] Shibusawa convinced Inoue Kaoru, who followed Itō as vice minister of finance, of the importance of establishing paper and pulp industries. After receiving government permission and limited finances, Shibusawa convinced several *zaibatsu* – Mitsui, Ono, Furukawa, and Shimada – to help capitalize the venture. Shibusawa was not alone in his interest in paper manufacturing. Corresponding to a temporary decline in the silk trade,[35] Western merchants sought additional sources of revenue, and paper manufacturing seemed attractive.[36]

The project began in much the same way as Tomioka, and Shibusawa's experiences at Shōshi Kaisha, the company that would become Oji Paper in 1893, only reinforced his understanding of the relationships between technology, "modernity," and technical knowledge. Established in 1873, Shōshi Kaisha was Japan's first successful venture in machine production of Western-style paper.[37] After making the proper contacts, Shibusawa imported paper-making machinery from a British firm, James Bertram & Son, Ltd., with the help of Walsh, Hall, & Company, the leading American trading company operating in Yokohama.[38] Upon its arrival at Oji, a Tokyo suburb, the machinery was installed by a British mechanic and an American mechanical engineer with Japanese assistants – a pattern familiar to early Japanese industrial ventures, whether public or private. The foreign workers proved unable to properly install the machinery for some time, and the mill's Japanese workers were too inexperienced to be of much help. Legend has it that Shibusawa called the foreigners to his office with the intention of firing them. The pair pleaded and eventually convinced Shibusawa that they would get the job done correctly and in short order. They appear to have been successful, but following their departure, the mill still struggled to produce quality paper.

Shōshi Kaisha failed to be profitable for its investors for several reasons, including high production costs, little domestic demand, and technological inefficiencies.[39] Even as demand grew, the mill continued to produce paper of poor quality and failed to improve production efficiency.[40] In an effort to develop Japan's own source of "modern" technological knowledge, Shibusawa sent Ōkawa Heizaburō to the United States and Europe to study the latest paper manufacturing technologies in 1879.[41] Within two years of his return to Japan, Ōkawa developed a process for substituting and/or blending rice straw pulp with the cotton rags typically used to make paper that had become harder to obtain.[42] Ōkawa continued to experiment and innovate, this time with chemical processes for pulping wood for paper production. Technically more difficult than other methods of pulping wood, Ōkawa's first attempts failed. Like contemporaries in Europe, however, he continued to experiment with the process and was eventually successful. By 1890, as Japan's foremost authority on paper manufacturing, he had turned the company around. Within a few years, however, Shibusawa and Ōkawa left the company following a power struggle with investors over company management.

The struggles to make the mill technologically successful made Shibusawa a firm believer in the value of indigenous human capital. He learned firsthand that although "modern" machines may make one appear "modern," knowledge was the key. The difference between the "great civilized and enlightened" countries, the *"daibunmei daikaika no kuni,"* like Britain and France, and the "uncivilized" countries of the world was more than technological artifacts. To be truly "modern," one had to have the right technologies *and* the knowledge to create and sustain them. As a result of this experience, when Shibusawa looked to transform Japan's cotton spinning industry, one of his first steps was to "create" his own source of indigenous knowledge in the form of Yamanobe Takeo, a promising student who at the time was studying economics at University College, London.

The New Paradigm, Technology Transfer, and Osaka Cotton Spinning

Developing alongside, but not as rapidly as, the silk reeling industry, the cotton spinning industry was also rooted in tradition and had a "modern" face. Traditional spinning wheels, *itogurumi*, closely resembled their Western counterparts. A completely manual operation, *itogurumi* required a skilled operator to draw out consistent amounts of cotton to produce a relatively uniform thread. At best, the process produced a course yarn that was nonetheless favored by local consumers well into the nineteenth century.

Modern British spinning machinery was introduced to Japan in Kagoshima through the auspices of the Satsuma *daimyō* Shimazu Tadayoshi. Several Satsuma retainers journeyed to England and purchased machinery from Platt Brothers of Oldham, Lancashire, which was then installed by a team of British mill engineers/mechanics and several Satsuma retainers. In 1867, the mill opened with great promise. By the following year, the British mill workers returned to England, leaving operations in the hands of their eager yet inexperienced Japanese counterparts. Despite having some of the most modern machinery available, the mill soon encountered problems, achieving neither technical nor economic efficiency. Struggling on, Satsuma opened a second mill in Sakai in 1871. Although benefitting from its experience in Kagoshima, the Sakai Mill fared no better and proved to be a second economic drain on Shimazu resources. This time, however, the Meiji government stepped in and, in 1872, bought the mill. In addition to alleviating the former *daimyō* of further financial responsibility, officials turned the mill into the government's first model "modern" cotton mill.

The pattern of importing British spinning machinery with mixed results continued in other parts of Japan as entrepreneurs tried to break into the potentially lucrative cotton industry. Seeing some private sector success, the government opened ten 2000-spindle mills in Aichi and Hiroshima prefectures in 1878. Ushering in the "period of 2000-spindle mills," the government purchased ten sets of British-made 2000 spindle-spinning frames for sale to the private sector at very favorable terms – no money down, ten years to repay, interest free.[43] The government's new mills and private sector operations, *jukki bōseki* or ten cotton spinning mills, however, were plagued by technical difficulties and economic inefficiencies. Much like Shibusawa's experience at Ōji Paper, the Meiji government was able to transfer the "modern" artifacts of the spinning industry but lacked the expertise to use them effectively.

One thing that differentiated the government's efforts in Aichi and Hiroshima from the private sector was the physical mill space. Whereas the Kagoshima mill tried to approximate Western-style mill buildings, using stone for one and a stucco facade on the superintendent's quarters, all other buildings were wooden structures where traditional spinners and weavers worked side-by-side. The government's mills were brick and of Western design, part of the continued effort to be differentiated from the former domains and introduce an aura of "modernity" to the countryside. As will be discussed later, especially in its early days, masonry construction made little sense for Japan.

As with silk reeling, there were alternative spinning technologies between *itogurumi* and steam/water-powered British spinning frames. The *garabō*, an indigenous spinning frame, was invented in the early 1870s and improved throughout the decade. Its public introduction came at the First National Industrial Exposition in Ueno, Tokyo, in 1877.[44] Rather than garner praise as a completely indigenous invention that simplified the spinning process, Tokimune Gaun, the *garabō's* inventor, received advice that he should replace the machine's wooden gears with iron.[45]

Nonetheless, the *garabō* was improved and spread in popularity. By 1880, there were 150 *garabō* mills in the Tokyo area, 25 in Aichi prefecture, and dozens more in the Kansai area. According to the company that manufactured the *garabō*, there were 585 machines sold after the Ueno exposition.[46] Demand for the machine continued beyond initial sales. By the end of the decade there were 483 *garabō* in Aichi prefecture alone, as well as a 500-spindle, water-powered *garabō* mill. These numbers do not take copies into account. Because of the *garabō's* relative simplicity, craftsmen were able to fabricate reasonable facsimiles of Gaun's invention.[47] *Garabō* became the mainstay of small and medium-sized cotton mills throughout Japan. They were more readily available, less expensive, and less alien to anyone who wanted to open a spinning mill. Made of wood, however, they were not "modern."

Despite the popularity of the *garabō* and the coarse-textured thread it produced, it faced a significant problem – "modern" British technology. The *garabō* was the latecomer that attempted to challenge the superiority of British industrial might. As Eugene Choi argues, it "was not a transitional spinning technology that bridged the gap between traditional schemes and British-style spinning.... It was an independent and spontaneously developed technology to cope with local needs in spinning."[48] By the time the *garabō* made its debut, British mule frames had largely become the basis of Japan's modernizing cotton spinning industry.[49] The *garabō* had none of the aura of British machinery. Wood versus iron, a seeming lack of precision versus scientific complexity – the name *garabō*, which means "rattling spindle," detracted from its appeal to "modernizers." If the Meiji government opted for *garabō* over British spinning frames for its mills, it would have done nothing to distinguish the government from the rest of the field.[50]

Even a British alternative spinning frame was rejected by Meiji modernizers. For many overseas cotton mill projects, British firms such as Platt Brothers manufactured and sold manually operated spinning machinery. In many ways these machines "made sense" for developing economies because they were less expensive, could be competitive, and avoided the constraints associated with hydro and steam power. Yet these, too, were rejected by Japan. Although

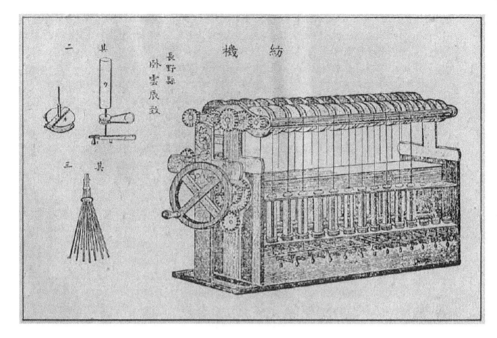

Figure 3.6. *Garabō* or "Rattling Spindle" Spinning Frame

Source: Nakamura Tsutomu, *Nippon garabō shiwa* [Story of the Japanese *garabō*] (Tokyo: Keio Shuppankai, 1942), 42.

manual operations would have been cost effective in Japan, they were not fully "modern," and thus rejected.[51]

Japan's first truly "modern" spinning mill was built under the direction of Shibusawa Eiichi. The story of the founding of Osaka Cotton Spinning Company is well known, but several points related to technology and technology transfer are worth discussing for several reasons. First, there is a positive correlation between the Osaka Spinning Mill and Shibusawa's vision for Tomioka Silk Filature. Second, Shibusawa's experience opening Shōshi Kaisha had a direct impact on his ideas about industrialization. Finally, the factors usually identified as the reasons for the mill's success – the number of spindles, steam power, and twenty-four-hour-a-day operation – were perhaps less important than who ran the mill.

Following in the footprint of Tomioka filature, Osaka Spinning was large, occupying more than six acres of land.[52] Constructed of brick and stone, the mill was a faithful reproduction of an Oldham mill, which according to one author was a standard Platt Brothers design. Even the bricks were imported from England![53] Osaka Spinning relied on the latest British spinning technologies. With

Figure 3.7. Shibusawa Eiichi, ca. 1883 (*left*) and Yamanobe Takeo (*right*)

Source: Courtesy of the Shibusawa Eiichi Memorial Foundation Museum.

more than four times the number of spindles of its nearest competitors, Osaka Spinning boasted 10,500 spinning mules. Some economic historians point out that Shibusawa was simply considering economies of scale when he and his British trained engineer,[54] Yamanobe Takeo, envisioned the mill, but if one wanted to be truly "modern," size mattered.

Osaka Spinning was a size anomaly. It was physically larger, stories taller, and housed more spinning machinery than any other cotton mill in Japan. Its masonry construction was representative of modernizing mills that in some ways demonstrated a trend in brick mill construction that, as mentioned, made little sense for Japan. Although considered more solid than traditional wooden architecture and thus better able to withstand earthquakes, the collapse of several mills in a major 1891 earthquake debunked this fallacy. Japan's humidity also worked against the logic of brick buildings, as did a general scarcity of brick, mortar, and artisans' lack of familiarity with the materials.[55]

Yet throughout the country and well into the early twentieth century, mill owners built brick mills with towering chimneys, creating their own modernity, even though masonry construction had few technological advantages and made little economic sense. Mill construction in Japan was an expensive proposition

Figure 3.8. Osaka Spinning Mill, Building 3

Source: http://tenyusinjo.web.fc2.com/osaka_walk/osakabouseki/bousekibirudai.jpg.

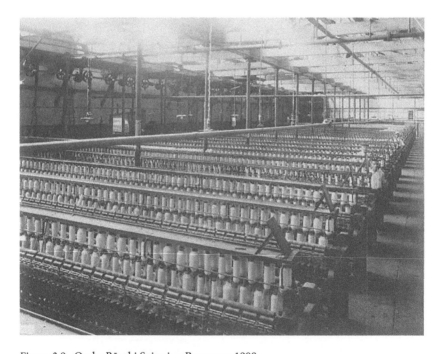

Figure 3.9. Osaka Bōseki Spinning Room, ca. 1908

Source: https://www.toyobo-global.com/discover/story/img/detail1882.jpg.

with higher initial investments than in other "modern" nations. An average cotton mill in Japan cost approximately $25 per spindle. Half of this expense was for machinery, with the remainder divided between building and land costs at an approximate ratio of 1:1.5, respectively. In comparison, a comparable mill in England was approximately $7.91 per spindle; $11 per spindle in the United States; and $13 per spindle in Germany.[56] Most Japanese mills were sprawling single-story structures located in relatively rural areas.[57] In cities such as Osaka, mills were two or more stories tall. Part of Japan's additional expense was for building worker dormitories. Expansive single-story mills were theoretically less prone to collapse in an earthquake – or at least to collapsing in a less spectacular way than three-story buildings – which also contributed to the expense. When the Naniwa Mill collapsed in Osaka in October 1891 during the Mino-Owari (Nōbi) earthquake, the third floor, stressed by the massive quake and weight of the textile machinery, pulled free from the walls and plummeted to ground level, taking down the entire building.[58] The Aichi Mill, although a single story, similarly collapsed during the same seismic event.[59]

Simply put, brick buildings and chimneys fared poorly when the ground shook. This was partly due to Japanese masons' unfamiliarity with the materials and Western masonry techniques, and partly because of architectural design and the limitations of the material.[60] Small earthquakes or tremors may have left a brick building with little or no structural damage. A major quake such as the Nōbi Earthquake, however, quickly reduced brick buildings to piles of rubble. In Osaka, several mills, including the Sangenya and Naniwa Mills, were completely destroyed. Western-style buildings throughout the city lay in rubble, as did all of Nagoya's "modern" brick buildings. And although Japanese buildings were also damaged by the quake, local perceptions – backed by reality – fed a newfound disdain for masonry buildings. While falling wooden buildings admittedly caused injuries such as broken bones, bricks gave rise to new classes of crushing and lacerating injuries that wrought infection and ultimately death.[61] Ironically, or perhaps by design, Tomioka silk mill was left virtually unscathed by earthquakes. Supposedly part of the reason for Tomoika's site selection was being in an area that was not prone to earthquakes. Additionally, its hybrid timber frame and brick curtain wall construction tended to be more elastic than traditional Western mill or factory construction.[62]

Unlike the 2000-spindle mills, Osaka Spinning was steam powered. This was a deliberate decision, contrary to the original plans that called for a 140- to 150-horsepower waterwheel. In fact, the mill's Osaka location was based in part on the availability of water.[63] While admittedly more practical in the long run, Yamanobe's and Shibusawa's understanding of the cultural symbolism of technological artifacts cannot be ignored. Steam engines were the hallmark of the Industrial Revolution and indicated "modernity." Their use is what separated "modern" nations from the less "civilized." Although there were practical considerations that could have led to the choice of steam power, Yamanobe's and Shibusawa's abandonment of tradition was so thorough and on so many fronts that raising Japan's "level of civilization" was also a motivating factor.[64]

Japan was walking the tightrope of "modernization" and industrialization. In the process of industrializing, the nation would also become "modern" and thus ascend within the hierarchy of nations if the government and/or entrepreneurs chose the "right" technologies. Making the "right" technological choices spelled the difference between value-free industrialization and value-laden "modernization." In "modernization" it mattered little whether Japan made technological choices that were economically or technologically appropriate. What mattered was that Japan opted for technological artifacts that would impart the right kind of cultural values. What makes Osaka Spinning particularly interesting in technological choice is that Yamanobe and Shibusawa made the correct technological choices for the right reasons *and* simultaneously demonstrated the mill's and thus Japan's "modernity" through technological artifacts. Also interesting is that Osaka Spinning was built at a time when the movement for "civilization and enlightenment," *bunmei kaika*, was giving way to concerns over national security and military preparedness.[65] And while Shibusawa's attitude toward "modernizing" Japan is clear, motivation for his more than 400 economy and industry building projects is more so – to bring about technological self-reliance and release Japan from the bonds of expensive foreign goods. In short, he was motivated by national economic security.

Shibusawa's vision for Osaka Spinning included something that would move Japan further within the realm of "modern" Western nations: technological independence. As a patriot and nationalist, Shibusawa believed it was essential that Japanese industry be fully under Japanese control.[66] He understood that if Japan was to be equal to or better than the West, it needed its own basis of expertise and should not rely on foreign advisers.[67] Perhaps more than anything else, this demonstrates the degree to which Shibusawa understood the Victorian world in which he lived. Only technological and scientific nations were "modern." All others, even countries that adopted foreign technologies – but were reliant on foreign advisers – were lesser nations in the European mind.[68]

There were other mills that employed several of Osaka Spinning's methods such as steam power and twenty-four-hour-a-day operation. The Aichi and Mie Mills are two examples. Neither, however, had an experienced manager who was able to contend with the technical problems that arose daily. The Shimomura Mill, which opened one month before Osaka Spinning, had a fifty-four-horsepower steam engine and ran round the clock yet failed because of technical inexperience. Struggling throughout its existence, the mill eventually closed its doors in 1899.[69] Yamanobe and Shibusawa understood that having the technology and knowing what to do with it were two different things. Knowing how to adapt to changing technical demands required a greater level of knowledge that came only with experience and training. And this is what separated Osaka Cotton Spinning Mill from all others.

When Japan reopened its doors to the West, it quickly learned that technology and science were required to build a *Rich Nation and Strong Army*. American, British, and French industrial and military might were brought to bear on Japan several times before the collapse of the Tokugawa *bakufu*. Overseas experiences during the Bakumatsu and Meiji eras only confirmed for some Japanese – men such as Shibusawa Eiichi, Itō Hirobumi, and Sugiura Yuzuru – what the Western powers already "knew." A country's mastery of the natural world and degree of technological proficiency – measured in accumulated "modern" technologies – determined where one fit into the grand hierarchy of nations.

"Modern" technologies were ones made of "modern" materials – iron, brick, and glass. Machines were powered by steam engines, men and materials moved by rail, buildings were masonry and massive. All demonstrated precision and permanence, which in turn demonstrated one's "level of civilization." Believing steadfastly in this progress ideology of materials, Meiji leaders sought to import only the most "modern" technological artifacts, ones that would provide evidence that the new government was "enlightened" and that the nation was, if not "modern," then "modernizing."

Technological choice and technology transfer to Tomioka Silk Filature followed this belief. French technologies became part of Japan's technological repertoire based on the government's and Shibusawa's beliefs in their "modernity." The government's choice of technique largely had its desired effect. Foreign observers and domestic producers praised the government's efforts at modernizing the silk reeling industry. Tomioka Filature was a showcase, a "modern" factory whose symbolic value often surpassed its economic utility.

In its quest to become "modern," Japan adopted numerous technologies from the industrialized West. Under government guidance, technologies were chosen and imported largely on the basis of their symbolic values of "progress" and "modernity." As such, officials often paid little attention to economic and technical evaluations of the artifacts they sought and relied more often on appearance and the perceived reputation of an artifact's country of manufacture. The government's efforts thus often met with mixed results; technologies took longer to be absorbed into Japan's industrial landscape, and there was a relatively high degree of reliance on foreign advisers during this initial period. Tomioka Silk Mill exemplifies this stage of industrialization. Although eventually highly successful, Tomioka's technologies and methods were initially slow to spread because silk reelers lacked requisite capital and knowledge.

As ideas about industrial modernization and Japan's relationship to the West evolved, we see a similar evolution in technological choice and a growing trend in technological self-reliance. On the basis of his experiences at Tomioka and

Shōshi Kaisha, Shibusawa sought to curtail Japan's reliance on foreign engineers. Through the lens of Odaka Atsutada, he saw Tomioka's myriad problems, which were solved only when "modern" Western technologies were replaced with more practical, yet symbolically neutral alternatives, and when foreign advisers were replaced with Japanese experts. Shibusawa considered education essential for building a modern nation – the belief that led him to venture into the paper industry in the first place. It was his experience at Shōshi Kaisha, however, that fueled his belief in Japan's need to create and rely on indigenous knowledge for industrialization, among other things.

Following the same developmental model as Tomioka, i.e., foreign machinery, foreign knowledge, Shōshi Kaisha struggled to produce quality paper and failed to be profitable. After six years of tribulations, Shibusawa sent Ōkawa Heizaburō overseas to learn Western-style paper manufacturing. Despite initial setbacks, Ōkawa was able to make Shōshi Kaisha a technologically sound and profitable business. When Shibusawa set his sights on the cotton spinning industry, he followed what would become Japan's new paradigm for industrial development – the creation of indigenous knowledge first, technological choice second. Unlike previous ventures, Shibusawa largely left Osaka in the hands of his engineer and manager, Yamanobe. Decisions about Osaka Spinning's technologies and design were based on Yamanobe Takeo's practical experience and industry knowledge. Whereas Ōkawa replaced Shōshi Kaisha's machinery and invented his process for utilizing domestic materials after the fact, i.e., post-design and construction, Yamanobe ordered modified spinning machines capable of using Japanese short staple cotton *before* they were shipped from Britain. Later, he developed an innovative process for blending Japanese cotton with Indian long staple cotton that helped launch Japan on its trajectory to become one of the world's largest producers and exporters of cotton yarn.

The cases of Tomioka Filature, Shōshi Kaisha, and Osaka Spinning demonstrate that ideas about symbolic modernity influenced technology transfer and choice of technique for much of the first two decades of the Meiji era. More importantly, accumulated experience, even among dissimilar industries, transformed the way entrepreneurs such as Shibusawa Eiichi established modern, Western-style industries in Japan.

NOTES

1 My basis for technological systems comes from Hughes's "complex system," which he describes as "coherent structures comprised of interacting, interconnected components that ranged from relatively simple machines to regional electric supply networks." See Thomas Parke Hughes, *Networks of Power: Electrification in Western Society, 1880–1930* (Baltimore, MD: Johns Hopkins University Press, 1983), ix.

2 The financial ramifications of poor quality reeled silk and exporting the country's best quality silkworm eggs predates the rise of the Meiji government in 1868. Tokugawa officials were also faced with foreign complaints before their demise in 1867. Put in perspective, raw silk accounted for nearly half the value of all exports in 1868. See Stephen McCallion, "Silk Reeling in Japan: The Limits to Change" (PhD diss., Ohio State University, 1983), 70.

3 Ōtsuka Ryōtarō, *Sanshi* [Silk history], 2 vols. (Tokyo: Fusōen, 1900), 1:249–50. The directive also blamed merchant greed and poor production methods for the declining quality of raw silk.

4 Shibusawa was the head of the finance ministry's Bureau of Taxation and the only government official with experience in the silk industry.

5 Odaka was Shibusawa's first cousin, brother-in-law, and earlier his tutor.

6 Brunat described the facility as Swiss in design and out of date. Swiss factories, however, used Italian methods. One author identifies Hayami's Swiss factory as based on a facility in Turin. See Yoichi Shimatsu, "Japan's Silk Reelers Blazed an Asian Path of Economic Development," Chichibu, http://www.chichibu.com /CHICHIBUSILKHISTORY.html.

7 Odaka Atsutada, "Seishi no hōkoku," *Ryūmon zasshi* 60 (15 May 1893), 5.

8 Odaka, "Seishi no hōkoku," 5.

9 The text of Brunat's proposal can be found in Tomioka Seishijōshi Hensan Iinkai, ed., *Tomioka seishijōshi* [The history of Tomioka Silk Mill] (Tomioka: Tomioka-shi Kyōiku Iinkai, 1977), document 4, 1:147–50. Hereafter *TSS*.

10 *TSS*, 1:147.

11 *TSS*, 1:148.

12 *TSS*, 1:147–8. By "locally available materials" Brunat meant wood. Although Japan had an infant iron industry, manufacturing machinery out of iron was impractical on a local level and too expensive if the iron needed to be imported.

13 McCallion, *Silk Reeling in Japan*, 82; David G. Wittner, *Technology and the Culture of Progress in Meiji Japan* (London: Routledge, 2008), 50.

14 Ōtsuka, *Sanshi*, 319.

15 Odaka, "Seishi no hōkoku," 5.

16 Giovanni Federico, *An Economic History of the Silk Industry, 1830–1930* (Cambridge: Cambridge University Press, 1997), 111–14.

17 Federico, *Economic History of the Silk Industry*.

18 Federico, *Economic History of the Silk Industry*, 106–7; Wittner, *Technology and the Culture of Progress*, 59.

19 Kiyokawa Yukihiko, "Transplantation of the European Factory System and Adaptations in Japan: The Experience of the Tomioka Model Filature," *Hitotsubashi Journal of Economics* 28, no. 1 (1987): 33.

20 Michael Adas, *Machines as the Measure of Men: Science, Technology, and Ideologies of Western Dominance* (Ithaca, NY: Cornell University Press, 1989), 144.

21 Adas, *Machines as the Measure of Men*, 146.

22 Adas, *Machines as the Measure of Men*, 146.

23 This was not Sugiura's first trip to Europe. He had been to Europe twice before and became a proponent of importing Western civilization to Japan prior to his trip with Shibusawa. Igarashi Akio, *Meiji isshin no shisō* [The mental world of the Meiji restoration] (Kanagawa: Seori Shōbō, 1996), 184–5. Sugiura Yuzuru is also known as Sugiura Aizō.

24 Sugiura Yuzuru Iinkai, *Sugiura Yuzuru zenshū* [The complete works of Sugiura Yuzuru] (Tokyo: Sugiura Yuzuru Iinkai, 1979), 5:364–88. Hereafter *SYZ*.

25 *SYZ*, 5:373–81.

26 Shibusawa Hanako, *Shibusawa Eiichi Pari banpaku e* [Shibusawa Eiichi at the Paris International Exposition] (Tokyo: Kokusho Kankōkai, 1995), 85.

27 Shibusawa, *Shibusawa Eiichi Pari banpaku e*, 85–95.

28 When Tomioka was in the planning stages, many domains were still under the authority of *daimyō*. Although some domains had already been "returned" to the emperor, the official decree that abolished *han* (domain) and created *ken* (prefectures) was issued in August 1871.

29 The first mill had only three reeling frames, the expanded mill, according to Ōtsuka, had thirty-two. See Ōtsuka, *Sanshi*, 1:257, and Odaka, "Seishi no hōkoku," 5. Odaka stated that there were thirty-six frames.

30 Kiyokawa, "Transplantation of the European Factory System," 33.

31 Although a debate would ensue for years between the British expatriate communities in Yokohama and Shanghai, early observers of Japan's technical progress identified the Japanese as superior to Chinese for their willingness to adopt the trappings of Western "civilization." See, for example, *Japan Weekly Mail*, "Japanese Progress," 15 October 1870, 490–1; and *Japan Weekly Mail*, "Progress: Japan and China," 23 September 1871, 545–6.

32 Sano Tsunetami, *Ōkoku hakurankai hōkokusho: sangyōbu* [Report on the Austrian Exhibition: Industry section], 2 vols. (Tokyo, 1875), vol. 1, s. 6:7.

33 Henry Dyer, *Dai Nippon: The Britain of the East* (London: Blackie and Son, 1904), 134; and Wittner, *Technology and the Culture of Progress*, 30.

34 Ogura Ichio, ed., *Ōji Seishi no kiseki* [The history of Oji Paper Company] (Tokyo: Ōji Seishi Kabushiki Kaisha, 2004), 163.

35 On the origins of Oji Paper, see Shinomiya Toshiyuki, *Kindai Nihon seishigyō no kyōsō to kyōchō: Ōji Seishi, Fuji Seishi, Karafuto Kōgyō no seichō to karuteru katsudō no hensen* [Competition and coordination in modern Japanese paper industries: Ōji Paper, Fuji Paper, Karafuto industry growth, and transition to cartel activity] (Tokyo: Nihon Keizai Hyōronsha, 1997); and Johannes Hirschmeier and Tsunehiko Yui, *The Development of Japanese Business, 1600–1973* (London: Routledge, 1975, 2006), 106. Here I am referring to the collapse of the Kobe silk trade.

36 At first merchants began shipping cotton rags from Japan to Europe and the United States for paper manufacturing. After a few ships caught fire because the rags spontaneously combusted, merchants decided to try producing the paper

in Japan as an alternative. See Peter Ennals, *Opening a Window to the West: The Foreign Concession at Kōbe, Japan, 1868–1899* (Toronto: University of Toronto Press, 2014), 168–9.

37 Some sources say 1872; see Shinomiya, *Kindai Nihon seishigyō no kyōsō to kyōchō*, for an example.

38 Ernest Satow, *Records of a Diplomat* (Tokyo: Oxford University Press, 1968), 27; Fujihara Gingiro, *The Spirit of Japanese Industry* (Tokyo: Hokuseido Press, 1936), 4–8.

39 Shinomiya Toshiyuki, "Competition and Cooperation among Paper and Pulp Enterprises in Modern Japan Prior to World War II: The Rise of Prominence of a Powerful Triumvirate of Enterprises, and Transitions in Cartel Activity," *Japan Yearbook on Business History* 14 (1997): 116–17.

40 Johannes Hirschmeier and Tsunehiko Yui, *The Development of Japanese Business, 1600–1973* (London: Routledge, 1975, 2006), 106.

41 Most sources state that Ōkawa was Shibusawa's nephew, who had originally come to work at the mill as a mechanic.

42 Takafumi Kurosawa and Tomoko Hashino, "From the Non-European Tradition to a Variation on the Japanese Competitiveness Model: The Modern Japanese Paper Industry since the 1870s," in *The Evolution of the Global Paper Industry 1800–2050: A Comparative Analysis*, ed. Juha-Antti Lamberg, Jari Ojala, Mirva peltoniemi, and Timo Särkkä (Dordrecht: Springer, 2012), 142.

43 A "set" refers to a cotton opener and a beater lapper, both of which beat, draw out, and clean the cotton fibers. Eight carding machines that untangle and align the cotton fibers create a continuous strand called a sliver. A drawing machine or frame is used to put the fibers in parallel alignment and reduce the number of fibers in a sliver. A slubbing frame begins the process of twisting the fibers into a roving (a long narrow bundle of fibers); two roving frames further twist and refine the roving, and four spinning frames. See Kōzaburō Katō, "Yamanobe Takeo and the Modern Cotton Spinning Industry in the Meiji Period," in *Papers on the History of Industry and Technology of Japan*, vol. 2, *From the Meiji Period to Postwar Japan*, ed. Erich Pauer (Marburg: Fördervereing Marburger Japan-Reihe, 1995), 6; https://www.dover.nh.gov/government/city-operations/library/history/the-cloth-manufacturing-process-drawing-frame.html; http://www.glencoenc.com/library/doc1.htm; http://www.cottontown.org/Resources/Glossary/Pages/Textile-Terms.aspx.

44 Eugene K. Choi, "Another Path to Industrialisation: The Rattling Spindle, *Garabō*, in the Development of the Japanese Spinning Industry" (paper presented at the Asia-Pacific Economic and Business History Conference, Gakushuin University, Tokyo, 18–20 February 2009), 5–6.

45 Choi, "Another Path to Industrialisation," 12.

46 Choi, "Another Path to Industrialisation," 26.

47 Tessa Morris-Suzuki, *The Technological Transformation of Japan: From the Seventeenth to the Twenty-First Century* (Cambridge: Cambridge University Press, 1994), 90.

48 Choi, "Another Path to Industrialisation," 16.

49 Choi, "Another Path to Industrialisation," 15.

50 There were factors that worked against the *garabō*'s diffusion, including the texture of the thread it produced. Although a local selling point, the *garabō*'s coarse thread was not desirable for export. Then again, the same can be said for the quality of much of the thread produced by British machinery in Japan.

51 In all fairness, the manually operated machines would have also made it harder for Japan to fully stem the flow of imported cotton through domestic production, a purported goal of cotton modernization.

52 Wittner, *Technology and the Culture of Progress*, 38.

53 D.A. Farnie, "Four Revolutions in the Textile Trade of Asia 1814–1994: The Impact of Bombay, Osaka, the Little Tigers and China," in *Asia Pacific Dynamism, 1550–2000*, ed. A.J.H. Latham and Heita Kawakatsu (London: Routledge, 2000), 54; Gary Saxonhouse, "A Tale of Japanese Technological Diffusion in the Meiji Period," *Journal of Economic History* 34, no. 1 (March 1974): 153.

54 See, for example, Saxonhouse, "Tale of Japanese Technological Diffusion," 151.

55 William H. Coaldrake, *Architecture and Authority in Japan* (London: Routledge, 1996), 238.

56 W.A. Graham Clark, *Cotton Goods in Japan and Their Competition on the Manchurian Market* (Washington, DC: Government Printing Office, 1914), 212.

57 Location was part of the problem for the 2000 spindle mills. Being far from the economic center of the cotton industry, these mills were engineered with an economic disadvantage.

58 Josiah Conder, "An Architect's Notes on the Great Earthquake of October 1891," *Seismological Journal of Japan* 18 (1893): 77.

59 F. Omori, "Earthquake Measurement in a Brick Building," *Publications of the Earthquake Investigation Committee in Foreign Languages* 4 (1900): 11 and fig. 5.

60 Conder, "Architect's Notes," 74–81; W. Hague Harrington, "The Japanese Earthquake," *Science: A Weekly Newspaper of all the Arts and Sciences* 18, no. 464 (25 December 1891): 356.

61 Gregory K. Clancey, *Earthquake Nation: The Cultural Politics of Japanese Seismicity, 1868–1930* (Berkeley: University of California Press, 2006), 114–16.

62 Tests conducted on a scale model of Tomioka as part of its UNESCO application demonstrated this characteristic of its construction. See Toshikazu Hanazato, Yoshiaki Tominaga, Tadashi Mikoshiba, and Yasushi Niitsu, "Shaking Table Test of Full Scale Model of Timber Framed Brick Masonry Walls for Structural Restoration of Tomioka Silk Mill, Registered as a Tentative World Cultural Heritage in Japan," *Historical Earthquake-Resistant Timber Frames in the Mediterranean Area* (Switzerland: Springer Publishing, 2015), 83–93.

63 Janet Hunter, "Regimes of Technology Transfer in Japan's Cotton Industry, 1860s to 1890s" (paper presented at ninth conference of the Global Economic History Network, Kaohsiung, Taiwan, 9–11 May 2006), 19.

64 Ono Ken'ichi, *Globalization of Developing Countries: Is Autonomous Development Possible?* (Tokyo: Tōyō Keizai Shimpōsha, 2000), 53. By choosing to rely on steam power, Shibusawa and Yamanobe were able to locate the Osaka mill in the heart of an industrial area rather than select a site based on reliability of water supply alone. Minami notes that there were insufficient water resources to power the 140–150 horsepower water wheels Osaka Mill required. See Minami Ryōshin, "Mechanical Power in the Industrialization of Japan: A Case Study of the Spinning Industry," *Hitotsubashi Journal of Economics* 21, no. 1 (June 1986): 22n14. However, one identifying feature of a "modern" or "civilized" country was the ability to control or disregard the forces of nature. Steam power allowed Shibusawa and Yamanobe to build a mill while not having to consider these factors.

65 See Wittner, *Technology and the Culture of Progress*, 109.

66 Ohno Kenichi, *Tojokoku no globalization: jiritsuteki hatten wa kanoka* [Globalization of developing countries: Is autonomous development possible?] (Tokyo: Tōyō Keizai Shimpōsha, 2000), English translation (2003), http://www .grips.ac.jp/forum-e/pdf_e01/eastasia/ch5.pdf, 53.

67 This was one area where Shibusawa and Hayami Kensō were in perfect agreement. Hayami was also a proponent of technological independence, recommending that the government rely on "men of talent" who could move the silk industry forward. Perhaps the Tomioka experience helped shape Shibusawa's vision of technological independence.

68 Throughout the 1870s and into the 1880s foreign observers living in Japan frequently criticized the Japanese penchant for "imitation." While some observers praised Japan's willingness to adopt Western ways, others saw fault in what they perceived as Japan adopting the technology or science without understanding the (enlightened) thought with which it was created.

69 Katō, "Yamanobe Takeo and the Modern Cotton Spinning Industry," 6.

4 The Evolution of the Exposition Form and Its Transfer from the West to Japan

JEFFER DAYKIN

The explicit goal of international expositions was to exhibit the best of human achievement in order to encourage continued development. With the exposition's roots in the events held by scientific and technological societies, the educative purpose of exhibiting the latest innovations was vigorously promoted. The guiding philosophy of the exposition form was that people, be they trained engineers or common laborers, could learn and be inspired to produce new and better products and processes by viewing exhibits of high-quality goods and the technologies that manufactured them. The promise of international expositions was that by assembling exhibits from all over the world and directly comparing them, even greater improvements in production could be realized through competition.

Providing the arena necessary for the study and direct comparison of the world's products, however, was difficult to realize. Attempts to physically organize hundreds of thousands of exhibits in a meaningful way commonly resulted in relegating the facilitation of direct exhibit comparison to the fair's rhetorical instruments such as catalogs and guidebooks and its jury awards system. The actual organization of structures where products of the same class were exhibited side-by-side was seldom achieved. Yet as expositions continued to be justified in the West for their value in providing opportunities for the direct comparison of goods and technologies, new configurations in exposition arrangement emerged as organizers wrestled with how to manageably realize this goal.

Similarly, late-developing nations such as Japan came to see the value of these events in fostering their industrial potential. The Japanese participated in many of the international expositions held abroad and came to hold their own expositions in the long nineteenth century. Through tracing the evolution of the international exposition form as it changed in response to practical issues of exhibit organization, I identify a clear trend in Western expositions that was followed and readily adopted by Japan's national expositions, but one that was adapted by Japan in ways that reveal an even greater commitment to the goals of comparison and stimulating domestic innovation than what was generally seen in the West.

Before considering the evolution of the exposition form and its adoption in Japan, it is important to specify the approach taken in this study as well as its scope. The captivating architecture of exhibitions is commonly examined in exposition research for its semiotic value in suggesting the messaging of fairs. This approach is often emphasized by studies considering the participation of countries outside the core of Western nations, as the choices made in design illuminated key themes in perceived/asserted cultural uniqueness relative to the universalizing pressures of modernity.[1] Where such analyses yield insight into the cultural milieu in which these events took place, studying the overall layout of exhibitions and the internal arrangement of exposition buildings independent of their exterior design elements is the approach taken here, as the aim is to analyze the practical functioning of the exposition form.

In scope, this study focuses on the evolution of the exposition form in its international configuration: those events held with international participation that are commonly referred to as the Great Exhibitions, *Expositions Universelles*, or World's Fairs.[2] There are, however, challenges to this methodology when considering the study of expositions held in the long nineteenth century. First, there was no formal agreement to determine the official status of world's fairs prior to 1912, when the International Convention of Berlin (ICB) was signed by fifteen countries supporting limitations on the number of these events. It was not until the 1928 Convention Regarding International Exhibitions, which formed the Bureau of International Expositions (BIE), that a commonly recognized set of ground rules and criteria for fairs was finally established.[3] What certified an international exposition during this period, then, was its de facto reception as such, evidenced by extensive foreign participation and informal consensus on meeting the general expectations of fairgoers and the international community in including requisite exposition components and features. This amorphous definition is far from ideal in establishing a subject of analysis, but the BIE has retroactively established a listing of international expositions, and these are used by this study to trace the form's evolution in the West.

A second issue arises when considering the transfer of the exposition form to Asia in that no "international" expositions were held in the period under consideration save the 1902 Tonkin Exposition in Hanoi, which was organized by the colonial government of French Indochina. Where this detail would seem to preclude the legitimate study of the international exposition's transference to the region, the Japanese did host several "national" expositions prior to the First World War. Though far smaller in every respect than the Great Exhibitions hosted in European capitals and major cities of the United States, Japan's 1903 Fifth National Industrial Exposition held in Osaka was quite comparable to many of the lesser-known but self-proclaimed (and BIE listed) international expositions in terms of attendance, physical size, and received foreign participation. Using Japan's national expositions as the unit of analysis for the transfer of the international exposition form is therefore justifiable and necessary for generating a more complete picture of the institution's spread outside of the West.

It is also important to specify that this study focuses on the transfer of the international exposition itself, which is expanded to include the national expositions of Japan, and not local or provincial expositions or other elements of what Tony Bennet has termed the "exhibitionary complex," which would include institutions such as museums and department stores.[4] All were concomitant developments and essential in creating opportunities to develop expertise in the principles of display and generating a process for exhibit selection, but this study looks to the object that was transferred – the international exposition – rather than the process by which it was implemented, and therefore focuses on the most-fully realized models of the form.

Japan's local-level expositions demonstrate, as Tessa Morris-Suzuki has noted, that the national government followed the lead of local areas in its effort to hold expositions.[5] Moreover, local-level expositions played a more significant role than national expositions as agents of technology transfer in that they reached a broader range of people, and the holding of area expositions and prize competitions motivated entire regions to improve their practices and spawned subsequent innovations. Yet a study focused on the structural components of Japan's national expositions can provide specific insight into what was envisioned as the highest achievable structure of the international exposition form. These events demanded intensive study, significant allocation of resources, and coordination of public and private efforts to achieve and so make clear statements about the nation's specific interests in holding them. The choices made in form and function may not account for *how* the exposition was transferred to Japan or whether it was successful in promoting innovation, but exhibitions clearly define *what* was transferred and how this technology of modernization evolved and was adapted to meet the needs of the countries hosting them, which is the aim of this work.

Emergence and Evolution of the Exposition Form in the West

There has been a great deal of research on the origins of the modern exposition form, stemming from scientific and technological societies in Europe as early as the first decade of the nineteenth century, but the Great Exhibition of the Works of Industry of All Nations (commonly referred to as the Crystal Palace Exhibition) held in London in 1851 is widely understood as the seminal international exposition.[6] In contrast to earlier events, the creators of the Crystal

Palace sought to provide an entirely comprehensive exhibition of all manner of products and technological innovations. The more than 100,000 exhibits from Britain, its colonies, and foreign nations were classified into four broad categories: (1) Raw Materials, (2) Machinery, (3) Manufactures, and (4) Fine Arts, which were subdivided into more specific classifications to generate what historian Jeffrey Auerbach describes as a "taxonomy of all things."[7] This all-inclusive approach represented an entirely new conception of the exposition form and immediately came to define it.

The form inaugurated by the Crystal Palace endeavored to place the entirety of exhibited items within one enormous structure. This arrangement, referred to in this chapter as the "amalgamated" format, made a lasting impression for how expositions and the related institution of museums should be configured but did not remain the dominant approach. As other nations hosted these events, practical challenges such as the need to manage and accommodate overwhelming demands for exhibit space pressed exposition organizers to move beyond the confines of a single building. The question of how to facilitate the comparison of products and technologies in one structure, given the complex classification schemes and logistical demands, also challenged a format that limited exhibits to a singular exhibition structure.

The Crystal Palace's four-part division of exhibits was subdivided into thirty classification categories that, if followed in consecutive order, were intended to provide a guided and comprehensive view of the processes of industry from raw materials, to the machines that extracted and used them, to finished products, and ultimately to the finest artistic creations. Of course, such an organizational scheme was easier to construct on paper through an exhibition catalog than in actual space. For example, structural requirements necessitated heavy machinery be located on the ground floor nearest to their power sources and that the lightest exhibits be sited in the galleries to avoid structural stress on an ephemerally sited building. The Crystal Palace's deliberate classification scheme therefore existed more as a theoretical intention than a practical reality in guiding the experience of fairgoers within the exhibition structure.[8] Moreover, the desire of foreign exhibitors to maintain a consistent section where they could best arrange their own products undermined the overarching design. This conflict between arranging by exhibitor or by item classification was a challenge that subsequent exposition organizers needed to address.

The next international exposition was held in Paris (1855), and though the event's planners originally intended to follow the Crystal Palace's amalgamated format, they found themselves so overwhelmed by requests for exhibit space that they made an ad hoc determination to create two additional structures for housing the Fine Arts and Machinery categories of exhibits.[9] This segregation of particular exhibit classes became the basis for a new exhibition approach referred to in this chapter as the "semi-differentiated" format.

Figure 4.1. Great Exhibition of the Works of Industry of All Nations (London, 1851)

Source: Joseph M. Wilson, *The Masterpieces of the Centennial International Exhibition, Illustrated* (Philadelphia: Gebbie and Barrie, 1876), 3:xx.

That arrangement was first intentionally employed from the outset at the 1873 exposition in Vienna and can be understood as an attempt to maintain a main exhibition building(s) for the majority of exhibit categories while erecting additional buildings for specific classifications.[10]

Prior to this intentional shift in format, the amalgamated model continued at London's expositions and found perhaps its most celebrated configuration at the 1867 Paris *Exposition Universelle*. The approach taken in Paris that year was to construct a massive exhibition building to allow the arrangement of exhibits both by classification as well as producing nation. This double-classification effect was accomplished through an elliptical-shaped structure comprising concentric rings (that displayed the same types of products) divided by radial aisles (that demarcated the different exhibiting nations). In this way, a visitor could pass down a given aisle and see all that a particular nation contributed to the exposition or choose to walk along a concentric ring and see all exhibits of a particular classification.[11] The achievement in finding a practical way to integrate the interests of exhibiting nations that wished to keep their exhibits together with the broader public interest of allowing for the direct comparison of similar classes of articles was widely hailed as an ideal approach for the structure of exposition spaces.

Despite the triumph of the 1867 Paris *Exposition's* design, the notion that a single event, let alone single exhibition structure, could effectively exhibit all the world's products in a meaningful way came to be doubted. An alternative concept of the exposition form was proposed in which only a select set of industries were to be assembled at a time to maximize focused comparison of like exhibits.

Figure 4.2. *Exposition Universelle* (Paris, 1867)

Source: Joseph M. Wilson, *The Masterpieces of the Centennial International Exhibition, Illustrated* (Philadelphia: Gebbie and Barrie, 1876), 3:xlvi.

This approach was attempted in what was to be a series of ten annual exhibitions in London, each dedicated to specific item categories, that was to provide an up-to-date survey of the world's innovations over the course of a decade. From the series' initial 1871 event, which focused on Fine Art and Art-Industry, this down-sized formulation was criticized in England and abroad. Beyond the financial consequences of hosting events that were, by design, limited in their scope and appeal, both fairgoers and participating nations found the approach to arranging exhibits simply by item-type unappealing. Though fostering education and competition were the ostensible purposes of these events, the spectacle of exhibiting international cultures in addition to their products was apparently what most enthused the fair-going public and inspired exhibitors.

The 1872 and 1873 installments were held, but competition with Vienna's full-scale 1873 exposition and overall lack of interest ultimately ended the series after the fourth exhibition in 1874 with a total loss of £150,000 – a sum that had to be supplied by the royal commissioners overseeing the endeavor.[12]

As if to highlight the shift in taste characterized by the response to the London series of exhibitions, the organizers of the 1873 Vienna Exposition diverged from prioritizing the comparison of like exhibits. Rather, its massive main exhibition building was simply organized by exhibiting nation, with each arranging displays as it wished. Though this confounded those who continued to view the exposition form as a singular opportunity for the direct comparison of all manner of products and technologies in a given year, one can understand the challenges. International exhibitors began to develop sophistication in the principles of display and had a strong desire to keep their exhibits together and arrange them to the best effect. By the same token, the coordination of display space within an organizational scheme involving the thirty or more exhibit classifications expected as part of the comprehensive exposition format was a daunting task. It was far easier to apportion space to each exhibiting nation and allow exhibitors to arrange the contents of their area in the manner best-suited to their needs.

That said, not all categories of exhibits were displayed in Vienna's main exhibition building. By employing a new semi-differentiated format, the planners of the Vienna Exposition made allowance for the localization of all exhibits for three specific categories of articles: Fine Arts, Machinery, and Agriculture. Though these exhibit buildings were also internally organized by exhibitor, as opposed to specific item classification, the segregation of particular categories of exhibits into dedicated pavilions created arenas where all goods of a general type could be housed and roughly compared. Moreover, Vienna's exhibition was able to present this arrangement in a cohesive manner because the semi-differentiated format was specifically planned rather than being an improvised approach to accommodate unexpected participation.[13]

The organizers of the 1876 Philadelphia Exposition, the first international exposition held in the United States, carefully studied both the 1867 Paris and 1873 Vienna models. They concluded Vienna's geographic approach to organization was fundamentally "retrograde" in that it inhibited the direct comparison of exhibits, and recommended that the double-classification arrangement pioneered in Paris be preserved in their event.[14] Despite this intention, those charged with realizing the exposition were confronted with the realities of a limited budget and challenges in arriving at a design for a massive structure with a unified classification system. The internal organization of exhibits was ultimately modeled on the less-favored but logistically easier geographic arrangement.[15] Yet, by also following Vienna's model of employing a semi-differentiated format, this event was similarly able to generate some localized areas where products of a particular class could be viewed and compared.

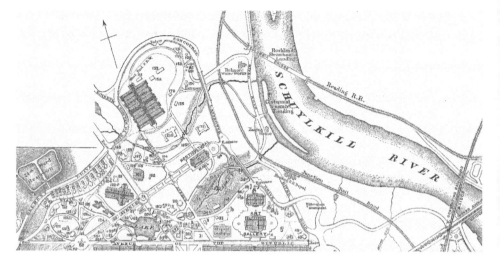

Figure 4.3. Centennial International Exhibition (Philadelphia, 1876)

Source: Joseph M. Wilson, *The Masterpieces of the Centennial International Exhibition, Illustrated* (Philadelphia: Gebbie and Barrie, 1876), 3:cxix.

The first three categories of the exposition's seven-part classification system (Education and Science, Mining, and Manufactures) were housed in a common Main Exhibition Building with the final four categories of Art, Machinery, Agriculture, and Horticulture allotted dedicated pavilions. Though far from the ideal modeled in the 1867 Paris *Exposition's* innovative amalgamated structure, the semi-differentiated format was a simple and cost-effective way to recapture some of the educative benefits of comparison on which expositions were premised. Where many of the subsequently held international expositions continued to deploy the amalgamated format's single exhibition building – and these without the complexity of a double-classification scheme, as was uniquely seen in Paris – the semi-differentiated format became de rigueur for expositions in the United States and common for the *Expositions Universelle* held in Paris. A notable variance was the 1878 Paris *Exposition*, which returned to the amalgamated format at the request of Prince Napoleon III, who had personally devised an organizational theory for the massive exhibition structure. His grid design was ultimately deemed a total failure for being too confusing and unwieldy and perhaps best serves as the exception that proves the rule of the overall trend away from the amalgamated format of exposition design.[16]

It was likely inevitable that the partial differentiation of exhibits into dedicated pavilions would give way to the abandonment of a "main" exhibition

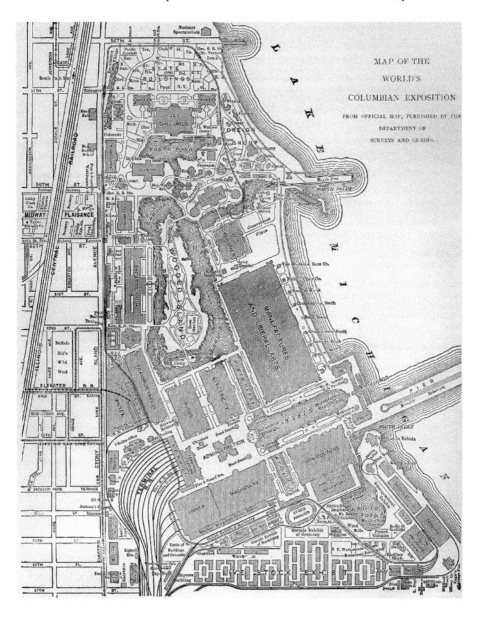

Figure 4.4. World's Columbian Exposition (Chicago, 1893)

Source: Jeffery Howe, Boston College.

building in favor of complete specialization for each structure on the exposition grounds. This approach, referred to in this chapter as the "fully differentiated" format, was pioneered by the planners of the 1893 World's Columbian Exposition in Chicago. Though arguably cheaper and easier to construct several relatively smaller buildings than a primary exhibition hall, the choice to establish dedicated pavilions to categories such as Manufactures and Liberal Arts, Fine Arts, Machinery, Mines and Metallurgy, Transportation, Agriculture, and Electricity had additional benefits to note. First, it allowed visitors to grasp the exposition's overall classification of exhibits by merely looking at a map of the grounds, so one could readily locate particular categories of interest. Second, although the organization within these buildings was generally based on exhibitor, as opposed to the particular classification of specific items, the fully differentiated format's localization of narrow categorical ranges within a single structure generated a reasonably easy way to facilitate comparison of like exhibits across the entire series of classifications. Such advantages became embedded in the form with the continued use of the fully differentiated approach.

After the 1893 Chicago Exposition, international expositions held in England, France, and the United States employed the fully differentiated format, as did many smaller-scale international events held throughout the world, and the establishment of this pattern can clearly be seen as established by the 1912 ICB (see table 4.1). The rapid spread of the evolving exposition form was enabled by the high degree of international participation garnered by the largest of these events. The intended purpose of stimulating technological innovation had strong appeal to nations beyond the initial core of Western exposition holders. Late-developing nations like Japan had compelling reasons to experiment with holding exhibitions in this period of European imperialism and American Manifest Destiny. That they should look to the latest trends in exposition design and adapt them to meet their unique needs is unsurprising, and their choices can be highly instructive for what they reveal about the functions of these events.

Japan and the Exposition Form

Japan was nearing the end of roughly two and a half centuries of Tokugawa rule and its policy of *sakoku* (seclusion) when the first international exposition was held in 1851. Within three years, Japan was forcibly opened to trade with the West by American gunships and, as the country became engaged in foreign commerce and its nationals were permitted to undertake foreign travel for study and diplomacy, the Japanese quickly began to learn of this recently developed Western institution. Japan's first self-representation at an international exposition was at the 1867 Paris *Exposition Universelle*, where the ruling Tokugawa *bakufu* and domains of Satsuma and Hizen participated.[17] Where the *bakufu* was in fact sovereign at the time, events culminating in the Meiji

Table 4.1. International Expositions 1851–1913 and Their Configurations

International Exposition	Amalgamated	Semi-Differentiated	Fully Differentiated
1851: London	*		
1855: Paris		*	
1862: London	*		
1867: Paris [J]	*		
1873: Vienna [J]		*	
1874: London [J]	*		
1875: Santiago, Chile	*		
1876: Philadelphia [J]		*	
1877: Cape Town	*		
1878: Paris [J]	*		
1878: Sydney, Australia [J]	*		
1880: Melbourne, Australia [J]	*		
1883: Amsterdam [J]	*		
1883–4: Calcutta		*	
1884: New Orleans [J]		*	
1885: London [J]	*		
1886: Edinburgh, Scotland	*		
1888: Barcelona [J]		*	
1889: Paris [J]		*	
1891: Kingston, Jamaica	*		
1891: Tasmania, Australia	*		
1893: Chicago [J]			*
1894: San Francisco			*
1894–5: Antwerp		*	
1897: Guatemala	*		
1897: Brisbane, Australia		*	
1897: Brussels	*		
1898: Omaha			*
1900: Paris [J]			*
1901 Glasgow [J]		*	
1901: Buffalo			*
1902: Hanoi (Tonkin), Fr. Indochina [J]		*	
1904: St. Louis [J]			*
1905: Liege, Belgium [J]		*	
1905: Portland, U.S.A. [J]			*
1906: Milan [J]			*
1907 Dublin		*	
1907: Hampton Roads, U.S.A. [J]			*

(*Continued*)

Table 4.1. (Continued)

International Exposition	Amalgamated	Semi-Differentiated	Fully Differentiated
1909: Seattle [J]			*
1910: Brussels	*		
1910: London, Japan-British Exhibition [J]			*
1911: Turin, Italy		*	
1913: Ghent, Belgium		*	

Source: List of international expositions derived from John Allwood, *The Great Exhibitions* (London: Cassell & Collier Macmillan, 1977), 181–3.

Note: *J* indicates known participation at the event by Japan.

Restoration were undertaken just days after the fair's closing on 31 October 1867, ultimately leading to a new Japanese state that invested great energy in quickly modernizing the country.[18]

Through their travels abroad, men like Fukuzawa Yukichi, who attended the 1862 London Exposition, Shibusawa Eiichi, who was part of the *bakufu* delegation for the 1867 Paris *Exposition*, and Sano Tsunetami, a member of Satsuma's delegation to the 1867 Paris *Exposition* and later a representative for the Meiji government at the Vienna Exposition of 1873, determined that these events were an important component of Western industrial, commercial, and educational strength. As their experiences were woven into the policies of the new Meiji state and shared with the Japanese public, efforts to continue the nation's participation in expositions abroad and hold them domestically were considered essential.

In order to prepare for the state's participation at the 1873 Vienna Exposition, the first full-scale international exposition held following the Meiji Restoration, Japan's Ministry of Education held a Western-style exposition in 1872.[19] Though the event followed the dominant amalgamated format encountered by Japanese delegations to Paris and London, there was no attempt at a systematic classification system for exhibited objects within the building beyond a small five-aisle section purporting to demonstrate the evolution of Japanese culture.[20] As Japan continued to participate in expositions abroad, however, the nation's awareness of both the purposes and practices of expositions became highly refined and was subsequently applied in future domestic expositions.

Following the nation's participation at Vienna, the Japanese government undertook a series of national expositions. The First National Industrial Exposition (*Daiichi Naikoku Kangyō Hakurankai*) of 1877 was held at Ueno Park in Tokyo. Historian Noriko Aso notes this event occurred as planned, despite

Table 4.2. Japanese National Expositions and Their Exposition Buildings

Exposition buildings	First (1877)	Second (1881)	Third (1890)	Fourth (1895)	Fifth (1903)
"Main" Exhibition Hall(s)	*	*	*		
Machinery	*	*	*	*	*
Fine Art	*	*	*	*	*
Horticulture	*	*			
Agricultural Production	*				*
Agriculture and Forestry			*	*	
Foreign Samples			*		*
Animals			*	*	*
Marine Products			*	*	*
Industrial				*	*
Forestry Production					*
Education					*
Transportation					*
Taiwan (colonial exhibit)					*

Note: Buildings that initially contained two designations of items but later specialized in one are treated separately.

Japan being embroiled in the Satsuma Rebellion, which, beyond the significant loss of lives, cost the Japanese government the very large sum of ¥42 million (approximately 80 percent of its annual budget) to suppress.[21] This clearly demonstrates the importance placed in hosting expositions to help realize the goals of *shokusan kōgyō* (*increase production, promote industry*).[22] This first national exposition was modeled on the semi-differentiated format encountered at both the 1873 Vienna and 1876 Philadelphia Expositions and, as many other exposition planners had done around the world, emulated specific components of previous expositions by adopting virtually the entire classification scheme used at Philadelphia and choosing to similarly distinguish the categories of Fine Arts, Machinery, Agriculture, and Horticulture for dedicated pavilions (see table 4.2).[23]

Though the government emphasized the importance of comparison as an essential purpose for expositions, objects exhibited at Japan's first national exposition were arranged by prefecture. This, of course, was not unique to Japan. The Vienna and Philadelphia Expositions had similarly organized exhibits this way, despite the earlier 1867 Paris exposition's highly touted arrangements. Beyond this, however, opportunities for comparison at Japan's first national exposition were nearly restricted further as Interior Minister Okubo Toshimichi initially banned the display of foreign exhibits out of concern their presence would showcase Japan's inadequacies in industrial development. He later relented, with the provision foreign articles be exhibited by Japanese officials, but in many ways the intention of comparison at this first national exposition was, as historian Angus Lockyer observed, "compromised by official design."[24]

Japan's Second National Exposition, held in 1881, continued to reflect the cutting edge of exposition design by once again employing the semi-differentiated format encountered in Vienna, Philadelphia, and Paris (1878), and by bringing in resident British architect Josiah Conder to design its primary exhibition building, which later became the gallery of the Tokyo National Museum. Though modeling the format and architecture of Western expositions, the organizers of Japan's second national exposition found a novel way to address the traditional conflict between arranging exhibits by exhibitor with the higher purpose of arranging articles by classification for direct comparison. The method devised was to arrange all exhibits by specific item classification except in the "First Main Building," which served as a dedicated structure for the arrangement of items based on exhibiting prefecture. In this way, the interests of exhibitors in arranging their own display space could be met while also maximizing the opportunity for the direct comparison of specific types of products, which was seen as indispensable for generating competition and promoting improvements and innovation.

The Third National Industrial Exposition, held in 1890, continued the previous domestic exposition's striking effort to arrange exhibits by classification in the various exposition structures, with the exception of the Machinery Building, which seems to have had its limited exhibits purely arranged by exhibitor.[25] Similarly, the 1890 event followed the semi-differentiated format, which had been well-established and most commonly used by the large-scale international expositions. One novel feature, at least in terms of Japan's domestic expositions, was that the Third National Exposition included a dedicated Foreign Samples Building. This, of course, maximized comparison, since Western products and technologies could be referred to on site, but the arrangement within this pavilion was surprisingly also organized by item classification rather than exhibitor. As noted, such an approach was rather rare in Western expositions but had the obvious benefit of sparing fairgoers the experience of wading through eclectic displays of foreign exhibitors to find specific types of items to compare with Japan's domestic offerings.

The Fourth National Exposition held in Kyoto's Okazaki Park, in 1895, did not include a Foreign Samples Building, but this can be explained by the fact that the Sino-Japanese War erupted the previous year and continued, even through the first weeks of the exposition. Indeed, the government's decision to continue with the event, despite the conflict, demonstrates again how essential these events were considered. Despite the failure to include foreign exhibitors, the

Fourth National Exposition can illustrate how attuned Japan continued to be with international exposition format trends.

The movement toward the fully differentiated configuration occurred only two years earlier by the organizers of the 1893 Chicago Exposition. This approach was immediately followed at the 1894 Midwinter Exposition in San Francisco and at all subsequent fairs in the United States. International expositions held abroad continued to use the amalgamated or semi-differentiated formats until the 1900 *Exposition Universelle* in Paris (see table 4.1). Japan, a participant at the 1893 Chicago Exposition, was the first foreign nation to organize its own exposition, albeit domestic, on the fully differentiated model, suggesting how closely Japan followed developments in the exposition form. Moreover, the now fully dedicated pavilions at Japan's Fourth National Exposition continued to be arranged by exhibit classification, maintaining Japan's unique emphasis on direct comparison (see table 4.2).

Japan's Fifth National Industrial Exposition held in Osaka's Tennōji Park, in 1903, was vastly different from the nation's previous expositions. With an area of 105,000 *tsubo* (roughly eighty-five acres), it was more than twice as large as any of the previous events. Within this massive area the products of the nation's post-Sino-Japanese War industrialization boom were showcased to its almost 4.5 million visitors, which was more than four times the attendance of Japan's previous 1895 exposition.[26] Although the fair's planners did not originally intend for the Osaka Exposition to be broadly open to international participation, they received so many applications from foreign nations and companies that they were moved to accommodate them. As was done for the 1890 exposition, a Foreign Samples Building was constructed. When it was fully booked, companies and nations that still desired to exhibit were left to construct their own pavilions, which Canada and several Western companies were obliged to do. Ultimately, fourteen foreign nations and many private Western firms participated in the Osaka Exposition and helped transform what was officially billed as a domestic exposition into something closer to a world's fair.

The Osaka Exposition's organizers continued to employ the fully differentiated format and constructed its dedicated pavilions to distinguish a wide range of categories (see table 4.2). Also continued at the Fifth National Exposition was the specific regulation in exhibit organization that goods be grouped by classification in all of the ground's dedicated pavilions, with the exception of the Machinery and Foreign Samples Buildings.[27] The Osaka Exposition in its size, scope, and physical arrangement can well be considered Japan's first international exposition. As such, the choices regarding aspects of the exposition form that were to be adopted and adapted reveal much about Japan's particular interest in holding these events.

Figure 4.5. Grounds of the Fifth National Industrial Exposition (Osaka, 1903)

Source: Courtesy of John Wilson Special Collections, Multnomah County Library, Portland, Oregon.

Lessons from Japan's Adoption and Adaptation of the Exposition Form

Several conclusions can be drawn considering how the form of the international exposition evolved and the ways this process was reflected in Japan's national expositions. First, even Japan's initial national event was at the cutting edge of exposition organization in its overall site plan. Held in 1877, it was modeled on the Vienna (1873) and Philadelphia (1876) Expositions' semi-differentiated format, not followed by other period "international" expositions such as Chile (1875), Cape Town (1877), Australia (1878 and 1880), Amsterdam (1883), and Edinburgh (1886). International expositions were events where nations asserted their relative level of progress and strength on the world stage, and the Japanese were highly attuned to such signals and used those highest in the perceived hierarchy as their guide. England, France, the United States, and Austria were seen as among those representing the highest levels of "civilization," and thus their approaches to the international exposition were naturally influential.[28] That being said, one may also gauge the relative value Japan placed on each nation's exposition by looking to the amount expended for participation. Using ¥100,000 as a baseline, all events supported at least at that level by Japan – with the exception of the 1878 exposition in Paris, which was widely regarded at the time as a complete failure in design – were ones that employed the ascendant semi-differentiated approach. We can therefore conclude that the expositions Japan valued most in terms of its own participation were consequently those that exhibited the latest in exposition design (see table 4.3a).

Second, Japan continued to be at the cutting edge of exposition arrangement. By its Fourth Domestic Exposition in 1895, Japan moved to the fully differentiated model first used in Chicago just two years earlier. Although this approach immediately became the standard for all expositions held in the United States,

Table 4.3a. Japanese Expenditures for Participation in Expositions with Advent of New Semi-Differentiated Format (1873–1893)

International Exposition	Amalgamated	Semi-Differentiated
1873: Vienna		¥520,858
1874: London	¥8,932	
1876: Philadelphia		¥359,545
1878: Paris	¥213,242	
1878: Sydney, Australia	¥29,817	
1880: Melbourne, Australia	¥33,014	
1883: Amsterdam	¥19,980	
1884: New Orleans		¥15,500
1885: London	¥27,517	
1888: Barcelona		¥23,000
1889: Paris		¥130,000

Table 4.3b. Japanese Expenditures for Participation in Expositions with Advent of Fully Differentiated Format (1893–1915)

International Exposition	Semi-Differentiated	Fully Differentiated
1893: Chicago		¥630,766
1900: Paris		¥1,319,559
1901 Glasgow	¥57,718	
1902: Hanoi (Tonkin), Fr. Indochina	¥11,900	
1904: St. Louis		¥800,000
1905: Liège, Belgium	¥40,000	
1905: Portland, U.S.A.		N/A
1906: Milan		N/A
1907: Hampton Roads, U.S.A.		¥12,768
1909: Seattle		¥100,000
1910: London, Japan-British Exhibition		¥2,080,000
1915: San Francisco		¥1,500,000

Source: Japanese expenditures to exhibit at international expositions derived from Ayako Hotta-Lister, *The Japan-British Exhibition of 1910: Gateway to the Island Empire of the East* (Richmond, Surrey: Japan Library, 1999), 221–2.

many international expositions continued to employ both the amalgamated format, such as Brussels (1897), Liège (1905), and New Zealand (1906–7), or the semi-differentiated approach employed at Antwerp (1894–5), Glasgow (1901), Turin (1902), Dublin (1907), and Brussels (1910). Again, these nations were not seen as among the highest in the global hierarchy, in contrast to the events where Japan spent at least the ¥100,000 baseline to participate, and these were ones that used the fully differentiated approach (see table 4.3b). Japan recognized and valued the most current trends in exposition design and applied them to their own domestically held national expositions without delay.

Third, though the 1867 Paris exposition modeled an approach that was seen as ideal for permitting the direct comparison of like articles by displaying them together, exhibits at subsequent international expositions were commonly organized by exhibitor. Classification systems existed on paper but were generally not manifest in the layouts of specific exhibition buildings. This was not the case for most of the Japanese expositions. From the nation's Second National Exposition onward, exhibits were arranged in the various pavilions by item classification. Although this regulation did not seem to apply to Japan's machinery buildings, that this approach was maintained once implemented in most of Japan's exhibition structures demonstrates the nation's strong commitment to the educational purposes of these events beyond what was seen in the West.

Conclusion

From its inception, the international exposition was idealized as an ephemeral event that could bring the world's best products and inventions together to help educate and stimulate the progress of "civilization," but the challenges of generating structural organizations to permit the side-by-side comparison of like exhibits ultimately superseded such high-minded ideals. The desire to advance the progress of civilization as a whole was tempered by the needs of exposition organizers and participating nations, which preferred easy source-focused arrangements, as opposed to the more challenging and technical exhibit-type approach. Structurally, despite the resulting emphasis on nation/exhibitor in organization, the exposition form evolved to accommodate at least proximate areas of exhibit comparison through increased specialization of pavilions, as seen in the transitions from the original 1851 Crystal Palace's amalgamated format, to the semi-differentiated format of the 1873 Vienna Exposition, and finally to the 1893 Chicago Exposition's fully differentiated approach.

For late-developing nations like Japan, the event of an international exposition offered the occasion to view and learn from the latest technologies, and as the host of these events they were afforded the ability to alter the features of the exposition form to best suit their needs. The latest trends in exposition arrangement as encountered abroad were adopted by the Japanese but were not blindly followed. Where Western expositions moved away from organizing exhibits by item classification, despite the educative value of direct comparison, Japan bucked this trend and came to consistently arrange exhibits in this way. When considering the initial concept of international exposition as events that could educate and stimulate continued development and progress through the direct comparison of goods and technologies, it seems as if the manner in which Japan adopted the exposition form was most faithful to its original ideal.

NOTES

1 There are a number of works that deal with this topic generally, such as Robert W.
   Rydell, *All the World's a Fair: Visions of Empire at American International Expositions,
   1876–1916* (Chicago: University of Chicago Press, 1984); and Burton Benedict,
   "International Exhibitions and National Identity," *Anthropology Today* 7, no. 3 (1991):
   5–9; as well as more specifically focused on Asia, such as Carol Christ, "Japan's Seven
   Acres Politics and Aesthetics at the 1904 Louisiana Purchase Exposition," *Gateway
   Heritage* 17, no. 2 (1996): 2–15; and Abigail Markwyn, "Economic Partner and Exotic
   Other: China and Japan at San Francisco's Panama-Pacific International Exposition,"
   Western Historical Quarterly 39, no. 4 (2008): 439–65.

2 As a note, the French "exposition," British "exhibition," and U.S. "world's fair" or
   "fair" will be used interchangeably in this study.

3 John Allwood, *The Great Exhibitions* (London: Cassell & Collier Macmillan, 1977),
   179.

4 Tony Bennett, "The Exhibitionary Complex," *New Formations: A Journal of Culture,
   Theory, and Politics* 4 (Spring 1988): 78–82.

5 Tessa Morris-Suzuki, *The Technological Transformation of Japan: From the Seventeenth
   Century to the Twenty-First Century* (Cambridge: Cambridge University Press, 1994), 93.

6 Toshio Kusamitsu, "Great Exhibitions before 1851," *History Workshop* 9 (1980): 70–89.

7 Jeffrey Auerbach, *The Great Exhibition of 1851: A Nation on Display* (New Haven,
   CT: Yale University Press, 1999), 92–3.

8 Auerbach, *Great Exhibition of 1851*, 94.

9 Allwood, *Great Exhibitions*, 33.

10 Allwood suggests that it was in fact the Polytechnic Exhibition of Moscow in
   1872 that was the first to consciously move away from the tradition of a central
   exhibition hall, but the event is not explicitly mentioned by subsequent adopters
   of the semi-differentiated format. Indeed, Moscow's exhibition was downplayed
   by foreign countries because there were to be no prize competitions, which caused
   France, for example – which initially appointed an honorary commissioner – to
   ultimately refuse their participation. See Allwood, *Great Exhibitions*, 48–9; *Journal
   of the Society of Arts, of the Institutions in Union and Official Record of Annual
   International Exhibitions* 20, 17 November 1871 to 15 November 1872 (London:
   Bell and Daldy, 1872), 818.

11 Javier Monclus, *International Exhibitions and Urbanism: The Zaragoza Expo 2008
   Project* (Surrey, UK: Ashgate Publishing, 2009), 27.

12 Allwood, *Great Exhibitions*, 48.

13 Allwood, *Great Exhibitions*, 33.

14 W.P. Blake and Henry Pettit, *Reports on the Vienna Universal Exhibition, 1873, made
   to the U.S. Centennial Commission* (Philadelphia: McLaughlin Brothers, 1873), 4.

15 Joseph M. Wilson, *The Masterpieces of the Centennial International Exhibition,
   Illustrated* (Philadelphia: Gebbie and Barrie, 1876), 3:xci–cxi.

16 Wilson, *Masterpieces of the Centennial International Exhibition* 59, 62–3.

17 Noriko Aso, *Public Properties: Museums in Imperial Japan* (Durham, NC: Duke University Press, 2014), 25–6.

18 For greater detail on the Tokugawa *bakufu*'s participation in the 1867 Exposition (as well as the challenge presented by the domain of Satsuma at the fair), see Angus Lockyer, "Japan at the Exhibition, 1867–1970" (PhD. diss., Stanford University, 2000), 27–78. For insight into the indigenous types of expositions in Japan, see P.F. Kornicki. "Public Display and Changing Values: Early Meiji Exhibitions and Their Precursors," *Monumenta Nipponica* 49, no. 2 (1994): 167–96.

19 The purposes for this event were multiple, as the exposition's structure was to become a permanent museum, and the exposition's exhibits were collected in pairs where practical so they could both be sent on to Vienna for exhibition and also maintained for the new museum's collection. The connection between the permanent institution of the museum and the ephemeral institution of the exposition was well understood. Both were educational tools predicated on the assumption that people can learn by viewing purposefully arranged exhibits. Exposition buildings were commonly intended to serve as permanent museums once the period of an exposition had closed, and the occasion of an exposition was often prearranged to coincide with the construction of a museum. In fact, this was another value of the semi- and fully differentiated formats for expositions, in that the use of multiple buildings made it possible to cheaply construct a number of temporary pavilions while, if the exposition planner's wished, allowing for the construction of a permanent structure at a more modest sum than what would have been required for the massive amalgamated form of exhibition building. See Monclus, *International Exhibitions and Urbanism*, 30.

20 Lockyer, "Japan at the Exhibition," 86.

21 Aso, *Public Properties*, 36–7.

22 Noriko Aso, "New Illusions: the Emergence of a Discourse on Traditional Japanese Arts and Crafts, 1868–1945" (PhD diss., University of Chicago, 1997), 69.

23 Ayako Hotta-Lister, *The Japan-British Exhibition of 1910: Gateway to the Island Empire of the East* (Richmond, Surrey: Japan Library, 1999), 220.

24 Lockyer, "Japan at the Exhibition," 101.

25 The reasons for this are unclear, but it was in fact the typical arrangement at Western expositions and not necessarily significant.

26 Aso, "New Illusions," 67.

27 Though the choice to organize the Foreign Samples Building at Osaka by exhibiting nation is not surprising, given the likely pressure from foreign participants and the ease of space allocation, a topic that deserves further research is why Machinery Buildings were exempted from this regulation at Japanese expositions. Structural issues were likely a factor, and one can imagine that the

value of direct comparison would have been especially appreciated for this sector's exhibits. For example, the 1904 St. Louis Exposition held the following year in fact singled out its Machinery Pavilion to be arranged by specific classes of items rather than exhibitor, suggesting that this was a practical approach.

28 David G. Wittner, *Technology and the Culture of Progress in Meiji Japan* (London: Routledge, 2008), 104.

5 What the Eastern Wind Brings: Rickshaws, Mobility, and Modernity in Asia

M. WILLIAM STEELE

Technology transfer often involves a hegemonic movement of ideas, skills, and goods from the developed to the developing. Governments on both sides assume the initiative; foreign advisers are invited and students are dispatched overseas. In Asia this process is often referred to as "Westernization," a term that underlies the metanarrative of Asia's long nineteenth century. This is especially the case in the area of mobility. As a result of contact with the West, the pace of life sped up immensely. In 1885, Fukuzawa Yukichi, Japan's most famous Westernizer, argued that Japan had no alternative but to follow the lead of the West:

> Transportation has become so convenient these days that once the wind of Western civilization blows to the East, every blade of grass and every tree in the East follow what the Western wind brings. Ancient Westerners and present-day Westerners are from the same stock and not much different from one another. The ancient ones moved slowly, but their contemporary counterparts move vivaciously at a fast pace. This is possible because present-day Westerners take advantage of the means of transportation available to them.... If one observes carefully what is going on in today's world, one knows the futility of trying to prevent the onslaught of Western civilisation. Why not float with them in the same ocean of civilization, sail the same waves, and enjoy the fruits and endeavors of civilization?[1]

Accordingly, the locomotive emerged as a powerful symbol of Japan's (and Asia's) modernity, contributing to industrial development, national integration, and to social and physical mobility. In 1854, Commodore Matthew C. Perry, dispatched by the United States to bring Japan into communication with other nations, presented a working telegraph and a Lilliputian steam locomotive to the "partially enlightened" Japanese, thereby inviting them to partake of the fruits of "science and enterprise."[2] And partake Japan did: by the turn of the century, Japan was one of the dynamos of the world, with a surging industrial economy, a powerful army and navy, and a growing empire.[3]

Figure 5.1. Illustration from Fukuzawa Yukichi's *Seiyō Jijō* [On Conditions in the West], 1866, Depicting the New World Connected by Telegraph, Steamship, and Rail (International Christian University Library).

To be sure, new technology of transportation and communication – the steamship, the locomotive, and the telegraph – were harbingers of modernity. These new vehicles suddenly and fundamentally altered the relationship between time and space. But the story of Asia's modernity is more complex than a simple West-East transfer of new technologies. Success was not a matter of imitation – or relative skill in copying. Western winds were instrumental in forcing the new Meiji regime to lift long-standing political and practical restrictions on wheeled transport.[4] What followed was an explosion in personal mobility. The new government, with British financial and technological help, built Japan's first railroad, laying 29 kilometers of track between Tokyo and Yokohama. Over 300 British and European civil engineers, general managers, locomotive engineers, and drivers were involved in the project. Service began in 1872.[5] By 1900, Japan had a network of over 6,000 km of track connecting all parts of the country.[6]

Eastern winds were also bringing about Japan's mobility revolution. Modernity did not suddenly emerge after the Meiji Restoration of 1868, the culmination of civil wars that resulted in the collapse of the regime that had governed Japan since the early seventeenth century. The Restoration did not mark the victory of progress (in the form of Westernization) over retrogression. Indeed, in Japan, as in modernizing regimes elsewhere, traditional values and technologies played an important, if not decisive role in bringing about revolutionary change.

For ordinary people, it was the low-tech rickshaw (in Japanese, *jinrikisha*, human-powered car), invented in Japan in 1869, that provided their first glimpse into a new world of cheap effective transportation. By 1872, three years after the new vehicle made its appearance, there were 40,000, and by 1875 over 100,000 rickshaws on the streets of Tokyo. The number reached a peak in 1896 with 210,000 countrywide.[7] The rickshaw, as a sort of juggernaut of modernity, quickly spread throughout Asia (including Southeast Asia and South Asia), and even into parts of Africa. By 1900, Japanese rickshaws (and their cheap imitations) had become Asia's primary people mover. This chapter examines the transfer of rickshaw technology from Japan to the rest of Asia: what the winds of the East brought. It highlights the role played by Akiha Daisuke and his adopted son-in-law Akiha Daisuke II, men who developed the rickshaw industry in Japan for domestic and overseas consumption in the late nineteenth and early twentieth centuries.[8]

Local Knowledge and the Invention of the Rickshaw

The Tokugawa *bakufu*, or shogunate, the government of Japan between 1603 and 1868, imposed restrictions on travel as one means to exert and sustain its authority. Members of the samurai or warrior class were given the privilege of riding on horseback, and major roads were under the direct control of the government. Commoners were expected to travel on foot. Heavy cargo was transported by small boats on rivers and coastal sea routes, and overland by packhorse. Nonetheless, the description of Japan as a "nation in night-caps" is an exaggeration.[9] The Tōkaidō and other major highways were kept in excellent repair; social and physical mobility, while slow, was not uncommon. Indeed, the simile of the "beehive" describes both England and Japan in the early nineteenth century, bees being the symbol of hard work and acceptance of social order.

The demographic historian Hayami Akira dated Japan's "industrious revolution" and the birth of the "workaholic" Japanese to the middle of the eighteenth century.[10] Moreover, Constantine Vaporis has debunked the myth of pre-modern Japan as a "society frozen in place." In his book on "breaking barriers," he shows how a "culture of movement" developed in the late eighteenth and early nineteenth centuries, including substantial travel for leisure as well as business.[11]

What happened after the opening of Japan to the Western world was a speeding up of existing trends. Well before the coming of Commodore Perry, Japanese thinkers were calling for the end of attempts to limit contact with the West. As early as 1798, for example, the mathematician, ship captain, and economic thinker Honda Toshiaki called on the government to promote the domestic production of articles famed for their excellence and to open up the country to foreign trade, thereby transforming Japan into "the England of the East."[12]

Nonetheless, government permission to use horse-drawn carts in the city of Edo and on major roads was granted only in 1866, two years before the Meiji Restoration. Regular stage service between Yokohama and Edo began immediately. The boneshaker, introduced by foreign residents of Yokohama, made its appearance on the streets of the newly renamed city of Tokyo in 1868.[13] The invention of the rickshaw followed in 1869, one year after Japan's political revolution. Three men – Suzuki Tokujirō, Izumi Yōsuke, and Takayama Kōsuke – applied for and were granted permission to produce and operate rickshaws for hire on the streets of Tokyo.[14]

Human-drawn carts were not unknown in Japan and other parts of Asia. The wheelbarrow, for example, was in widespread use in northern China for the transportation of both goods and people. The Japanese *daihachi kuruma*, a two-wheeled man-driven cart, performed similar functions. Both relied on wooden wheels and lacked speed and maneuverability. The use of horse-drawn carriages in port cities such as Yokohama may well have inspired the "invention" of the rickshaw. Indeed, the rickshaw was more the result of creative adaption of existing technologies with those from the West. The new people-movers were hybrid "exotic commodities," technological innovations associated with foreign modernity, copied locally at low cost and quickly made available to large

Figure 5.2. New Wheels for New Japan (*Shinpan jinrikisha zukushi*), woodblock print, early 1870s (Waseda University Library)

segments of the population.[15] As Suzuki Tokujirō claimed in a leaflet advertising his new transport service, "It is now possible for everyone high and low
rich and poor, to move about here and there."[16] Compared with the palanquin
in which two men carried a passenger suspended from a pole, the rickshaw was
cheap, convenient, comfortable, and speedy. As noted above, the new conveyance was immensely popular; by 1875, more than 100,000 rickshaws were plying the streets of Tokyo.

The earliest rickshaw was like a small cart with a roof and bamboo blinds. An
enterprising merchant, Akiha Daisuke (1843–94), was responsible for improvements that resulted in the familiar rickshaw. He reduced the size of the cab and
added a cushioned seat, hood, footrests, mudguards, and elliptical leaf springs
for comfort. Above all, he made his machines stylish: lacquered and decorated
in gold leaf. As Richard Bulliet has noted, as in the European carriage revolution, "aristocratic display rather than technology" contributed greatly to the
success of "Daisuke's car," as the rickshaw came to be known.[17]

Akiha was born into a family that specialized in military armor and horse
trappings. In the late 1860s, he helped to set up an overland horse-drawn stage
service between Kawasaki and Tokyo, giving him familiarity with the construction of Western carriages. Seeing the growing demand for speedy, convenient,
and inexpensive transport, in 1872 he set up a shop in the Ginza selling carts,
carriages, and jinrikisha of his own manufacture.[18] The 1911 sales catalogue of
his company, Akiha Shōten, includes a description of those early days:

> The introduction of the Jinrikisha, in 1869, really opened a new era upon the mode
> of travel in Japan where social status was still in its infant stage. Soon after its
> debut, approbation followed appreciation, and its reputation spread like wild fire
> over the whole country, so that in the year 1872 saw the business growing in such
> flourishing a state as the customers often crowded in front of the store, and in
> some case, they were compelled to draw lots, in order to obtain a Jinrikisha.
> The same experience I had in Osaka, at the opening of my branch store in 1871.
> The customers were always impatiently waiting for the goods from Tokyo. Right
> on the arrival, all had gone, leaving nothing at the store, even the damaged in the
> transit being gladly accepted.[19]

Akiha Shōten produced a line-up of rickshaws, from a sturdy stripped-down
model for everyday taxi use, to rickshaws that qualified as works of art. The
Ginza address for his showroom was fitting for Japan's foremost producer of
rickshaws. As can be imagined, however, with demand so great, Akiha was not
alone; rickshaw workshops were quickly established in Osaka, Kyoto, and other
parts of Japan. In Tokyo, following Akiha's example, Itō Tekesaburō and Saiga
Fujisaburō set up rickshaw showrooms and workshops, aiming at domestic
and foreign sales. Akiha Daisuke, however, was the undisputed leader in the

Figure 5.3. Jinrikisha for One Person, Akiaha Jinrikisha Catalog, 1911. Description of
Construction: Lacquering, best NURITATE, clothed underneath; Trimming, leather
diagonally buttoned; Hood, open style, of cotton drills lined with rubber muslin;
Stretchers, fourfolded iron; Mud-guards, full length; Wheels, sixteen knotted spokes;
Springs, suspending style (Edo-Tokyo Museum)

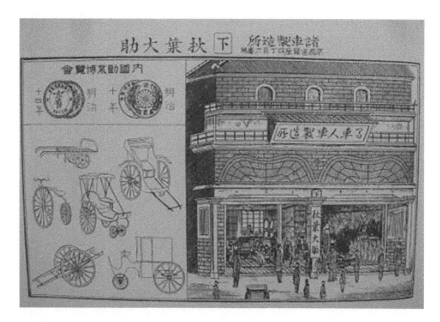

Figure 5.4. Akiha Shōten, Ginza Showroom and Manufactory, 1885 (National Diet Library)

field. His production method became the industry standard. At first, the process was simple, requiring the work of a few woodworkers, blacksmiths, and wheelwrights. By the end of the 1870s, however, rickshaws were more elaborate (lacquered body, hood, cushions, mudguards, springs, and other accessories designed to improve comfort and speed), requiring a more specialized labor force.[20]

Akiha's solution was to turn to subcontractors (*shita-uke*). His main workshop became more a place of assembly of parts produced elsewhere in small-scale workshops. The body was made in one shop, lacquered and decorated in another; hoods were assembled out of sailcloth and bamboo in another shop; axles and springs forged in other shops; and wheels with metal rims manufactured elsewhere. At the First National Industrial Exposition held in 1877, an event set up explicitly to encourage interaction between foreign and Japanese technologies, Akiha Daisuke was awarded the Hōmon (Phoenix) medal, the highest award, in the category of machinery relating to transportation. At the same time, however, recognition was given to a variety of workers who contributed to the rickshaw industry. At the Third National Industrial Exposition in 1890, for example, the products of several rickshaw-related subcontractors were selected for display, including those of spring-maker Nakano Torakichi, metalworker

Torii Bunjirō, lacquer artist Nishi Sagorō, hood-maker Takeuchi Keitarō, blacksmith Shingū Tōkichi, and others.[21] Akiha Daisuke continued to win awards in national industrial expositions, and before his death in 1894 was listed as one of the entrepreneurial heroes of new Japan.[22] He was able to offer mobility to the masses, but he did so by marshaling the skills and resources of a multitude of small workshops engaged in parts production.

Rickshaws to Asia and Beyond

Akiha Daisuke also gained a reputation as a pioneer in the export of rickshaws. As early as 1874, his cart company was shipping Japanese rickshaws to Shanghai and Hong Kong. By this time, the speed, convenience, and conferred status of riding in a rickshaw had attracted the foreign community in Yokohama and other port cities in Asia. In 1874, a French merchant known only as Ménard received permission from the French Concession to register the first rickshaw company in Shanghai and began to import rickshaws from Japan.[23]

According to Hanchao Lu, by the end of 1874, another nine companies, all Western-owned, had about 1,000 rickshaws in operation.[24] The numbers of rickshaws grew steadily, spreading out of the foreign concession, with the business devolving out of foreign hands. By the early twentieth century, replacing cumbersome wheeled pushcarts and sedan chairs, the Japanese rickshaw was the most common form of personal mobility, offering speedy, inexpensive, and convenient transportation to anywhere in the city. Their numbers peaked in 1930 with more than 23,000 vehicles, with an average of one public rickshaw for every 150 people.[25] The same story was repeated in the port city of Hong Kong, although, perhaps because of the hilly geography, the numbers were not as great. At their peak, in the 1920s, there were over 3,000 rickshaws in Hong Kong; in neighboring Canton, the numbers reached close to 6,000 in the 1930s.[26]

Rickshaws imported from Japan reached Beijing in 1886, but only after road conditions improved in the early twentieth century did their numbers began to rise significantly. David Strand reports that in 1923 there were over 30,000 rickshaws on the streets of Beijing, swelling to over 40,000 in the 1930s. "Rickshaw pulling was a public spectacle in Beijing in the 1920s. Sixty thousand men took as many as a half million fares a day in a city of slightly more than one million people."[27]

Rickshaws came to Singapore in 1880, but not directly from Japan. In the late 1870s, imported machines from Japan into Shanghai quickly had to compete with a multitude of local rickshaw workshops. It was these Chinese entrepreneurs who saw market opportunities in other parts of Asia, especially in areas where there were established settlements of overseas Chinese. The first machines to arrive in Singapore were from Shanghai, but more luxurious models were quickly ordered from Japan. According to James Warren, "Within a year of its advent, over a thousand of these two-wheeled vehicles were plying for hire in the city."[28] By 1906, there were 1,226 first-class, rubber-tired, and 6,138 second-class, iron-tired rickshaws in Singapore. Their numbers peaked in 1923 at just under 30,000.[29] The first-class machines were Japanese imports, as can be seen in the following newspaper advertisement:

> Rikishaws! Rikishaws! Rikishaws! The very, very best of Rikishaws just unpacked. The undersigned beg to inform their numerous constituents and the public in general that they have just received several kinds of Rikishaws from the best manufacturer in Japan.... Single or double seated rikishaws, fitted with English steel electro silver-plated, ball-bearing India rubber-cushion tyre wheels, with plain black colour and best velvet cushion.[30]

By the end of the nineteenth century, aided by networks of overseas Chinese traders and active sales campaigns by Japanese merchants, the winds of the East brought new forms of mobility to ordinary people in the then developing world. Akiha Daisuke relied on several Chinese merchant establishments in Yokohama, including Wing Tai Lung Importer and Exporters, Kwang Sing Woo and Co., and Wing Yee Who and Co.

Many merchants were originally involved in the export of Japanese marine products, including seaweed and dried squid, but gradually expanded into the export of Japanese silk, curios and handicraft products, and rickshaws. Overseas Chinese merchants in Yokohama, Kobe, and Nagasaki had close contact with trading partners in major port cities in China, Southeast Asia, and India. This intra-Asia Chinese commercial network facilitated the rapid spread of the rickshaw.[31] As the 1911 Akiha Shōten catalog noted, the rickshaw was not only the most convenient vehicle within Japan for the conveyance of persons, but enjoys "world wide fame as one of the chief exports from Japan." Moreover, its utility "has been gradually acknowledged throughout the East, especially in Singapore, Penang, Colombo, Hong Kong, Shanghai and Korea, and the trade so prospered that the vehicles are exported to as far as Zanzibar, Africa, contributing, to a certain extent, to the national wealth."[32] The streets of Durban, the busiest port in South Africa, thronged with more than 2,000 rickshaws, introduced first by Japanese traders in 1892.

Akiha Daisuke II – Mobility Merchant

After Akiha Daisuke died in 1894, his adopted son-in-law and successor, Akiha Daisuke II, sought to modernize rickshaw production and increase rickshaw exports to Asia. Under his leadership, Akiha Shōten, with its headquarters in Ginza and factory in the Honjo district of Tokyo, became the major producer, retailer, and exporter of rickshaws in Japan. Indeed, by the end of the nineteenth century, its assembly-line style of production, its use of subcontractors, its nationwide distribution network, its attention to overseas markets, and its

Figure 5.5. Rickshaws in Singapore (Postcard) (Author's Collection)

Figure 5.6. South African Ricksha [*sic*] Boys (Postcard) (Author's Collection)

attention to style, comfort, and quality, pioneered a style of industry that characterized Japanese modern economic growth: importing raw materials and producing a sought-after finished product for export.

In 1903, the company entered one of its elite models for display in the Fifth National Industrial Exposition held in Osaka, including a diagram of the assembly processes involved in the manufacture of rickshaws (see figure 5.7). The flow line emphasized the multinational origins of raw and finished materials (from India, Britain, Germany, China, Spain, and Japan) that would be used in the assembly of rickshaws in Japan.[33]

When Akiha Daisuke II became president of Akiha Shōten in 1898, production of domestic *jinrikisha* had peaked. In 1896, there were 210,688 rickshaws registered nationwide. By 1901, however, with numbers down to 200,000, it had become obvious to many, especially to a young graduate of Japan's most prestigious business school (the Tokyo School of Business, forerunner to Hitotsubashi University), that the future of the rickshaw business was clouded. Japan had an extensive and expanding national network of private and national rail for long distance travel. In Tokyo, as in other urban areas, commuter lines were in operation, and electric streetcars had replaced horse-drawn carriages; bicycle usage was also on the upswing.[34]

The new president determined that the future of Akiha Shōten lay in expanding exports, even though already more than 70 percent of its production was shipped overseas.[35] As can be seen in figure 5.8, rickshaw exports began slowly in 1880 (the first year for which official records are available) and peaked in 1910, with the export of 14,197 vehicles. Thereafter, in the face of motorization (competition with automobiles, buses, and streetcars) and competition with locally produced inexpensive imitations, exports gradually declined. For the twenty years between 1895 and 1915, however, precisely the years of the expansion of the Japanese empire, the Japanese rickshaw was king in the realm of Asian mobility.

The Akiha Shōten 1911 catalog is good evidence of the company's commitment to the export market (figure 5.9). It listed twenty-one different rickshaw models, some with variations according to climate.[36] Other of his catalogues included explanations in Japanese, English, and Chinese. Singapore was Akiha's largest customer in Asia, but in 1900 plans were announced to lay track for a new streetcar system in the British colony. Electric trams were also planned (or already in place) in Calcutta, Madras, Colombo, and Hong Kong. Akiha saw the need to open up new markets, and focused on China and its growing population, already at 415 million in 1900.[37]

In September 1901, the twenty-five-year-old entrepreneur embarked on a two-month inspection tour of China and Hong Kong. He kept detailed notes that he compiled in two travel diaries. His first stop was Tianjin, and from there

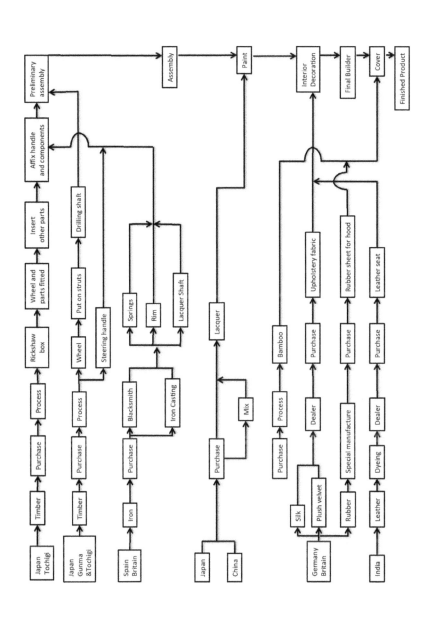

Figure 5.7. Jinrikisha Assembly Line – Akiha Shōten, 1903 (Edo-Tokyo Museum)

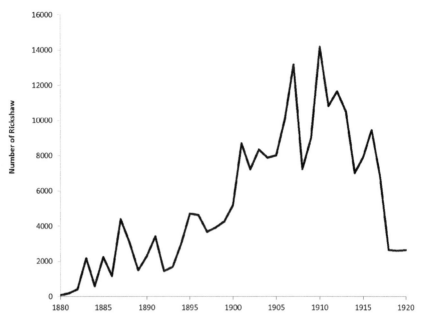

Figure 5.8. Exports of Japanese Rickshaws to Asia 1880–1920 (Compiled from Saitō, *Jinrikisha*, 222–3)

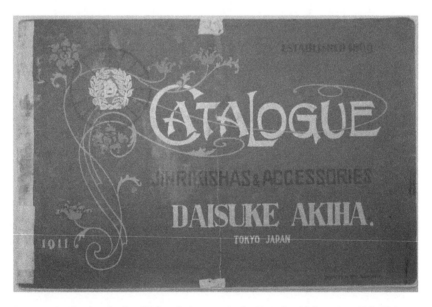

Figure 5.9. Catalog for Jinrikishas & Accessories by Daisuke Akiha, 1911 (Edo-Tokyo Museum)

he went to Beijing, Shanghai, and finally Hong Kong. Everywhere he inspected rickshaws: their structure, size, price, materials with which they were made, labor costs, taxes, import duties, and how local pullers pulled. He also took notes on local weather conditions, road quality, the size of the local rickshaw market and its growth potential. At the end of his inspection tour he declared that the seventy days and ¥500 was well worth the effort. A good general, he noted, knows his enemy and knows himself.[38]

In addition to carrying out market research on local conditions, Akiha set up local sales offices and sought to make direct contact with potential buyers. Japanese businessmen depended on Chinese merchants in Yokohama in order to gain access to the Chinese market. Akiha wanted to shift to direct sales. One year after his trip, for example, he sent a letter to all the company's overseas buyers in which he argued the advantages of dealing with his company directly. For example, in his 1903 letter to Whittal and Co., the firm that first imported rickshaws to Colombo in 1883, he promised an increase in profits if the company would agree to deal with Akiha Shōten directly.[39]

The young Akiha Daisuke II was a skillful and forward-looking businessman. He used advertisements in newspapers and magazines, introduced pneumatic tires and other innovations to improve rickshaw comfort and safety, and repeatedly won prizes in Japanese and overseas industrial expositions.[40] In the early twentieth century, newspapers extolled his entrepreneurial spirit as a pioneer in the mobility business.[41] In 1903, he remodeled the company's Ginza headquarters and built a state-of-the art factory in Honjo in order to expand production. He concluded a tie-up with Dunlop Rubber at a time when pneumatic tires were coming into general use on rickshaws, bicycles, and early automobiles. In the end, Dunlop pulled out, causing Akiha substantial financial loss. Nonetheless, he continued to diversify his operations.

In 1914, as representative of Ford and Chevrolet, he formed the Number One Auto Company (Daiichi Jidōsha Kaisha) and the Aoi Automobile Company. He even attempted to join with Hoshi Hajime, the head of Hoshi Pharmaceuticals, to start up a company to make airplanes, but this failed to materialize.[42] His company in 1909 employed 115 workers; in 1910 this was expanded to 250 workers, most of whom were put to work in new ventures including automobiles, rubber, coal, and asbestos. By the 1920s, however, Akiha's company was in trouble. Foreign demand for rickshaws shrank, in the end forcing him to reduce and eventually abandon rickshaw production. He was exploring the possibility of switching production from rickshaws to baby carriages when the Great Kanto Earthquake of 1923 delivered the final blow, destroying the Akiha shop and factory.[43] The new Tokyo that emerged from the rubble robbed the rickshaw of its modernity; in its place the bicycle, celebrated for its convenience, economy, and efficiency, emerged as "the speedy feet of the nation."[44]

Conclusion

While rickshaws nearly disappeared from Japan, they remained an essential part of urban mobility in other parts of Asia. In Hong Kong and Canton, for example, rickshaw usage actually increased alongside motorization in the 1920s and 1930s. Busses and trams were unable to offer the door-to-door service offered by rickshaws; moreover, and perhaps more importantly, the rickshaw, akin to the chauffeur-driven automobile, capitalized on the status it offered.[45] In Beijing, moreover, the rickshaw business not only benefited from the creation of European-style paved avenues, but opened new routes to urban modernity. As David Strand put it in his book on rickshaws in Beijing, "The rickshaw modernized urban transportation and speeded up the movement of people around the city in a manner comparable to the way in which telegraph wire hastened intercity communication and factories accelerated production."[46] Indeed, the introduction of streetcars did not immediately spell the end of pulled rickshaws, which were not only cheaper and faster, but offered access to Beijing's maze of narrow *hutong* alleyways.[47] Moreover, considerations of comfort and prestige gave the rickshaw significant advantages over more modern transportation systems.[48]

In other parts of Asia, the everyday mobility offered by the rickshaw gave way to various of its offspring: the cycle-rickshaw, *rintaku*, trishaw, pedicab, sidecar, cyclo, *becak,* and auto-rickshaw. According to Peter Cox, "No singular pattern of design or layout emerged, different cities and nations constructing distinctive styles and layouts, each reflecting local customs and practice, each having particular names."[49] The initial marriage of a bicycle with a rickshaw may have taken place in Singapore, but by the 1920s variations on this hybrid machine had become ubiquitous and by the end of the Second World War had largely replaced the pulled rickshaw. These cycle rickshaws continue even today to be an essential element of everyday mobility in many Asian cities. In India, for example, an estimated four to five million cycle rickshaws continue to play a valuable and irreplaceable role in urban and rural transport.[50] Dhaka, the capital city of Bangladesh, continues as "rickshaw capital of the world."[51]

This chapter focused on the rickshaw and the role it played as "wind from the East" in prompting Asia's mobility revolution. Westernization, involving the introduction (some would say the imposition) of foreign material goods, technology, and values, is the usual story of Asian modernization. In many cases this is true, but recent research suggests a more complex repertoire of possibilities and interactions between global and local initiatives and the existence of a multiplicity of modernizations.[52] The railroad may have impressed people in Japan and elsewhere in the "developing world" with its speed and power, but the low-tech rickshaw was equally attractive, if not addictive. And while the revolution in mobility that took place in late-nineteenth-century Asia was undeniably set in motion by new ideas, commodities, and technologies coming from the West, wind from the East demanded attention to different histories, cultures, geographies, climates, and population densities, producing different modes of movement. A fascination with power and speed preoccupied the vision of modernizing societies, and especially their governments.[53] Steam-engine speed came at a price beyond the reach of ordinary people; instead the rickshaw, a "bottom-up" industry that produced speeds only twice as fast as walking, helped set Japan and the rest of Asia on the path to modernity.

Akiha Daisuke was an active participant in Asia's creative appropriation of Western ideas and technologies of mobility and speed. The rickshaw he produced for domestic and overseas markets offered ordinary people the opportunity to buy mobility at an affordable price. Writing about everyday changes in the material landscape of modernizing China, Frank Dikötter questions theories of globalization that emphasize the alienation of local culture. He demonstrates that people in China not only embraced cheap imitations of foreign goods but also rapidly began to export them.[54] The story of the rickshaw follows a similar trajectory: made in Japan, this simple machine and the mobility it provided were exported to Asia, where even today it continues to confound simple narratives of modernity and technology transfer.[55] The rickshaw may be a sad reminder of a past best forgotten and overcome; but for others the rickshaw (or at least a solar-powered version of it) may be the green vehicle of the future.

This history and fate of the rickshaw can thus be used to complicate usual understandings of how technology transfer relates to local, regional, and global development (what we used to call "modernization"). First of all, the fact that the rickshaw was "made in Japan" is important. Asia's mobility revolution (and modernity in general) is marked by hybridity: winds from the East as well as those from the West were at work. Second is the importance of recognizing continuities. The 1868 revolution and the new government's commitment to Western "civilization and enlightenment" mask important areas of resistance and continuity with the past. The immediate success of rickshaw mobility was due only in part to imported technologies and ideologies of speed and convenience; fundamentally, it derived from and built upon an established "culture of movement" that encouraged (rather than hindered) popular participation in new modes of behavior made possible by contact with the West.

A related third point is the role and persistence of tradition, or what Tanimoto Masayuki calls "indigenous development" in Japan's (and Asia's) industrialization.[56] The workshops, contractors, and subcontractors that "manufactured" rickshaws were a world apart from the model factories set up by the central government in the 1870s and 1880s. The path followed by Akiha Daisuke and other entrepreneurs who developed indigenous industries (and relied less on technology transfer) complicate the prominence often given to factory-based industrial processes in the creation of "modern industry." Indeed, well into the 1920s, over 60 percent of Japan's industrial workforce was employed in workshops that employed fewer than five workers. Tanimoto concludes that the Western-style factory system played a comparatively limited role in Japan's industrialization and calls on scholars to look more closely at the role of small-scale and traditional/indigenous industry and their success in grafting rather than transplanting technology from outside.[57]

Finally, the rickshaw experience highlights the importance of subaltern perspectives on technology transfer and further complicates top-down or "state-led" models of industrialization. Ultimately, Japan's and Asia's modern experience is defined by both the rickshaw and the train, by bottom-up and top-down initiatives, by continuity and change, by grafting and transplanting technologies, by economies that respond to the demands of the state at the same time they seek to meet the desires of ordinary people. The history of the rickshaw in Asia is but a gentle reminder of the sometimes gale force of Eastern winds.

NOTES

1 Fukuzawa Yukichi, "Datsu-A ron" [On leaving Asia], *Jiji Shinpō*, 16 March 1885. For English translation, see David John Lu, *Japan: A Documentary History: The Late Tokugawa Period to the Present* (Armonk, NY: M.E. Sharpe, 1996), 35–53, translated as "Goodbye Asia."

2 On the Perry mission, see Francis L. Hawks, *Narrative of the Expedition of an American Squadron to the China Seas and Japan: Performed in the Years 1852, 1853, and 1854, under the Command of Commodore M.C. Perry, United States Navy* (New York: D. Appleton, 1856). For the interest excited by Japan's first encounter with the locomotive, see pages 415–16.

3 Readers unfamiliar with the history of modern Japan may wish to look at Andrew Gordon, *Modern Japan: From Tokugawa Times to the Present* (New York: Oxford University Press, 2003). Another recent general account is Elise K. Tipton, *Modern Japan: A Social and Political History* (London: Routledge, 2008). A collection of academic articles on the Meiji period (1868–1912) may be found in the four volumes edited by Peter Kornicki, *Meiji Japan: Political, Economic, and Social History, 1868–1912* (London: Routledge, 1998). See also Marius Jansen, ed., *The Emergence of Meiji Japan*, (New York: Cambridge University Press, 1995); and M. William Steele, *Alternate Narratives in Modern Japanese History* (London: Routledge, 2003).

4 The Tokugawa *bakufu*, or shogunate, the government of Japan between 1603 and 1868, imposed restrictions on travel as one means to exert and sustain its authority. As Constantine Vaporis notes, carts (pulled by horses, bullocks, or humans) "were kept off the principal roads as part of a conscious policy to maintain the roads in

good condition for pedestrian traffic." See Constantine Vaporis, *Breaking Barriers: Travel and the State in Early Modern Japan* (Cambridge, MA: Council on East Asian Studies, 1994), 11. After the opening of Yokohama to foreign trade in 1859, foreign merchants urged the Tokugawa regime to relax these restrictions. Finally, in 1866, two years before the Meiji Restoration, permission to use horse-drawn carts in the city of Edo and on major roads was granted. See Saitō Toshihiko, *Kurumatachi no shakaishi* [A social history of automobiles] (Tokyo: Chūō Kōronsha, 1997), 3.

5 On the revolution brought about by the introduction of the railroad, see Steven J. Ericson, *The Sound of the Whistle: Railroads and the State in Meiji Japan* (Cambridge, MA: Council on East Asian Studies, 1999), esp. 25–94.

6 Ericson, *Sound of the Whistle*, 9.

7 On the history of the rickshaw in Japan, the most important source is Saitō Toshihiko, *Jinrikisha* (Tokyo: Sangyō Gijutsu Sentaa, 1979). For rickshaw numbers, see chart 1, 223. I have written previously on the history of the rickshaw in Japan and Asia: M. William Steele, "Mobility on the Move: Rickshaws in Asia," *Transfers: Interdisciplinary Journal of Mobility Studies* 4, no. 3 (Winter 2014): 88–107. Much of the material in this chapter draws upon this earlier research.

8 Akiha Daisuke's name is more commonly written Akiba Daisuke. He spelled his name Ahiha in all of his English correspondence. The prime source of information on Akiha Daisuke and Akiha Daisuke II and their company, Akiha Shōten, is Saitō Toshihiko, *Jinrikisha*. I have also taken advantage of "Akiha Shōten Monjo" [Documents relating to the Akiha Shōten] in the archives of the Edo-Tokyo Museum of History.

9 Upon learning of the Perry mission to Japan, the *Times-Picayune* (New Orleans) wrote, "The fleet destined Japan will soon be ready to put to sea.... [T]he Japanese refuse all intercourse with other nations whom they look upon as beyond the pale of humanity. But humanity and the United States are progressive, and it thus happens that Japan is now in the way of civilization.... The world cannot stand still to accommodate a nation in night-caps" (28 March 1852, 2).

10 In English, see Hayami Akira, *Japan's Industrious Revolution, Economic and Social Transformation in the Early Modern* Period (Tokyo: Springer Japan, 2015).

11 Vaporis, *Breaking Barriers*, 14–15.

12 Donald Keene, *The Japanese Discovery of Europe, 1720–1830* (Stanford, CA: Stanford University Press, 1969), 109; Keene's book includes translations of excerpts of Honda Toshiaki's writings, including the conclusion of his *Seiiki monogatari* [Tales of the West], 175–229. See especially page 226. For the Japanese original, see Tsukatani Akihiro and Kuranami Seiji, eds., *Honda Toshiaki, Kaibose Iryō: Nihon shisō taikei* (Tokyo: Iwanami Shoten, 1970), 44:132.

13 On this history of the bicycle in Japan, see M. William Steele, "The Speedy Feet of the Nation: Bicycles and Everyday Mobility in Modern Japan," *Journal of Transport History*, 3rd ser., 31, no. 2 (December 2010): 182–209.

14 Later claims that an American missionary, Jonathan Gobel, invented the rickshaw
    have been discredited. See Calvin Parker, *Jonathan Gobel of Japan: Marine,
    Missionary, Maverick* (Lanham, MD: University Press of America, 1990). See also
    Richard Bulliet, *The Wheel: Inventions and Reinventions* (New York: Columbia
    University Press, 2016), 191–4.
15 Frank Dikötter, *Exotic Commodities, Modern Objects and Everyday Life in China*
    (New York; Columbia University Press, 2006), 261.
16 Tokyo-shi shi-kō (Tokyo: Rinsen Shōten, 1996), 51:168. For complete translation of
    the advertisement, see Steele, "Mobility on the Move: Rickshaws in Asia," 91.
17 Bulliet, *The Wheel*, 194.
18 For biographical details on Akiha Daisuke, I reply on Saitō, *Jinrikisha*, 158–62.
19 "A Short History of the Industry," *Catalogue: Jinrikishas & Accessories*, Daisuke
    Akiha, Tokyo, Japan (*Jinrikisha katarogu*), 1911, "Collection of Documents relating
    to Akiha Shōten," Archives of the Edo-Tokyo Museum of History.
20 For details on the process of rickshaw production, see Saitō, *Jinrikisha*, 194–216.
21 Saitō, *Jinrikisha*, 196–7.
22 Shinoda Shōsaku, *Shin-Nihon gōketsuden: jitsugyō risshin* [The lives of heroes
    of New Japan: Entrepreneurs who rose up in society] (Tokyo: Igyōkan, 1892),
    164–7.
23 Very little is known about the Frenchman Ménard. The primary source of
    information on his role in introducing Japanese rickshaw to Shanghai is Ch.
    B-Maybon and Jean Fredet, *Histoire de la concession française de Changhai* (Paris:
    Librairie Plon, 1929), 367–9.
24 Hanchao Lu, *Beyond the Neon Lights: Everyday Shanghai in the Early Twentieth
    Century* (Berkeley: California University Press, 1999), 68.
25 Hanchao Lu, *Beyond the Neon Lights*, 69.
26 Fung Chi Ming, *Reluctant Heroes: Rickshaw Pullers in Hong Kong and Canton,
    1874–1954* (Hong Kong: Hong Kong University Press, 2003), 65.
27 David Strand, *Rickshaw Beijing: City People and Politics in the 1920s* (Berkeley:
    University of California Press, 1989), 20.
28 James Francis Warren, *Rickshaw Coolie: A People's History of Singapore, 1880–1940*
    (Singapore: Singapore University Press, 2003), 14.
29 Warren, *Rickshaw Coolie*, 61.
30 Warren, *Rickshaw Coolie*, 52.
31 Despite the importance of intra-Asian trade networks dominated by overseas
    Chinese merchants, scholarship lags in the study of Western merchants in
    Asia. One excellent study is Linda Grove and Shinya Sugiyama, *Commercial
    Networks in Modern Asia* (London: Routledge, 2001). See also the "Conclusion"
    to Hitoshi Hirakawa and Hiroshi Shimizu, *Japan and Singapore in the World
    Economy: Japan's Economic Advance into Singapore, 1870–1965* (London:
    Routledge, 2002), 207–22. On Chinese merchants in Yokohama, see Sasaki Keiko,

"Yokohama kyōryūchi no Shinkoku-jin no yōsō to shakai-teki chi'i" [The character and social standing of the Chinese in the Yokohama foreign settlement], *Kanagawa University Graduate School Studies* 10, no. 10 (2008): 213–37, https://core.ac.uk /download/pdf/291680792.pdf. Biographical information on individual Chinese merchants is rare; one exception is the study by Itō Izumi on Ng Chuck Hon (Ng Jik Wun). See the special issue on the history of Yokohama Chinatown in *Kaikō hiroba* (Yokohama Archives of History News), 46 (11 June 1994), http://www .kaikou.city.yokohama.jp/journal/images/kaikouno-hiroba_46.pdf.

32 "A Short History of the Industry," *Catalogue: Jinrikishas & Accessories* (front matter, no page numbers).

33 See Peter James Rimmer, *From Rikisha to Rapid Transit: Urban Public Transport Systems and Policy in Southeast Asia* (New York: Pergamon, 1986), 46; original Japanese version in Saitō, 199–203. The source of figure 5.7, Jinrikisha Assembly Line, is a 1903 chart titled "Akiha Daisuke kōjō jinrikisha seizō kōtei" (The process of jinrikisha production, Akiha Daisuke Factory), included in the "Collection of Documents relating to Akiha Shōten" held in the Archives of the Edo-Tokyo Museum. A version of the chart may be found in Saitō, Jinrikisha, 200, and Rimmer, 49. I thank Jung Jaehoon, research assistant, Institute of Asian Cultural Studies, for his assistance in making the chart.

34 See Steele, "Speedy Feet of the Nation."

35 Saitō, *Jinrikisha*, 226.

36 *Catalogue: Jinrikishas & Accessories*, Daisuke Akiha, Tokyo, Japan (*Jinrikisha katarogu*), 1911, "Collection of Documents relating to Akiha Shōten," Archives of the Edo-Tokyo Museum of History. (Reference is to the entire catalogue, which consists of around forty-five pages).

37 Saitō, *Jinrikisha*, 218–19.

38 Akiha Daisuke II, "Shinkoku Ei-ryō Honkon manyō kikō" [Travel diary for a trip to the English colony of Hong Kong], 1902; "Tenjin Shanhai Honkon hanro kōchō shutchō nisshi" [Diary of an excursion to Tianjin, Shanghai, and Hong Kong seeking to expand sales (of Rickshaw)], 1903. "Collection of Documents relating to Akiha Shōten," Archives of the Edo-Tokyo Museum of History. See also summary of the activities of the "King of the Jinrikisha Industry" in China in *Shokanshō yōtatsu shōnin meikan* [Who's who of merchants associated with government offices and ministries], ed. Yamaguchi Shinichi (Tokyo: Unyo Nippōsha, 1910), 1:36–7.

39 Saitō summarizes the Whittal letter in *Jinrikisha*, 221–2. The English original of correspondence with Whittal and Company and with Seeroomul Topundas is included in "Tenjin Shanhai Honkon hanro kocho shutcho nisshi" [Diary of an excursion to Tianjin].

40 A short biography of Mr. Daisuke Akiba, *Jinrikisha Maker*, was included in the souvenir guidebook to the Japan-British Exhibition of 1910: "When Mr. Akiba succeeded to his father's business, he never for a moment relaxed his attention toward improvements. The demand for these vehicles [Jinrikisha] has rapidly

increased in British India, Straits Settlements, Hongkong, China and Korea. In the national exhibitions, they were awarded high class medals. It was in the year 1901 that a Grand Asiatic Exhibition was held in Hanoi, French territory, at which a silver medal of honour was awarded." Mochizuki Kotarō, "Japan To-day: A Souvenir of the Exhibition Held in London 1910" (Liberal News Agency, Tokyo 1910), 599.

41 Akiha copied newspaper and magazine articles that described him and his business. See "Akiha Daisuke kankei kiji utsushi" [Copies of articles relating to Akiha Daisuke], "Collection of Documents relating to Akiha Shōten," Archives of the Edo-Tokyo Museum of History.

42 Saito, *Jinrikisha*, 165.

43 See "Decline of the Rickshaw," *Mt. Ida Chronicle* 45, no. 2 (2 February 1923): 1. "Mr. Akiha, looking for other challenges to direct his enterprise and money, is of opinion that Japanese women are no longer satisfied with their lot of being wife, mother, nurse, and servant of the family; they desire, he says, to go out more and see more in order that they may have a broader outlook and more properly bring up their children.... Baby-carriages are the answer, he believes, and he is planning to flood the country with them" (https://paperspast.natlib.govt.nz/newspapers /MIC19230202.2.5).

44 In the 1920s, as the rickshaw declined, bicycles expanded dramatically. In 1920 there were 2 million bicycles in use, rising to over 5 million in 1930. In 1927, the Ministry of Commerce and Industry boasted that Japan was "the foremost bicycle country in the world." See Steele, "Speedy Feet of the Nation," 191–2.

45 Fung Chi Ming, *Reluctant Heroes*, 165.

46 Strand, *Rickshaw Beijing*, 26.

47 Strand, *Rickshaw Beijing*, 136.

48 Strand, *Rickshaw Beijing*, 137.

49 Peter Cox, *Moving People: Sustainable Transport Development* (London: Zed Books, 2010), 166.

50 Cox, *Moving People*, 169.

51 Rob Gallegher, *The Rickshaws of Bangladesh* (Dhaka: University Press, 1992). See the 3 August 2012 report from Bangladesh that continued to celebrate Dhaka's status as "the world's capital city of rickshaws": "Rickshaws of Bangladesh and Its History," http://weloveourbangladesh.blogspot.jp/2012/08/rickshaws-of -bangladesh-and-its-history_7522.html.

52 The introduction to Frank Diköttor, *Exotic Commodities*, elaborates on the usefulness of concepts such a hybridity, acculturation, and emulation in attempts to understand what happens when two cultural systems and their material objects come into contact with each other.

53 John Tomlinson, *The Culture of Speed* (Los Angeles: Sage Publications, 2007), esp. "The Cultural Significance of Speed," 1–14.

54 See the introduction to Diköttor, especially 7–12; his conclusion brings the story of "exotic commodities" into the twenty-first century: "If an intrinsic element of

a rapidly changing world is the capacity to overcome resistance to novelty, could China be more in tune with modernity than Europe?" 267.

55 See the Introduction (Steele) and four articles on rickshaws in South Asia in "Special Section on Rickshaws," *Transfers* 3, no. 3 (Winter 2013): 56–130, for recent studies on the history, present status, and future of rickshaw usage.

56 See the essays in Masayuki Tanimoto, ed., *The Role of Tradition in Japan's Industralization*, Japanese Studies in Economic and Social History, vol. 2 (Oxford: Oxford University Press, 2006).

57 Tanimoto Masayuki, "The Role of Tradition in Japan's Industrialization: Another Path to Industrialization," in Tanimoto, *Role of Tradition in Japan's Industralization*, 3–44, see esp. 4–5.

6 Zhang Jian and the Transfer of Western Business Practices through Japan into China

YU CHEN

Best known as an entrepreneur who promoted the modernization of Nantong, Jiangsu province, in the wake of China's defeat in the Sino-Japanese War (1894–5), Zhang Jian (1853–1926), a local gentry turned industrialist, provides a good example of local entrepreneurial initiative to transfer Western industrial technologies (through Japan) into the Chinese hinterland. Exhibiting great business acumen, Zhang established the Da Sheng Cotton Mill, China's only profitable, private, Western-style cotton mill. His achievements also included creating a Western filature, flour and oil mills, machine shop, and distillery – all of which relied on the successful transfer of advanced Western industrial technologies, technological know-how, and creation of an enterprise system.

To chronicle Zhang Jian's thoughts and actions, this chapter is divided into four parts. First, I will discuss the historical circumstances within which Zhang Jian was active. I am most interested in his transformation from a government official into a modern industrial entrepreneur. I will also examine his blueprint for local self-government. Part 2 examines Zhang's views on the transfer of Western technologies and business practices from Japan to China. In particular, I will explore his 1903 visit to Japan to uncover the origins of his ideas about local self-government from the perspective of knowledge acquisition. Part 3 illustrates Zhang's efforts to improve political conditions in Nantong City and introduce his concept of "people's or citizen's diplomacy," which was promoted by industrialists who sought local self-government and greater participation in the state. I will also show how Zhang tried to bring peace to his hometown during the Boxer Rebellion. The last part deals with Zhang's ideas concerning managerial systems in modern Chinese enterprises. I will focus on Zhang's particular form of business management as well as his views on how to distinguish between the concepts of "public" and "private."

Following China's defeat in the First Opium War and the conclusion of the Treaty of Nanjing, the Qing dynasty (1644–1912) was faced with the crisis of potentially becoming colonized by the West. To save the country, enlightened reformers, most of whom were government officials, adopted advanced Western technologies to strengthen China's military and preserve traditional culture in what is often referred to as "China's response to the West" – a concept that has been used to portray the process of social and political changes in late imperial China. Paul A. Cohen argues, however, that it is necessary to reconsider Western centralism by focusing on the Chinese context, and asserts that the gentry's reaction to Western intrusions was likely to be different from that of government officials.[1]

Local gentry reform initiatives should not be viewed as a reaction to the West because they reflected only local interests and problems. Moreover, the relationship between the central government and local gentry was so subtle that even in the aftermath of the Boxer Rebellion (1898–1900), the Qing government's new policies were seen by local gentry as threats that would deprive them of their interests and rights gained from local administrative management or businesses.[2] After the conclusion of the Boxer Protocol in 1901,[3] the Qing government initiated a series of political, economic, military, cultural, and educational reforms, among which was the adoption of a local administrative management system, which they called local self-government, to be implemented by local gentry. While the Qing believed that local self-government would strengthen the polity as a top-down reform, many local gentry and reformers saw this as an opportunity for greater local autonomy.

The decline of the Qing dynasty produced two main groups with differing opinions about how to cope with the Western crisis and the threat of being colonized. One group comprised people who attempted to overthrow the government through revolutionary movements. The other group – which proved to be more popular during the 1860s – was composed of so-called reformers who were opposed to violence. They preferred reform without destroying the old institutions of government and society. The Self-Strengthening Movement, which aimed to adopt Western military technology and armaments in the 1860s, reflected their ideals. At that time, the reformers emphasized the importance of military affairs because they thought it was simply a lack of modern military power that led to China's defeat at the hands of Great Britain in the Opium Wars. In order to acquire modern Western weapons, in 1865, Zeng Guofan (1811–72), a Qing statesman and later general, along with fellow reformer and high-ranking Qing official Zhang Zhidong (1837–1909), established the Jiangnan Manufacturing Bureau, the largest arsenal in China at the time, to produce rifles, canon, and gunpowder, as well as small armored naval vessels. The bureau relied on Western equipment and foreign technicians who played a crucial role in the manufacturing. Wu Chengming has argued that military industries, together with shipbuilding, mining, and railway construction during this period, failed to accelerate China's industrialization because technology transfer from the West was insufficient and based on moving machines, not knowledge.[4] However, China's low level of initial industrialization was partly due to the reformers' attitudes toward Western civilization.

Beyond military technology, when reformers attempted to transfer other artifacts of Western civilization, they abided by the famous dictum "Chinese learning for the foundation, Western learning for utilization." Chinese learning meant traditional social structure and Confucian philosophy. In other words, they never seriously questioned the basic Confucian precepts that formed the guiding principles of their lives. For a follower of Confucius, moral superiority was more important than technical knowledge. Between the 1870s and 1890s, however, reformers gradually realized that it was crucial to accelerate growth led by the private sector if China was to industrialize and modernize.[5]

Zhang Jian was more of a reformer than a revolutionary because he believed, like other reformers, that Confucianism was crucial for maintaining a stable state. He stated, "The principle will not change, the way to maintain the internal stability of the empire has to be changed."[6] By "principle" Zhang meant China's traditional social structure and Confucianism; the "way" referred to the adoption of advanced Western technologies.

Zhang's attitude toward Western civilization, however, was not exactly like that of other reformers, because he devoted himself to adopting not only the material aspects of the West, but also the political institutions of Western civilization. Zhang was aware that local self-government, with which he was most concerned, was derived from the West. He noted, "Because there were many different ethnic groups in Western countries, it was not very long since absolute monarchy was adopted in the West. Most governments placed great significance on local affairs and called it local self-government so as to distinguish from the administration of the central government. It makes local people become their own masters."[7] Zhang's knowledge of Western local self-government, however, came to him indirectly through Japan, as did his ideas regarding industrialization. Looking at Zhang's early life will help us understand why he followed a different path from that of other reformers and believed in the value of Western society within a Chinese Confucian context.

Zhang was born on 1 July 1853. At the age of four, he began to study the Chinese classics and spent most of his early days studying for the civil service examination. In an official-oriented society based on Confucianism, sitting for examinations and earning high positions proved to be the most efficient way to build a career as a government official.[8] By capturing and holding the loyalty of local elites, China's dynastic governments assured state control over the population for more than 1,300 years. The educated elite, including Zhang Jian – raised in Confucianism and taking civil service examinations – served as role models for the people.

After failing the primary level examination many times, Zhang finally gained his first government station in 1894 at the age of forty-one. In addition, he was appointed to the position of compiler of the first class at the Han Lin Academy, a sign of his academic achievement. Zhang, however, quickly abandoned his career as an official in the Qing government. Historian Wang Dunqin argues that Zhang left because of China's defeat in the first Sino-Japanese War and his father's death, both of which were great shocks to him.[9]

The more decisive reason, however, was Japan's victory over China. Zhang was aware of the economic dangers that resulted from the Treaty of Shimonoseki, which settled the war. The treaty permitted Japan to establish factories in several Chinese port cities. Weaving was Nantong's main industry, and the importation of Japanese cotton thread constituted a major threat to his hometown's economy. Zhang's transformation from bureaucrat to entrepreneur was motivated by more than ensuring Nantong's economic stability. Discussing his change of career, Zhang stated, "After a great deal of thought, I decided to condescend to take up business. My goal was to save our country rather than to achieve personal gain."[10] Rather than simply confronting potential economic pressure from abroad, Zhang was motivated by national patriotism.

Zhang Xiaoruo, Zhang Jian's son, too, has concluded that the primary factor that changed his father's career was China's weakness in the face of foreign military and economic aggression. Zhang's turn to practical affairs was also intended to challenge the stereotype of the useless scholar.[11] Zhang was concerned with not only the weaving industry in Nantong, but with the national crisis facing China. It was only through self-strengthening and enriching each locality that the nation could be saved.

In order to put his ideas into action, Zhang believed that he needed an overall plan.[12] He quickly drew up blueprints for local self-government in Nantong, which emphasized the importance of educational reforms. "Enlightenment is most important to undertake for local self-government. To enlighten the ignorant, we should give priority to education. Then, we have to collect funds first by developing industry to promote education. Industry and education should support each other. Based on the product resulting from both industry and education, I will then focus on charitable projects and the public good."[13]

In Zhang's mind, education was the highest priority, a point with which Zhang Xiaoruo concurred.[14] It is also clear that Zhang Jian regarded the development of the economy as a financial resource for educational reform, local charities, and even political change. Once satisfactory educational reforms and an ideal political system were realized, Zhang Jian might achieve more from his business management. Zhang's economic ideas and the Western business methods he transferred should not be viewed in isolation, because he combined business with all other social activities. In short, the methods Zhang introduced from Japan, including business management, were merged within a grand plan.

Zhang's dedication to developing Nantong's economy was also in accord with the central government's policy on local self-government. At the time, and in the face of a Japanese threat in the Yangtze delta area, Governor-General Zhang Zhidong encouraged local officials and gentry to establish industrial enterprises. Zhang Jian followed Zhang Zhidong's ideas and persuaded six other merchants – Pan Heqin, Guo Maozhi, Liu Yishan, Chen Chutao, Fan Shixun, and Shen Jingfu – to work with him to establish a modern, Western-style cotton mill, known as the Da Sheng Cotton Mill, in 1896.

Where Zhang Jian proved to be different from other reformers was in the methods he adopted to strengthen the country. Whereas many reformers were attaching greater importance to military power, Zhang believed that the basis of Western success came from the development of industry and education, not only military affairs.[15] In reality, and before starting in business, Zhang had little knowledge of Western ideas. Regardless, he was enthusiastic about learning from Japan because he believed that Japan had close cultural connections to China. When he advised the central government to implement constitutional reform, he noted, "China is culturally similar to Japan, so it is better to learn from Japan because Japan has taken much knowledge from Germany and the Kingdom of Great Britain."[16] Even at the early stages of his conversion from official to entrepreneur, Zhang exemplified the process by which technologies and technical know-how were transferred from the West through an East Asian intermediary, Japan.

Initially and for several years, Zhang had little first-hand knowledge of Japan. Most of what he knew was learned from a friend, Luo Zhenyu (1866–1940), a classical Chinese scholar. Between 1901 and 1903, Zhang read and proposed using Japanese education regulations, based on sources translated into Chinese from Japanese.[17] When the Nantong Normal School was opened in 1903, the school's regulations followed what he had learned from Japan.

After the Treaty of Shimonoseki was signed in 1895, Zhang proposed to the central government – on behalf of Zhang Zhidong – methods to reform the political and economic situation in which the late Qing dynasty found itself. It is clear that Meiji Japan's transformation served as the basis for much of his proposal.

The Qing Dynasty should accelerate the development of commerce. While Japan was trading with the West, the government provided necessary support to merchants if their businesses were operating in the red. In contrast, in China, there is a large gap between the upper class [government officials] and lower class [merchants]. The elite are less familiar with commercial affairs. The key to protect commerce is to join forces with all the merchants. It is necessary to establish commercial bureaus in each province. Also, meetings should be convened to discuss how to facilitate the people's lives and benefit the merchants. The government should order ministers abroad to investigate the commercial conditions in each country at any time and exchange information with those in China.

Generally, it was said that the foundation of Western countries is reinforced by commerce. People do not know the fact that the crucial element to enrich and strengthen the country is industry. Japan especially paid more attention to industrial affairs and set up industrial exhibits in almost all commercial cities. There, they collected all sorts of exhibits from the private sector and judged and compared their quality. This is a good example of imitating the West. The government should nominate an officer to take craftsmen to visit factories in the West and study there. When they return, they can be ordered to take leading initiatives in the improvement of industry.[18]

Nothing was more persuasive than Japan's first-hand experience. From 22 May to 27 July 1903, Zhang made his first trip to Japan. At that time, he had the chance to participate in the Fifth National Industrial Exposition in Osaka, where he saw firsthand the fruits of Japan's labors in transferring Western industrial technologies. During his stay, Zhang witnessed Japan's material civilization. Besides visiting the exposition, he traveled south to Nagasaki in Kyūshū and north to Hokkaidō. He had conversations with numerous teachers, school administrators, farmers, bankers, journalists, merchants, and industrialists.[19]

Nozawa Yutaka has argued that Zhang's visit was closely linked to his own ideas on business management and political reform in Nantong.[20] I am confident that the educational situation in Japan significantly influenced Zhang Jian. He showed keen interest in creating a modern educational system in China. In fact, before leaving for Japan, he hired two Japanese teachers, Kizukuri and Yoshizawa, to work at Nantong Normal School.[21] While traveling around Japan, he visited not only primary schools and middle schools, but kindergartens, and normal and vocational schools.

The way by which he visited the schools is important. He asked Kanō Jigorō (1860–1938), a judo expert and educationist, to show him small schools rather than large ones. With regard to the textbooks used in the schools, he liked to read the old versions. He was also eager to visit schools in the countryside, not the cities. He thought only by visiting schools that were still under construction could he acquire more knowledge. As far as the local economy in Japan was concerned, Zhang paid more attention to areas that were administered independently without financial aid from the central government.[22] Throughout his visit, he kept in mind Nantong's situation and compared it to Japan's. I believe that he was looking for an appropriate Japanese model on which to base Nantong's modernization. In other words, his learning from Japan was based on what Nantong demanded. He insisted, "I am trying to learn from all advanced things. I do not mind whether it is old or new. Nor do I care whether it is from abroad or not. Instead, I would just take into consideration what Nantong is eager to acquire."[23]

Zhang kept a detailed diary during his visits to schools in order to put into practical use what he learned following his return to Nantong. His notes include budgets, classroom descriptions, dormitories, even the dimensions of the rooms and the games students played. It is generally known that Japan's modern school administration system originated in France. Zhang selected what he needed and put that into practice when he returned to Nantong.

As an entrepreneur, Zhang did not miss a chance to visit industrial sites, confirming Japan's improved modern industry. There, he saw agricultural experimental field stations, banks, printing houses, libraries, museums, as well as many factories and workshops. In Osaka, he visited the Asahi Shimbun Company, Shimada Glassworks factory, the mint, a textile factory in Tenmabashi-kita, the Osaka port, the Hanta Ryutarō (Osaka) ironworks, and the Sanjūshi Bank.[24] In Kyoto he visited a hydroelectric plant; in Shizuoka he went to two paper-making factories. In Tokyo he visited a letter-press manufactory. When in Hokkaidō, he visited not only an experimental field station for marine products, but also farms for hemp production, seed propagation, and cattle breeding. Moreover, he paid a visit to a salt farm in Kurashiki.

Zhang discovered that Japan was a country that had adopted Western civilization without abandoning its traditional culture. He noticed, for example, that in contrast to China and the United States, lamb and pork were not the main foods in Japan. He concluded that Japan had preserved its traditions even though it was eagerly learning from the West. Thus he suggested that China should take account of its traditions while implementing social reforms.[25]

To practice what he had learned, soon after Zhang returned from Japan, he began making changes to Nantong's educational and industrial spheres. In 1904, the Tong-Hai Educational Bureau was created to design a universal school system from primary through higher education. After the abolition of the civil service examination in 1905, the bureau was renamed the Educational Association. From 1908 to 1910, sixty-seven lower primary schools were established in Nantong.[26] The year 1904 also saw the establishment of the Han Mo Lin Publishing House, Nantong's first modern printing factory, to provide textbooks for the rapidly increasing number of local schools.

Moreover, Zhang managed to start a number of enterprises including Tong Ren Tai Salt Company, Fu Sheng Sericulture Company, Zi Sheng Iron Company, Ze Sheng Waterway Company, and Da Da Pier Company, to name a few. At the salt company, he followed the methods by which Japan began its industrialization: hiring foreign advisors who would assist in the rapid transfer of advanced Western technologies. In this case, he hired Japanese experts to supervise the process of salt production.[27]

At the same time that Zhang sought to modernize industry in Nantong, he also emphasized the significance of moral education in school. He argued that since ancient times education in China consisted of three parts: morality, proper behavior, and technology. Because of declining national power and a fascination with Western science, the civil service examination system became increasingly irrelevant. Zhang believed, however, that technology (science) would not advance without stressing morality and proper behavior.[28] Zhang considered Confucian social norms, which he termed morality and proper behavior, as the "foundation," whereas Western technology was "utilization." His ideas followed the aforementioned dictum "Chinese learning for the foundation, Western learning for utilization." Zhang regarded moral education as the most important component in primary education.[29] He was firmly convinced that the essence of Confucian teachings should be the core spirit of all Chinese education.[30] Although he became an entrepreneur, Zhang remained a product of his classical Confucian training, reasoning that industry, technological development, and business – including management techniques – should be infused with Confucian morality.

Visiting Japan motivated Zhang to accelerate constitutional reform on the one hand, and to promote local self-government on the other. As pointed out by Samuel Chu, all that Zhang strived to accomplish was guided by his desire to achieve local self-government.[31] Zhang's impression was that Japan relied on local self-government: "The way Japanese govern their country is the same as the way a farmer works on his small rice field. Laozi has made an assertion that running a big country is like cooking a small fish.[32] The Japanese have grasped the essence of how to cook a small fish."[33] "Cooking a small fish," i.e., local self-government, was his top priority.

Perhaps recalling the Taiping Rebellion, which had significant impact on Jiangsu province even before his visit to Japan, Zhang recognized that Nantong needed a stable environment in order for local self-government to develop through the creation of Western-style industry and promotion of education. His concerns for local affairs are illustrated by his actions toward maintaining peace in east-central China during the Boxer Rebellion. In June 1900, when a joint expeditionary force consisting of troops from eight countries entered Beijing to fight the Boxers, who had besieged the foreign legation compound, the Qing government declared war on all foreign nations. Realizing that internal upheavals and external aggression would follow the declaration of war, Sheng Xuanhuai (1844–1916), a government official who wanted to negotiate with the foreign powers, asked Governor-general Zhang Zhidong and Liu Kunyi (1830–1902) to formulate plans to resolve the crisis. Knowing that negotiations with the West were nothing but a rejection of the Qing government's instructions, Zhang Zhidong and Liu Kunyi (especially the latter) were hesitant to pursue negotiations.

Throughout this process, Zhang Jian played a crucial role in persuading Liu to advocate for actions that would protect east-central China from the ravages of the Boxers and the foreign troops. Consequently, consensus was reached by provincial officials in the Yangtze delta and coastal areas that a declaration of war should not be followed. Later, the prefect of Shanghai, Yu Lianyuan, signed a formal agreement with the foreign consuls in Shanghai promising to protect foreign lives and property. In return, the Western powers agreed not to send troops into east-central China, sparing Nantong from a possible war and subsequent foreign occupation.

Zhang Jian believed that China's economic climate was closely connected to its political situation, but all of his attempts to gain official support for industry and business failed.[34] On the basis of this experience, he concluded, "A bad government is more fearful than a tiger. So far, there are only rules concerning how to squeeze merchants without any regulations supporting them."[35] As he criticized the Qing dictatorship, he looked toward the East for a solution to better government.

Zhang long admired Meiji Japan's constitutional monarchy, and his appreciation was reinforced during his trip to Japan. In 1901, in a proposal to the central government, Zhang evaluated Japan's constitutional reform after the Meiji Restoration and gave it high ratings.[36] His respect for Japan's constitutional government grew following Japan's 1905 victory over Russia during the Russo-Japanese War, which he saw as a victory of constitutionalism over autocracy.[37] He believed a constitutional monarchy in China was appropriate for local self-government, especially in Nantong, where he sought to industrialize, following Western business management practices, and to initiate educational reforms. It is likely that his trip to Japan provided a timely opportunity to see directly how a constitutional monarchy functioned – or so Zhang believed.

During his stay, Zhang paid particular attention to the relationship between Japanese entrepreneurs and government officials. He observed that these two groups carried out their professional duties respectively in developing Japanese industry.[38] In contrast, there were no clearly assigned roles for these two groups in China. Zhang complained that government officials were not willing to support industrialists and used them only to extract bribes. In this context, Zhang perceived a need for political reform in China, especially constitutional reform.

After returning to China in 1904, Zhang Jian helped Zhang Zhidong draft a petition entitled "A Request for Constitutional Reform" and sent it to the central government. He and his associates also published "An Interpretation of the Japanese Constitution" and distributed copies to other concerned persons, achieving a consensus among them on the need for constitutional reforms.[39]

As a result, the efforts of Zhang Jian and his associates contributed to the Qing government's subsequent policy change. In 1905, the central government dispatched five ministers to Japan, Great Britain, the United States, Germany, and France to find out how their governments operated, and to investigate the possibility of constitutionalism for China.[40] After the mission returned, all members proposed a constitutional government.[41] Then, in 1906, the Qing government was forced to establish a nine-year period to prepare for constitutional reform. Encouraged by this move, Zhang, along with colleagues Zheng Xiaoxu (1860–1938) and Tang Shouqian (1856–1917), immediately founded the Constitutional Preparation Association in Shanghai; Zhang was nominated vice-president.

The wave of constitutional reform quickly spread to other parts of the country. Urged by local gentry in 1907, the Qing government had to set up a national consultative council. Two years later, Zhang and leaders of consultative councils from the other provinces established combined provincial consultative councils and urged the central government to reduce the preparatory period from nine to six years.[42]

In June 1910, the Nanyang Industrial Exhibition was held in Nanjing. In August, the commercial commissioners of the Associated Chamber of Commerce of the Pacific, headed by Robert Dollar (1844–1932), founder of the Dollar Steamship Company, visited China. To honor Dollar, Zhang held a grand banquet and discussed developing cooperative agreements between China and the United States. In essence, Zhang sought to transfer Western banking techniques and shipping technologies. Zhang called this type of cooperation between China and the United States "Sino-American People's Diplomacy." Judging from Zhang's speech, it is clear that the cooperation he expected was not confined to the economy. Importantly, Zhang showed an interest in the political efforts of industrialists in China to contribute to political reforms throughout the country.[43] Historically relegated to the sidelines, however, Zhang foresaw a new role for entrepreneurs in a new China. Understanding the limitations of a Confucian government bent on supporting the status quo, and despite agreeing to some changes, Zhang believed that entrepreneurs – industrialists – would be the people to bring the latest Western technologies to China and support their expanded use throughout society.

Zhang visited several factories while he was traveling in Japan. What he witnessed greatly influenced his ideas for the adoption of Western/Japanese business management techniques. According to Li Yu, Chinese enterprises that employed Western-style managerial techniques were established by the group of Westernizers, including the reformers mentioned previously.[44] Enterprises owned and operated by private merchants, however, operated primarily in a traditional manner termed "he-huo."

Management methods within modern, i.e., Western-style, Chinese enterprises, while related to Western-style management at the time, can be divided into three types: guan ban (government-run enterprises); guandu shangban (government-supervised, merchant-operated enterprises); and guanshang heban (government-merchant supervised enterprises). The latter two types of enterprises tended to have much in common. Decision-making authority in these enterprises was dominated by government officials, and although most enterprises were organized by imitating a Western-style joint-stock company, management proved to be quite different. Directors failed to regularly hold shareholder's meetings and typically ignored the rights of shareholders.

The China Merchants Steamship Company, founded in 1873, is an example of a *guandu shangban* enterprise and paved the way for the creation of greater numbers of Western-style enterprises throughout the country.[45] Established by the Qing government and supervised by Li Hongzhang, governor-general of Zhili Province, the China Merchants Steamship Company was intended to take back some of the profits gained by British shipping companies in Chinese waters. Although succeeding in the short term, the company went the way of other *guandu shangban* enterprises and failed to expand at the same rate as British (and Japanese) firms. By the mid-1880s the company was suffering from government exactions and corruption. Albert Feuerwerker summarized the impediments as foreign competition, governmental weakness, inadequate capital, technical backwardness, and deficient motivation.[46] It proved difficult for *guandu shangban* enterprises to smoothly adopt Western technology, a point consistent with Wu Chengming's argument. Wu emphasizes that for China to industrialize, it was necessary to combine advanced Western technology with the principle of adaptation to local conditions.[47] In short, early enterprises transferred technological artifacts and some of the techniques of Western business management but failed to fully embrace the totality of their methods.

Motivation to learn from the West is an extremely important factor when we reevaluate technology transfer from the West to the East. In the case of the China Merchants Steamship Company's management, Sheng Xuanhuai, the director-general was said to have strived to obtain private profits, a factor that contrasts with Zhang's pursuit of profits for the "public good."[48]

Like other entrepreneurs at that time, Zhang found it difficult to raise construction funds for industrial projects. When he tried to collect the funds promised for the Da Sheng Cotton Mill, for example, two Shanghai shareholders, Pan Heqin and Guo Maozhi, ultimately betrayed Zhang's trust and left the would-be Nantong entrepreneur empty handed. Zhang had no alternative but to seek help from government officials. Subsequently, the local government agreed to provide spinning machines for the cotton mill rather than become a shareholder. Later, Zhang consulted with Sheng Xuanhuai, who was working in the weaving industry, too; consequently, the government allocated Zhang and Sheng each half of the spinning machines. According to an agreement signed by Zhang and Sheng, the government did not get involved in the management of the Da Sheng Cotton Mill except for receiving *guan-li*, a kind of profit shared regularly among stockholders without losses or gains being taken into consideration. In this way, Zhang is known for creating a new managerial system that was called *shenling shangban* – firms run by gentry who had left official positions.[49]

Zhang also sought to redefine the way joint-stock companies, *gong-si*, were run. He defined the principal of *gong-si* as follows: "According to the *Zhuangzi*,[50] the mountain results from an accumulation of small hillocks and the river was formed from little streams. Thus, *gong* [equivalent to 'public' in English] surely means mergers."[51] Zhang's understanding of the essence of joint-stock companies, *gong-si*, was superficial. What he grasped was nothing more than the idea of gathering shareholders and raising funds. According to Li Yu, the distinguishing characteristics of the joint-stock company is the separation of the rights of owners and managers,[52] which can be contrasted to a *he-huo* (partnership), a traditional management style in which the owners practically run the business by themselves. It was hard for merchants to understand shareholders' rights, as confirmed by their strict adherence to *he-huo* when they started new businesses.[53]

Zhang continued to operate under *he-huo* management style. Although the Da Sheng Cotton Mill began to take shape in 1896, and started operations in 1899, it was not until 1907 that a shareholder's meeting was held for the first time. Before that, all decisions were made by Zhang alone. In short, Zhang acted as the Da Sheng Cotton Mill's owner and general manager. He had absolute authority in purchasing, production, marketing, financing, and human affairs at the mill.

In later years, Zhang expanded the mill, building the number 2 mill in Chong Ming in 1907, the number 3 mill in Hai Men in 1915, and mill number 8 in 1921. In addition to several other enterprises mentioned earlier, Zhang established other companies, including Tong Hai Farming and Husbandry Company, Guang Sheng Oil Company, Da Xing Flour Mill, and the Da Da Inland Navigation Company. These enterprises were amalgamated into one corporate entity, the Da Sheng Capital Group. It is said that Zhang built all of his enterprises according to local conditions, i.e., making full use of local natural resources,[54] and most all of his enterprises were related. The products and waste of one enterprise tended to become resources of another. For example, Tong Hai Farming and Husbandry Company was established to increase sources of raw materials for Da Sheng Cotton Mill, and Guang Sheng Oil Company was built near the mill to recycle production waste.[55]

Da Sheng Capital Group's businesses developed quickly and prospered until 1922, when the Da Sheng Cotton Mill suffered a financial loss of 390,000 taels. For the first time, the company and Zhang ran into cash-flow problems; the market price of raw cotton rose while the price of cotton gauze declined. After the First World War, foreign commodities were being dumped into Chinese markets, and Zhang's business was not able to weather the competition.[56] That same year also saw the loss of 310,000 taels at the number 2 mill. Compounding Zhang's problems, the Da Sheng Cotton Mill had loaned more than 1,300,000 taels to the Farming and Husbandry Company, which the latter was unable to repay.

In 1925, the Da Sheng Capital Group was insolvent and put in a claim with the Jiang-zhe Financial Group to clear its accounts and pay its debts. In July, all Da Sheng businesses were taken over by a creditor group comprising four Shanghai banks – the Bank of China, Bank of Communications, Jin-cheng Banking Corporation, and Shanghai Bank, as well as the Yong-feng Group and Yong-ju Bank.[57]

The cause of Da Sheng's misfortunes was identified as a shortage of capital and, in many cases, Zhang's arbitrary business decisions and execution.[58] Zhang Jian was also accused of siphoning off too much of the company's funds to invest in projects for his dream of building a new world in Nantong without maintaining normal operations at the mills. Facing such charges, Zhang defended himself by asserting that the Da Sheng Capital Group had a moral obligation to promote the other Nantong projects.[59] Wang Dunqin argues that Zhang was not really an entrepreneur because he paid more attention to the improvement of society than to the management of his enterprises.[60] In fact, Zhang was likely to invest in non-profit activities in support of the public good, even in years when his businesses showed a loss.[61]

In 1929, Hu Shi, a leading May Fourth intellectual and later diplomat, wrote in his foreword to Zhang Jian's biography, "No one can deny that in the history of modern China, Zhang Jian was a great but ultimately unsuccessful hero. He single-handedly blazed innumerable new trails and played the part of a pioneer for thirty years. He provided a livelihood for millions, benefitted an entire region, and influenced the whole country. Yet because he embarked on so many projects and took upon himself such enormous tasks, he died with many plans uncompleted."[62]

Patriotism was part of Zhang's underlying motivation to undertake his projects. If this was his basic motivation, however, how did he reconcile the relationship between (national) patriotism and regionalism? This question is closely linked with Cohen's assumption that central government control sometimes conflicted with local self-government. A further answer to this question lies in Zhang's ideas about the word "public."

Zhang stated that all of his efforts were for the public good, not for his private interest. He distinguished between "public" and "private" by defining the role of ideal corporate leadership. He divided the nature of corporate leaders between public servants and private servants. The former referred to one who was chosen and entrusted by the masses in a local area. In contrast, Zhang considered a private servant to be a corporate leader chosen by capitalists, and the one who was obligated to create profits for the capitalists.[63] Zhang continued that a public servant should be a corporate leader who collects funds from the local area and serves as a model, while the private servant only serves shareholders and pleases them without doing anything for the local community. Zhang claimed that he would rather be a public servant.[64] In all likelihood, the concept of public for Zhang meant local, and in this case, local meant Nantong. Accordingly, public good referred primarily to wealth and prosperity in a particular place rather than to national prosperity.

One can also argue that Zhang saw no conflict between national and local. In truth, the impulse for his actions also came from two famous philologists, Huang Zongxi (1610–95) and Gu Yanwu (1613–82). One of Gu's most noted phrases, "Everybody is responsible for the fate of *tianxia*," was an ancient Chinese cultural concept that formed the basis for China's world view.[65] Gu criticized the so-called public and concluded that it was nothing but an excuse of the Chinese emperor who was concerned only with his own private interests. In other words, Gu's image of an ideal public did not refer to a country "owned" by an emperor, but referred to a large community of the people.

Zhang likewise argued that even the word "public," while being propagated by the emperor, represented the central government and had to take the local as its starting-point.[66] From this we may conclude that the public good Zhang pursued included the interests not only of the nation, but also the local. His ideas on local self-government corresponded with this notion of public good. As such, it is not surprising to see that, in 1913, invited by Yuan Shikai (1859–1916), president of the new Chinese republic, Zhang Jian became a member of Premier Xiong Xiling's (1870–1937) cabinet and served as the director general of the National Water Conservancy and the minister of agriculture. During his tenure in office, Zhang promulgated more than twenty laws or regulations related to the management of companies, commerce, finance, currency, and the mining industry, as well as promoting the development of economic modernization in China based on the transfer and development of Western technologies.

Conclusion

More than simply being a modern entrepreneur, Zhang Jian is also considered to be a modern distinguished politician, educationalist, and social activist. In addition to industrial growth, his goals included the creation of a modern system of education, as well as a constitutional government in Nantong. Zhang spared no effort in taking up philanthropic projects too; he established a foundling home, a medical clinic, a home for the disabled, a school for the vision and speech impaired, homes for the aged, as well as workshops for the poor. As Zhang noted, "I did all that I could so as to deliver a strong counter-balance to some foreign countries' claims that the Chinese people were not able to accomplish local self-government projects."[67]

Zhang Kaiyuan argues that although Zhang Jian grew up in the traditional environment of Qing China with classical Confucian training, he became a hero, breaking down the old customs that "the student, having completed his learning, should apply himself to be an officer."[68] Zhang Jian abandoned his official career, chose the path of a merchant, industrialist, and philanthropist, but never lost sight of his Confucian roots. He remained steadfast in his belief that only through developing modern industry and education could China be saved. It is clear that to save the entire country, Zhang believed that local self-government in Nantong was a first step. Although he confined most of his activities to the local level, he never lost sight of the larger purpose of modernizing China.[69] Also, he suggested that traditional gentry were responsible for building a strong state. To strengthen the state, he insisted, they should concentrate primarily on the development of their hometowns.[70] In this sense, Zhang sought national modernization through local self-government.

Wei Chunhui argues that Zhang Jian was not a true capitalist because he failed to follow the rules of capitalism, i.e., he was inclined to use profits from his enterprises to undertake social reform.[71] This explains why Hu Shi elevated Zhang to the status of unsuccessful hero. It also shows that Zhang neither viewed enterprise as the subject of profit maximization, nor did he run his businesses to maximize personal wealth.

As for the "Western impact" and "Chinese response," Zhang knew not only the importance of trying to understand the state of global economics, but also the need to learn from the West. Zhang did not, however, consider business methods, even those from the West, in isolation from China's or Nantong's political and educational situation. Except for transferring industrial technologies, i.e., equipment and machinery, directly from the West,[72] Zhang adopted advanced technologies and business management techniques through Japan. His visit to Japan had far-reaching influence on his entrepreneurial activities. Most importantly, he adapted what he learned abroad to fit local conditions and his ideas about society. Above all, his ambitious goal of realizing local self-government comported with the so-called public good he pursued. His efforts benefited not only Nantong, but the country as a whole.

On the basis of the failure of technology transfer in the *guandu shangban* enterprises, Wu Chengming insisted that, in response to Western incursions, China, as an economically backward country, should not simply copy patterns and theories from the West; changes must be based on local conditions. It is not hard to see why all of Zhang's efforts in adopting Western knowledge were closely associated with promoting local self-government in Nantong. Although adopting Western-style managerial systems, Zhang most often operated his businesses in his own way. Not only did he consider business management to be one part of his plan for local self-government, he also emphasized the importance of education and constitutional reform.

The decline of the Da Sheng Capital Group can be blamed on the juxtaposition of Zhang's blending of Western and traditional business techniques, an ambitious local social program, and the transfer of foreign technologies – but not necessarily management techniques – into China's generally unstable political environment of the 1920s.

NOTES

1 Paul A. Cohen, *Discovering History in China: American Historical Writing on the Recent Chinese Past* (New York: Columbia University Press, 1984), 36.
2 Cohen, *Discovering History in China*, 160.
3 The full name of the protocol is the Austria-Hungary, Belgium, France, Germany, Great Britain, Italy, Japan, Netherland, Russia, Spain, United States, and China – Final Protocol for the Settlement of the Disturbances of 1900.
4 Wu Chengming, "Zao qi Zhongguo jindaihua guocheng zhong de waibu he neibu yinsu: jianlun Zhang Jian de shiye luxian" [External and internal factors in the process of early Chinese modernization: Zhang Jian's industrial route], *Collected Papers of the International Symposium on Zhang Jian* (1993), 157–8.
5 Guo Yuming, ed., *Zhongguo jindaishi jiaocheng* [A course of modern Chinese history]. (Shanghai: East China Normal University Press, 1997), 134.
6 Cao Congpo and Yang Tong, eds., *Zhang Jian quanji* [Complete works of Zhang Jian] (Nanjing: Jiangsu Guji Publication House, 1994), 1:76.
7 Cao and Yang, *Zhang Jian quanji*, 4:467.
8 During the Qing dynasty, except through the civil service examination, obtaining an official post by economic means such as donations became popular. For more details, see Xu Daling, *Qingdai juanna zhidu* [The system of taxes and levies of the Qing dynasty] (Beijing: Yenching University, 1950).
9 Wang Dunqin, *Chuantong yu qianzhan: Zhang Jian jingji sixiang yanjiu* [Tradition and prospect: Zhang Jian's economic thought] (Beijing: People's Publishing House, 2005), 20.
10 Cao and Yang, *Zhang Jian quanji*, 3:115.
11 Zhang Xiaoruo, *Nantong Zhang Jizhi xiansheng zhuanji* [The biography of Zhang Ji in Nantong] (Shanghai: Shanghai Bookstore Publishing House, 1989), 68.
12 Cao and Yang, *Zhang Jian quanji*, 1:235.
13 Cao and Yang, *Zhang Jian quanji*, 4:468.
14 Zhang, *Nantong Zhang Jizhi xiansheng zhuanji*, 90.
15 Cao and Yang, *Zhang Jian quanji*, 1:35–7.
16 Cao and Yang, *Zhang Jian quanji*, 1:103.
17 Marianne Bastid, *Educational Reform in Early Twentieth-Century China*, trans. Paul J. Bailey (Ann Arbor: Center for Chinese Studies, University of Michigan, 1988), 46.

18 Cao and Yang, *Zhang Jian quanji*, 1: 36–9.
19 Cao and Yang, *Zhang Jian quanji*, 6:480–515.
20 Nozawa Yutaka, "1903 no Ōsaka hakurankai to choken no rainichi" [The 1903 Osaka Exposition and Zhang Jian's visit to Japan], *Keiri kenkyū* [Accounting research] (Tokyo: Chuo Daigaku Keiri Kenkyūjo , 1971), 14:131.
21 Nozawa, "1903 no Ōsaka hakurankai to choken no rainichi," 14:131.
22 Cao and Yang, *Zhang Jian quanji*, 6:502.
23 Cao and Yang, *Zhang Jian quanji*, 4:468.
24 Cao and Yang, *Zhang Jian quanji*, 6:486–96.
25 Cao and Yang, *Zhang Jian quanji*, 6:506.
26 Qin Shao, *Culturing Modernity: The Nantong Model, 1890–1930* (Stanford, CA: Stanford University Press, 2004), 32.
27 Cao and Yang, *Zhang Jian quanji*, 3:512–13.
28 Cao and Yang, *Zhang Jian quanji*, 4:191.
29 Yu Chen, *Shibusawa Eiichi to "giri" shisō: kindai higashi Ajia no jitsugyō to kyōiku* (Tokyo: Perikansha, 2008), 253.
30 Samuel C. Chu, *Reformer in Modern China, Chang Chien, 1853–1926* (New York: Columbia University Press, 1965), 109.
31 Chu, *Reformer in Modern China*, 162.
32 Laozi is the purported founder of Daoism.
33 Cao and Yang, *Zhang Jian quanji*, 6:482.
34 Cao and Yang, *Zhang Jian quanji*, 1:271.
35 Cao and Yang, *Zhang Jian quanji*, 1:37.
36 Cao and Yang, *Zhang Jian quanji*, 1:49.
37 Cao and Yang, *Zhang Jian quanji*, 6:522.
38 Cao and Yang, *Zhang Jian quanji*, 6:494.
39 Wei Chunhui, *Zhang Jian pingzhuan* [A critical biography of Zhang Jian] (Nanjing: Nanjing University Press, 2001), 82–3.
40 The members were Zai Ze, Dai Hongci, Duan Fang, Shang Qiheng, and Li Shengduo.
41 Dennis Twitchett and John K. Fairbank, *Cambridge History of China*. Vol. 11, *Late Ch'ing, 1800–1911*, part 2 (Cambridge: Cambridge University Press, 1980), 389.
42 Qin, *Culturing Modernity*, 23–4.
43 Ma Min, *Shangren jingshen de shanbian: jindai Zhongguo shangren guannian yanjiu* [The evolution of merchant spirit: Research on the concept of "businessman" in modern China] (Wuhan: Huazhong Normal University Press, 2001), 267.
44 Li Yu, *Wan Qing gongsi zhidu jianshe yanjiu* [The construction of the company system in the late Qing dynasty] (Beijing: People's Publishing House, 2002), 2.
45 Wang Dunqin, *Chuantong yu qianzhan*, 90; Li Yu, *Wan Qing gongsi zhidu jianshe yanjiu*, 16.
46 Albert Feuerwerker, *China's Early Industrialization: Sheng Hsuan-huai (1844–1916) and Mandarin Enterprise* (New York: Harvard University Press, 1970), 245.

47 Wu, "Zao qi Zhongguo jindaihua guocheng zhong de waibu henei yu yinsu," 163.

48 Feuerwerker, *China's Early Industrialization*, 250.

49 Cao and Yang, *Zhang Jian quanji*, 3:81–3.

50 The *Zhuangzi*, along with the *Daodejing*, are the two core texts of Daoism.

51 Cao and Yang, *Zhang Jian quanji*, 3:212.

52 Li Yu, *Wan Qing gongsi zhidu jianshe yanjiu*, 292.

53 Li Yu, *Wan Qing gongsi zhidu jianshe yanjiu*, 43.

54 Wang Dunqin, *Chuantong yu qianzhan*, 125–7.

55 Cao and Yang, *Zhang Jian quanji*, 3:782.

56 Zhang Jizhi xiansheng Shiye shi bianzhuan shu, *Da Sheng fangzhi gongsi nianjian: 1895–1947* [The annals of Da Sheng cotton mill] (Nanjing: Jiangsu People's Publishing House, 1998), 187.

57 Wang Shengyun, "Zhang Jian yu Da Sheng shachang de xingshuai" [Zhang Jian and the rise and fall of Da Sheng cotton mill], *Journal of Wuhan Institute of Science and Technology* 14, no. 4 (2001) 54–9.

58 Wang Dunqin, *Chuantong yu qianzhan*, 286–99.

59 Chu, *Reformer in Modern China*, 35.

60 Wang Dunqin, *Chuantong yu qianzhan*, 298–9.

61 Yu, *Shibusawa Eiichi to "giri" shisō*, 217–18.

62 Zhang, *Nantong Zhang Jizhi xiansheng zhuanji*, 3.

63 Cao and Yang, *Zhang Jian quanji*, 1:99.

64 Cao and Yang, *Zhang Jian quanji*, 3:73.

65 *Tianxia* can be translated as "under heaven."

66 For Gu Yanwu and Zhang Jian's discussion of public and private, see Yu, *Shibusawa Eiichi to "giri" shisō*, 182–5 and 188–91.

67 Cao and Yang, *Zhang Jian quanji*, 3:396.

68 Yoshida Kenkō, *Shinshaku kanbun taikei* [A newly interpreted compendium of Chinese classics], vol.1 "*Rongo*" ["The Analects"] (Tokyo: Meiji Shoin, 1985), 422.

69 Cao and Yang, *Zhang Jian quanji*, 4:644.

70 Cao and Yang, *Zhang Jian quanji*, 3:390.

71 Wei, *Zhang Jian pingzhuan*, 332.

72 For example, the spinning machines at the Da Sheng Cotton Mill Number 2 were purchased directly from Great Britain. Cao and Yang, *Zhang Jian quanji*, 3:203.

7 Shibusawa Eiichi and the Transfer of Western Banking to Japan

KIMURA MASATO

This chapter analyzes the leadership provided by Shibusawa Eiichi in the establishment of Japan's modern banking system, and the role that system played in encouraging the transfer of technology and business practices – essential elements in the country's emergence as a modern industrial power during the nineteenth century. Centrally involved in the establishment and management of some 500 companies and 600 non-profit organizations during his lifetime, Shibusawa often is described as the father of modern Japanese capitalism.[1] However, the business management philosophy and practice that guided his leadership, and in particular his role as a financial entrepreneur who strategically encouraged technology transfer, is less well known.[2]

The organization of this chapter is as follows. First, I clarify the historical context for technology transfer as a strategy for Japan's development. Second, I address why Shibusawa Eiichi paid special attention to the modern bank and banking system as a means to facilitate technology transfer. Third, I focus on Shibusawa's *gappon* method, which guided his practice of business management, in concept and practice. In the fourth section, I examine Shibusawa's leadership on the establishment of Daiichi National Bank (First National Bank) as a case study. The chapter then shares several conclusions.

The Historical Context for Technology Transfer in Nineteenth-Century Japan

The transfer of modern technologies and ideas as a feature of nineteenth-century Japanese modernization needs to be understood from the outset in its historical context. From the middle of the nineteenth century, advanced national economies such as Britain, France, and Germany transferred their ideas and production systems to developing regions of the world through their colonial administrations. Japan was an exception as a result of its historical and geographic isolation from Asia. From the mid-nineteenth century, the country adopted a strategy, led by the government and business sector, to selectively import Western ideas and technologies such as railways, electronics, and the banking system. Such technical and intellectual collaboration promoted and accelerated Japan's rapid modernization and industrialization, and the pace of such activity increased from the late nineteenth century until the First World War.

As many Japanese and international scholars have pointed out, modernization and industrialization of Japanese society was not just selective importation of advanced Western technologies; rather, it was the dynamic development of combining technical assistance from Western companies and entrepreneurs and traditional Japanese technologies that came to maturation through the efforts of industrial artists and craftsmen beginning in the Edo period. In order to accomplish the goals of industrial and social development, a prerequisite was the support of the modernization movement by national and local governments. Japanese political leaders such as Ōkubo Toshimichi and Itō Hirobumi, and entrepreneurs such as Shibusawa Eiichi, Godai Tomoatsu, and Iwasaki Yatarō well understood the role of the government in the promotion of Japan's economic growth, the need to cultivate modern industries, and the importance of promoting discussion about and openness to accepting, selectively, advanced technology and social systems. Godai established many companies in Osaka in the early Meiji period and served as the first president of the Osaka Chamber of Commerce. Iwasaki started a shipping company in the 1860s and also forged a close relationship with the Meiji government. He and his younger brother, Iwasaki Yanosuke, established the Mitsubishi *zaibatsu* and the Mitsui Financial Group in the early Meiji period, becoming strong rivals of Shibusawa Eiichi.

The ideas of these leaders served as the basis for the important strategy of *shokusan kōgyō* (cultivating industry and promoting trade and commerce). Shibusawa Eiichi, as one of Japan's important business leaders, in particular articulated an objective of this strategy as a focus on acquiring not only technology per se, such as rail stock or advanced manufacturing equipment, but also the practices associated with finance that facilitated the importation of monetary and fiscal policy.

It is important to note that Shibusawa's leadership during Japan's Meiji period grew out of his sojourn in Europe, when he served as representative of the Tokugawa Mission to the Paris *Exposition Universelle* in 1867. Between 1867 and 1868, Shibusawa quickly developed a respect for and interest in Western financial practices, investing and profiting from investments in French bonds designed to finance the rail industry, for example. Shibusawa's initiative to explore and develop financial skills earned him the respect of the delegations' members, indicating an early insight into the need to adapt political, economic, and social systems from Europe in order to modernize Japanese society upon returning to Japan in 1868.

Technology Transfer and the Modern Bank and Banking System

Shibusawa Eiichi's position on technology transfer in general was threefold. First, he clarified the rationale for why Japan should promote technology transfer. He explained the importance for Japan to conduct technology transfer in order to modernize and industrialize Japanese society while at the same time maintaining its independence. Prior to assuming a key business leadership role, Shibusawa served briefly as a high-ranking bureaucrat in the Meiji government who sought to drastically alter the old social and economic systems and customs of the feudal Tokugawa period, including encouraging the adoption of a new monetary system, national calendar and modern notions of time, weights and measures, and so on. In short, Shibusawa promoted reform in order to establish the economic and social infrastructure needed to import select aspects of advanced Western technology.

Second, Shibusawa invited several distinguished Western engineers to Japan in order to introduce advanced technologies. As discussed in David Wittner's contribution to this volume, these individuals helped establish Western-style manufacturers such as the Tomioka Silk Mill and the Oji Paper Company in collaboration with the Japanese government. He also cultivated emerging Japanese industry leaders such as Yamanobe Takeo and Takamine Jokichi, encouraging them to study abroad in order to better understand advanced technology and transfer such knowledge to Japanese society. Yamanobe Takeo, for example, moved to Manchester to study spinning technology in 1878. Shibusawa financially supported Yamanobe's study there. After returning to Japan, Yamanobe worked for the Osaka Spinning Company as a principal engineer and became the first president of Toyo Spinning Company in 1914.[3] Takamine Jokichi studied chemistry in Glasgow. Shibusawa supported him in the establishment of the Tokyo Jinzo Hiryo Company (Tokyo Artificial Fertilizer Company) in 1887. Takamine discovered several important medicines, allowing him to become a New York millionaire. He served as the first president at the Nippon Club in New York and played an important role supporting Japan-U.S. private diplomacy, in collaboration with Shibusawa, after the Russo-Japanese War (1904–5), until his death in 1922, just after the Washington Disarmament Conference.[4]

Third, Shibusawa thought that banks and the emerging Japanese banking system should take the initiative for promoting technology/knowledge transfer as a core practice and management activity. Japan did not have elements comparable to the Western-style bank and banking system prior to Shibusawa's introduction of them. Of note is that although many *ryōgaeshō* (money exchangers) and many *kanekashi* (moneylenders) had been conducting financial business in the Tokugawa and early Meiji eras, their practice was based on *daifukucho* (an old-fashioned account bookkeeping system) rather than double-entry bookkeeping. Traditionally, Japanese financial organizations such as

Mitsui, Kōnoike, and other small *ko* (mutual financing associations) did not make their assets and business activities open to the public.

To reform the traditional financial system, Shibusawa introduced several key changes: the necessity of collecting money from unspecified numbers of people as stockholders; recognition that banks must have the right to issue money; public disclosure of the details of bank assets and loans; and the practice of double-entry booking. Shibusawa believed that such practices, as features of a modern bank and banking system, were of critical importance to facilitating business activities and the creation in Japan of a level of prosperity equal to that of Europe. He also recognized that the banking industry is a type of corporation (*gappon kaisha*) that could stimulate the creation of civil society in Japan by challenging traditional practices such as granting excessive deference to the upper class or the government (*kanson minpi*), an obstacle to Japan becoming a democratic society. We will explore this point in more detail in the next section through analysis of the *gappon* method.[5]

Gappon Business Management Methods and Contributions to Technology Transfer

Shibusawa did not use the term "capitalism" to describe his entrepreneurial economic and business activities. Instead, his thinking about the optimal system for running businesses was described as the *gappon* method, *gappon* organization, and the *gappon* company. In order to better understand his leadership role facilitating technology transfer, it is necessary to explain the concept of *gappon*. The Japanese word *gappon* refers to binding two or more books together to form one. The roots of Shibusawa's thinking about the *gappon* method can be traced to his time in Europe and closely parallels the joint-stock trading system. According to discussions and speeches by Shibusawa, the *gappon* method can be defined as a business practice that assembles the best possible people and funding to achieve the mission of pursuing profit as well as contributing to the public good.[6] It is important to note that scholars have yet to clarify the exact origins of his use of the term *gappon*, and that despite the concept's similarity to the joint-stock trading system, Shibusawa did not use the two terms interchangeably.[7]

The *Gappon* Method

A *gappon* business is typically understood as similar to a joint-stock company. According to the *Kōjien*, joint-stock companies conduct business based on stock finance, where the funds necessary for starting a business or establishing or expanding a company are supplied by having stock issued and accepted or purchased. These companies are also organized by shareholders who own the company's stock, and have limited liability. However, the *gappon* method advocated by Shibusawa is quite different in several ways from the behavior of joint-stock companies and shareholders in today's capitalist societies. For example, companies that Shibusawa took part in establishing also included unidentified companies and limited partnerships, in addition to joint-stock companies. This is because the *gappon* method is distinguished by three characteristics: purpose and mission, human resources and networks, and capital.

For Shibusawa, the mission of *gappon* organizations was to attain benefits for the entire nation and society as well as to increase public benefits. Therefore, it was essential that shareholders and administrators fully understood the company's intents and mission when they invested in or managed businesses. There is a difference between Adam Smith's invisible hand and Shibusawa's thoughts. As Tanaka Kazuhiro points out,

> The characteristic peculiar to *gappon-shugi* is the … aspect of morality (passive morality) that advocates that self-interest should not be put first. It is a general understanding that in the market economy, as Smith also believed, pursuit of self-interest can be given priority as long as one conducts business without deceiving others and in a way consistent with justice. However, Shibusawa was not satisfied only with "justice" that prohibits dishonest conduct. He placed importance also on "beneficence," that is, behavior that tries to bring benefits to others. For Shibusawa, not putting self-interest first was also among the norms not to be deviated from. He noted "without indulging in self-centeredness" when he tried to present the "rule of Right in the business world" as the appropriate concept shaping *gappon-shugi*. It is fine to pursue self-interest, but it should be done by placing benefits for others first, instead of self-interest…. [C]onducting business based on such reasons and norms is how *gappon-shugi* operates.[8]

In other words, Shibusawa, as his first priority, believed that the purpose of business included a public-oriented value system as commended in the *Analects* of Confucius.

As such, a corporate organization was not necessarily a joint-stock company but could be any type of organization suited to the purposes of *gappon* organizations. Shibusawa established not only joint-stock companies but also limited partnerships as well as mutual-aid societies.[9] He also invested significant amounts of money in *tokumei kumiai* (anonymous companies and silent partnerships).[10] We should pay attention to the fact that these latter investments surpassed those that Shibusawa directed as joint companies in terms of the amount of money in some years such as 1897, 1898, and 1907.[11]

Shibusawa also regarded as critically important the value of human resources engaged in company management and business activities. An administrator, in particular, must be a person who understands the company's purpose and mission and pursues public benefit. As is clear from Shibusawa's famous argument with Iwasaki Yatarō, Shibusawa regarded securing profits from business activities as important, but ensuring that the benefits were distributed among all investors was more important.[12] He was firmly against monopolization of businesses and profits, or the formation of conglomerates.

In this regard, Shibusawa expected business administrators to have not only the ability to suitably conduct business, but also a broad perspective and cooperative disposition that made them willing to seek partners among a wide range of those collaborating through human networks. Shibusawa himself was deeply engaged in the establishment and operation of educational institutes such as the Tokyo Higher School of Commerce (now Hitotsubashi University), for example, with the hope of eventually hiring graduates with the skills he found desirable in organizing human resource networks.

Sufficient capital is needed for starting and developing businesses. In order to effectively utilize unused capital in Japan, Shibusawa established the First National Bank and many other private banks throughout the country, as further discussed in a later section of this chapter. At a deep personal and professional level, Shibusawa understood that the banking system enabled capital to be gathered from a wide range of people, beyond Japan's traditional class system of samurai, farmers, artisans, and merchants. Shibusawa precisely described his intent, as found in an advertising text for banks:

> To begin with, banks are like a great river. There are infinite ways banks prove themselves useful. However, money not yet collected at a bank is no different than water pooled in a ditch or water drops that keep falling. Sometimes money is hiding in a warehouse of a rich merchant or a farmer, or being kept in a day worker's or grandmother's shirt pocket. In such cases, money cannot serve the people or help make the nation affluent. Water cannot flow forward even if it has the force to do so if it is blocked by an embankment or a mound. But if we make a bank, and skillfully open a channel for letting the water flow, money that was kept in warehouses or shirt pockets can come together in great amounts. This will help trades to prosper, products to increase, industries to develop, studies to advance, roads to improve, and the entire situation of our country can be renewed.[13]

As Shibusawa presciently observed, the supply of funds through banks led to public benefit, that is, the creation of something new. Financial aid should be supplied to generate tangible wealth out of intangible resources and allow for its effective utilization. This is the role performed by banks and representatives of the activity found in *gappon* organizations.

Daiichi Bank: Transferring Banking Technologies and Business Practices

The well-known story of Shibusawa's establishment and management of Daiichi National Bank (and later Daiichi Bank) also serves as a valuable case study of his leadership promoting the transfer of technical know-how and business practices. My analysis illustrates the ways in which management practices are features of technology transfer when one considers technical know-how, methods, and the creation of managerial and technical systems.

Shibusawa resigned from the Meiji government and became a private businessman in 1873. Thus began the process of establishing the Daiichi National Bank from 1874, an initiative that identified the owners and managers of Mitsui-gumi and Ono-gumi, important financial leaders from the Edo period, as executive board members. Shibusawa's goal was to establish the bank as a joint-stock company because, in his view, modern financial institutions should be open to individual capital investment. Accordingly, Shibusawa established the Daiichi National Bank as a private bank, organized according to the *gappon* method, to promote technology and knowledge transfer from the West, as well as other activities in support of modern Japanese economic development.

As related in his autobiography, *Amayogatari*, the reason for Shibusawa's resignation from the Finance Ministry in 1873 was over conflicts with Ōkubo Toshimichi, the most influential leader in the early Meiji government. His disagreement stemmed from differing ideas about the management of national finances. Ōkubo was more likely to support a positive fiscal policy and insisted on increased support for military expenditures, even beyond maintenance of a balanced budget, in order to promote the policy of *fukoku kyōhei* (rich nation, strong army). Shibusawa and Inoue Kaoru, head of the Finance Ministry where Shibusawa was employed, strongly opposed Ōkubo's policy because of their commitment to a balanced budget. They held the view that overly large military expenditures would cause huge budgetary deficits, contributing to the possibility of a financial crisis that the Meiji government could not manage. Ōkubo, with his strong political power base in the Satsuma and Chōshū factions, prevailed. Inoue and Shibusawa resigned from the government, but not before publicizing their opinion in the press. Parenthetically, it is reasonable to propose that Shibusawa's resignation also represented his pessimism about his future as a political leader and bureaucrat as long as anti-Tokugawa factions, such as Satsuma and Chōshū, were in control of the government.

A second reason for Shibusawa's resignation was his commitment to conducting business as a private-sector leader in order to modify the notion of *kanson minpi*. From the *gappon* viewpoint, this second reason is the most important, and one that can be further explained through an examination of several challenges facing the establishment of the Daiichi National Bank.

The first challenge facing Shibusawa and Japan was which banking system model should be introduced to Japanese society – that of the Bank of England, or of the Bank of the United States. In the 1870s, Britain was militarily and economically the most powerful country in the world on the basis of its world trade and financial position. The Bank of England, the central bank, played a key role in the formulation of monetary policy in collaboration with the British government. In particular, the Bank of England contributed to social and economic progress by issuing paper currency based on the gold standard system. Yoshida Kiyonari studied the banking system of the Bank of England in London for several years and tried to introduce it into Japan.[14] Initially, Shibusawa supported this plan, paralleling Ōkuma Shigenobu's and Inoue Kaoru's position.[15]

Itō Hirobumi, who would be inaugurated as the first prime minister with the enactment of the Meiji Constitution in 1889, insisted that Japan introduce a national bank system modeled on the United States, specifically the U.S. National Currency Act of 1863. As embodied in the Act, the National Bank was chartered by the federal government as a commercial bank for the purpose of issuing new paper money and liquidating war loans associated with the Civil War (1861–5). The main difference between the British and American banking systems was whether new paper money issued by each national bank should be banknotes convertible to gold. In other words, private banks could issue their own paper money; in Britain, only the Bank of England had such authority. The two perspectives represented fundamentally different views on monetary policy. Yoshida attached importance to currency stability. Itō, on the other hand, was partial to creating a money supply in order to meet Japan's goal of becoming a "rich nation."

After intensive and contentious discussions, the Meiji government established the *Kokuritsu ginkō jōrei* (National Bank Law) in 1872, based mainly on the U.S. National Currency Act of 1863, but also including several aspects of the British banking system. The law had the merit of abolishing older paper money issued by the Tokugawa government and local *han* (feudal domains) during the 1860s, allowing new paper money to be issued by the National Bank in each of Japan's major cities. The National Bank Law was expected to encourage entrepreneurs to start new businesses as well as disseminate new paper money by making it exchangeable for gold at 60 percent of its value.

The main reason the Meiji government decided to introduce the U.S. National Bank system was that high-ranking government leaders and officials thought that it was too early to establish a central bank like the Bank of England because the government did not have enough political and economic power to support a central bank or to introduce the gold standard system.

The United States and Japan shared several apparent similarities. First, both countries had large amounts of diversified paper money after civil wars that occurred in the 1860s. Both also shared several commonalities in the industrialization process, despite major differences between their natural and cultural endowments. In the late nineteenth century, textile companies and food suppliers played major roles at the local level, reflecting small-scale and entrepreneurial business activity. Those businesses needed stable operating funds that previously had been supplied by local financiers. A national bank system in which each local bank had the power and authority to issue banknotes, therefore, played a critical new role in support of business development.

It is important to clarify at this point that Shibusawa's evolving thinking on the *gappon* concept played a role in influencing his decision to endorse the U.S. National Bank system. Shibusawa's change in thinking occurred during the spring of 1871, in the midst of discussions between major Meiji government leaders, including Itō and others. Shibusawa concluded that Britain's monetary model was too advanced to introduce into Japan, even though it closely resembled the ideal for a developing maritime state (*kaiyō kokka*) whose economy could prosper on the basis of worldwide trade.

Shibusawa concluded that for Japan's early modern development, the U.S. National Bank system would more easily meet the need to issue banknotes and supply money for local entrepreneurs. He based his thinking on the circumstances of a Meiji government, which in contrast to Britain, did not have sufficient power to establish a solid central bank based on the gold standard. He also observed that political and business leaders in rural areas possessed significant assets, including former clans such as the Tokugawa, Maeda, and Date families, wealthy farmers such as the Honma family in Sakata, and other entrepreneurial merchants. Since the Meiji government budget was still very small, access to those assets and funds through government-issued national bonds was particularly attractive. Ultimately, common interest was identified between government leaders and those who emerged as presidents of the early local branches of the national banks, the so-called *chihō meibōka*, comprising political and economic leaders in rural areas.

The second challenge for establishing a new banking system in Japan was how to communicate the concepts and practices of a Western-style banking system to the Japanese people. During the Edo period (1600–1863), *ryōgaeshō* played a role as financiers in Japan supplying money to both *han* and samurai who were not directly involved in the production of goods, trade, or commercial activities. *Ryōgaeshō* conducted financial business between merchants, engineers, and farmers as well. Mitsui, Konoike, and other old *ryōgaeshō* exerted tremendous influence on the Tokugawa government as well as on many of the aforementioned clans in financial and monetary policy in the nineteenth century. In the principle and theory of monetary policy, their activities were well understood; however, the key difference in the functioning of a Western-style banking system was the public nature of assets held. The traditional Japanese system, where funds were based on closed, private relationships between lenders and borrowers, a feature also true of the *ko*, represented a way of thinking that worked against the importation and adoption of a Western banking system.

Shibusawa thought that the transparency associated with a Western banking system was of crucial importance for the public's willingness to take the initiative to build a modern economy and society, as well as to change the traditional mindset of *kanson minpi*. He aggressively promoted the idea, concept, and practice of banking, and persuaded politicians and wealthy people to accept its openness through his articulation of the value of *gappon*-style business organization. The new banking law served to support his efforts, as paper money became more widely available.

Shibusawa was one of the few leaders in the early Meiji period who could understand at a deep level the essence of Western banking systems. This can be explained in part because of his own past business experiences. Through helping his father's indigo trade and other farming activities, Shibusawa learned how to manage businesses and the key role of money. During his stay in Paris and his trip to several other European cities in 1867, he was impressed by new forms of technology and the political and economic systems found there.[16] On the advice and suggestions of the French banker Paul Flury-Hérard, he bought railroad bonds in France, benefitting from their subsequent appreciation. In combination, these experiences contributed to Shibusawa's ideas about acquiring advanced technologies and management systems from the West and his ability to lead and manage Japan's emergent finance and banking systems as the country modernized after the Meiji Restoration.[17]

After returning to Japan from Europe, Shibusawa established in Shizuoka a *shōhō kaisho*, a combined bank and trading company. This company was one of the early *gappon* organizations in Japan, a first step in linking banking and the rice trade as well as other agricultural commerce. The company got off to a good start but did not continue after Shibusawa was recruited to serve as a bureaucrat in the Meiji government's finance ministry. Nonetheless, Shibusawa's early experience in the private sector, although interrupted, formed the foundation upon his return to the private sector for the tremendous leadership he provided as inspector for the Daiichi National Bank, leading to his realization of numerous benefits for the country as the wealthy of Japan came to invest their money in newly established national banks.

The final challenge in establishing the Daiichi National Bank was how to manage the relationship between the Finance Ministry and the National Bank. This brings this chapter's analysis to the question of public–private relationships in the emergence of a national banking system in Japan. In the nineteenth century, every advanced Western nation, as defined by the military and economic achievements of such countries as Britain, France, and Belgium, had its own central bank and the power to issue paper money. These central banks were not directly managed by the government because the practice of banking included, as their primary role, the activation of the market economy. Therefore, management responsibility rested with the private sector in order to maintain political neutrality. Issuance of paper money is one of the crucial rights of the nation-state; in the Japanese case, every national bank had such currency privileges, as regulated by the Meiji government's National Bank Law.

Shibusawa was not in favor of establishing banks managed by the government. His position was that governmental management would be overly preoccupied with the shadows cast by the Tokugawa era and that, in general, a management role would result in inefficiencies and improprieties. Shibusawa's economic philosophy was that there were public obligations inherent in the country's monetary policy that should inform not only the money collected through taxes but also the goals and commitments of those participating voluntarily in *gappon* or joint-stock-type companies. Competition was the preferred approach; at the same time, basic fairness led to a need for a legal role by the national government. Thus, Shibusawa's position was that independence from the government was essential for the Daiichi National Bank, as was maintaining a good working relationship with the Finance Ministry. He paid attention to the role of nurturing human networks between reliable and trustworthy leaders such as Ōkuma Shigenobu, Matsukata Masayoshi, and Takahashi Korekiyo, all of whom were deeply involved in the development and execution of Japan's financial and monetary policy.

Shibusawa's conceptualization of the public–private relationship was very broad and profound. Although he confirmed that a suitable distance between them was absolutely necessary for the new banking system to function, for the sake of the country and society (*kokka shakai no tame*) he came to realize his own role was as a private rather than a public leader. The respect Shibusawa garnered from his work in government allowed him to collaborate as a business leader with the Finance Ministry and other political leaders. Shibusawa was also uniquely suited to be in charge of collaborating with former *daimyō* (feudal lords) such as Maeda, Shimazu, and Date, and with large private money changers such as Mitsui and Konoike, who had substantial assets and became important early supporters of the banking system as it took hold throughout the country. In particular, Date Munenari, *daimyō* of the Date clan in Uwajima, Shikoku district, and his main family in Sendai, the largest clan in the Tohoku region since the early seventeenth century, greatly appreciated Shibusawa's talent and spirit. Date Munenari supported the establishment of the national bank in Uwajima and also asked Shibusawa to manage Date family assets.

Conclusion

Shibusawa recognized that technology transfer through technical assistance obtained from Western countries, in combination with Japanese entrepreneurial leadership, would be crucial for the nation's sustainable economic development. This point is well illustrated in the chapter's case study of the Daiichi National Bank.

Shibusawa followed two guiding principles in setting up the Daiichi National Bank. Each sheds light on the role of a banking system, in theory and practice, to open the country to embrace the role of banks in promoting technology transfer and technical assistance. Understanding technology as methods, procedures, and ideas – in addition to physical artifacts – we see Shibusawa's activities at the Daiichi National Bank as both supporting the transfer of industrial technologies from Europe through finance and the actual transfer of banking technologies through the adaptation of Western financial practices, i.e., methods and procedures, such as double-entry bookkeeping and investor-oriented financial reporting.

First, Shibusawa sought to raise capital from as many people as possible. As the National Bank Act was established, corresponding rules were specified. Since all banks based on the Act were private enterprises, Shibusawa tried to avoid allowing a single major capital investor to monopolize the bank. An example is his decision to decline Mitsui's offer to handle the management of all aspects of the bank. Many investors such as emerging companies like Ono-gumi were invited to join; as a result, the bank was supported by seventy-one stockholders, that included individual as well as major investors.

Second, Shibusawa decided to publicly disclose investor names and their investment amounts. From the Edo period, major money changers like Mitsui and Konoike had also undertaken financial activities such as *daimyōgashi* (lending money to *daimyō*). However, they never dared disclose the names of investors or the amounts received because doing so was at odds with tradition.[18] Ensuring transparency was not a practice that Shibusawa would compromise on, given that investor responsibilities were foundational to his thinking. After repeated efforts, he persuaded major investors, including Mitsui and Ono-gumi. As he was known to observe, "Bankers are positioned above other people engaged in commerce and industry. Bankers enjoy people's respect and honor. This is why they must always be willing to assume heavy responsibilities."[19] Insisting on transparency as a banking technique was extended to Daiichi National Bank's Korean expansion as well as its promotion of Western banking methods in Korea, as is noted in Kim Myungsoo's contribution to this volume. This kind of awareness-raising was needed in order to ensure that talented individuals from around the country were open to pursuing a career in commerce – individuals willing to identify, adopt, and adapt business ideas from throughout the world to promote Japan's economic development.

Pushing forward with awareness-raising among bankers and instilling a sense of responsibility in them required improvement of the status of banks in society. For this purpose, Shibusawa established *Takuzenkai* (later the Tokyo Bankers' Association) in the late 1870s with the aim of offering bankers opportunities to exchange information and develop relationships through friendly competition. A feature of these economic circles is that *Takuzenkai* cooperated with the likes of the Tokyo Chamber of Commerce in submitting recommendations and proposals to the government about such issues as finance and trade policy.[20]

We should also note that Shibusawa was adept at addressing serious crises that might have led to the bankruptcy of Daiichi National Bank, thereby undermining the potential of Japan's early efforts to establish a national banking system. Fundamentally, he understood that Daiichi National Bank and Daiichi Bank were very weak compared with Mitsui and other private banks that supported Japan's emerging industrial conglomerates (*zaibatsu*). In fact, the actual number of national banks to be established initially fell below expectations – just four – because early holders of banknotes decided immediately to convert them to gold. Nonetheless, Shibusawa was one of the few financial specialists who had practical experience in money matters in both Europe and Japan that allowed him to weather these challenges. He also had the skills to resolve the bankruptcies of both the Ono-gumi and Shimada-gumi companies in 1874, both of which had been functioning as money changers connected to the National Treasury since the early Meiji period.

Shibusawa demonstrated a capacity to selectively import ideas from outside Japan in this regard. Rather than the old-fashioned account system, he introduced double-entry bookkeeping into the operations of Daiichi National Bank, following the example of Alexander Allan Shand, a British financial officer serving as adviser to the Finance Ministry in the early Meiji period. He promoted industrial development and technology transfer from the West and to East Asia through banking activities, whether his own or by uniting financiers throughout Japan to support projects such as Shōshi Kaisha/Oji Paper and Osaka Spinning Mill. In short, Shibusawa saw banking as both a technology and a means by which to transfer physical technologies.

Finally, Shibusawa recognized the value of an extended period of leadership as president of Daiichi Bank, which allowed him to encourage and develop new enterprises that facilitated the transfer of technology for Japan's industrialization as well as the establishment of many educational, social welfare, and other institutions that improved the quality of peoples' lives. He well understood the role that a bank and the banking system could play in promoting such developments by directly gathering money from the private sector.

His actions affirmed his view that this approach would be the most important way for ordinary people to support, through personal investment, the development of a society rich in material and spiritual terms.

NOTES

1 For Shibusawa Eiichi's thoughts and activities, see Shimada Masakazu, *The Entrepreneur Who Built Modern Japan: Shibusawa Eiichi,* trans. Paul Narum (Tokyo: Japan Publishing Industry Foundation for Culture, 2017). See also the Japanese version, *Shibusawa Eiichi: shakai kigyōkano senkusha* (Tokyo: Iwanami Shoten, 2011). Miyamoto Matao, ed., *Shibusawa Eiichi: Nihon kindai no tobira wo hiraita zaikai ri-da-* [The financial leader who opened the doors for modern Japan], PHP Management Series (Kyoto: PHP Institute, 2016).
2 See Patrick Fridenson and Kikkawa Takeo, eds., *Ethical Capitalism: Shibusawa Eiichi's Business Leadership in Global Perspective* (Toronto: University of Toronto Press, 2017). See also its Japanese version, Kikkawa Takeo and Patrick Fridenson, eds., *Gurobaru shihonshugi no naka no Shibusawa Eiichi, Gappon kyapitalizumu to moraru* [*Gappon* capitalism: The economic and moral ideology of Shibusawa Eiichi in global perspective] (Tokyo: Toyo Keizai, 2014), v and 159–62.
3 For Yamanobe Takeo, see Miyamoto Matao, ed., *Toyobo 130 nenshi* [130-year history of Toyobo Corporation] (Tokyo: Toyobo, 2015); and Shibusawa Memorial Museum, *Special Exhibition: Kindai bōseki no susume: Shibusawa Eiichi to Toyobo* [The advancement of modern pinning: Shibusawa Eiichi and Toyobo] (Tokyo: Shibusawa Memorial Museum, 2015).
4 On Takamine Jōkichi, see Iinuma Kazumasa and Shigano Tomio, *Takamine Jōkichi no shōgai: Adorenarin hakken no shinjitsu* [The life of Takamine Jokichi: The truth of the discovery of adrenaline] (Tokyo: Asahi Shuppansha, 2000).
5 *Kanson minpi* can be translated as "respect officials and despise the people." It is less about actual hating or disliking but reflects the pre-modern attitude of obedience toward and favoring officials and the government and a general condescension toward merchants and merchant activity. For an extended discussion of *gappon* capitalism, see Kikkawa and Fridenson, *Gurobaru shihonshugi no naka no Shibusawa Eiichi*; or in English see Fridenson and Kikkawa, *Ethical Capitalism*.
6 Kikkawa and Fridenson, *Gurobaru shihonshugi no naka no Shibusawa Eiichi*, 3.
7 Regarding Shibusawa's thoughts on *gappon* from various points of view, see Kikkawa and Fridenson, *Gurobaru shihonshugi no naka no Shibusawa Eiichi*, 159–66; in the English version, 124–6.
8 Tanaka Kazuhiro, "Harmonization between Morality and Economy," in Fridenson and Kikkawa, *Ethical Capitalism*, 55–6.

9 See Shimada Masakazu, *Shibusawa Eiichi no kigyōka katsudō no kenkyū* [Research on Shibusawa Eiichi's activities as an entrepreneur] (Tokyo: Nihon Keizai Hyōronsha, 2007).

10 According to the Japanese Commercial Code, article 535, "[In] a *tokumei kumiai* arrangement, 'anonymous (or silent) partners' (*tokumei kumiai'in*) are composed of *tokumei kumiai* who invest in a venture operated by a manager."

11 Shimada, *Shibusawa Eiichi no kigyōka katsudō no kenkyū*, 233–7.

12 Shibusawa Hideo, *Shibusawa Eiichi* (Tokyo: Shibusawa Seien Kinen Zaidan, 1988), 41–2.

13 Shibusawa, *Shibusawa Eiichi*, 79–80. *Ryūmonsha* means "association at the gate of the dragon." "Seien" is Shibusawa Eiichi's pseudonym.

14 Yoshida Kiyonari (1845–91) was born in Kagoshima and studied in Britain and the United States for several years. He was one of the most talented financial bureaucrats in the Finance Ministry during the early Meiji period. He was also concerned with treaty revisions between Japan and Western countries such as Britain and the United States as assistant minister of finance in 1882, and later upon being nominated as vice minister of agriculture and commerce in 1886.

15 Regarding Shibusawa's attitude toward to the introduction of a Western banking system, see Shibusawa Seien Kinen Zaidan Ryūmonsha, eds., *Shibusawa Eiichi denki shiryō*, vol. 4 (Tokyo: Shibusawa Seien Kinen Zaidan Ryūmonsha, 1955).

16 Regarding Shibusawa's thoughts and activities during his stay in Paris and trips to other European countries such as Britain, Belgium, and Germany in 1867–8, see Nihonshiseki Kyōkai, ed., *Shibusawa Eiichi taifutsu nikki* [Shibusawa Eiichi's French diary] (Tokyo: University of Tokyo Press, 1967).

17 Regarding Paul Flury-Hérard (1836–1913), see Kashima Shigeru, *Shibusawa Eiichi I, sorobanhen* (Tokyo: Bungeishunju, 2011), 180–2.

18 To explain this point further, mutual aid organizations called *tanomoshiko* and *mujin*, dating back to the Kamakura period, handled small loans among commoners for financing. They were similar to the moneychangers in terms of anonymity. For this reason, many potential investors were reluctant to embrace public disclosure, as expected by Shibusawa, who sought to establish and manage banks according to the concept of *gapponshugi*.

19 *Shibusawa Eiichi denki shiryō*, 5:103.

20 The word *takuzen*, quoted by Shibusawa from the *Analects of Confucius*, means "lead the way and follow the good." After Shibusawa became chairman of the Tokyo Chamber of Commerce, the *Takuzenkai* met monthly at the Chamber's building.

8 The Transfer of Western Banking Systems to Korea's Hanseong Bank: The Path through Japan

KIM MYUNGSOO

This chapter continues the theme of methods, knowledge, and processes as technology through an examination of the means by which Western banking technologies were transferred between two East Asian countries during the late nineteenth and early twentieth centuries. Using a case study of the introduction of Western banking practices at Korea's Hanseong Bank and its relationship with Japan's Daiichi Bank, this chapter demonstrates that modernization of Korean banking was tied to Japanese imperialist ambitions and financial penetration of continental markets. Although modernization originated with an indigenous reform movement, political turmoil and financial necessity moved banking reform into foreign hands – or at least into a partnership with foreign ambition.

Prior to Korea becoming a Japanese colony in 1910, a variety of industrial technologies from the United States, Great Britain, China, and Japan were introduced into Korea such as railroads, tramcars, electricity, telegraphy, modern weapons, and Western medicine.[1] Western banking systems also entered Korea at that time. All were closely related to the colonization-modernization process that began with Korea becoming a Japanese protectorate in 1905, following the Russo-Japanese War, and subsequent annexation in 1910. Japan's financial penetration began much earlier, however, with the establishment of the Pusan branch of the Daiichi Bank 1878. This prompted the Korean government and high-ranking government officials to independently establish banks in order to protect Korea's financial system. There was little Korea could do against Japanese trade expansion, which, in contrast to antiquated and usurious traditional lending systems, was facilitated by prompt remittance and low-interest loans from Western-style Japanese banks.

The external shocks of Japanese colonial expansion and trade, coupled with internal necessity, awakened progressive Koreans to establish Western-style banks and modernize the country's financial system. In addition, enforcement of specie tax payments as part of the Gabo Reforms promoted the creation of a commodity money economy, which had been expanding since the late Joseon dynasty (1392–1897).[2] Korea's traditional systems of finance and usury, coupled with a lack of reliable financial institutions, led high-ranking government officials such as Lee Yongik and Kim Jonghan to promote the establishment of Western-style of banks on the model of Japan's Daiichi Bank.

Because of Korea's colonial status, it was difficult for Koreans to independently establish monetary and financial systems. In fact, the Hanseong Bank began as a byproduct of (Korean) colonization. From the start, Hanseong Bank relied on the Daiichi Bank's supervision and guidance; the process of dependent development came through the introduction of Western banking systems into Korea.[3]

The First Western-Style Bank in Korea: An Attempt to Independently Establish Korean Banks

It is well known that the first Western-style bank in Korea was the Pusan branch of Japan's Daiichi National Bank, established in June 1878, two years after the Treaty of Ganghwa (also known as the Japan-Korea Treaty of Amity) was signed in February 1876. Daiichi National Bank was founded in Tokyo three years earlier, in July 1873; its name was shortened to Daiichi Bank in 1896. The plan to establish a foreign branch of Daiichi National Bank resulted from the need to have a foreign exchange bank in Japan that was expected to support Japan's foreign penetration onto the East Asian continent.[4] When a plan to establish a Shanghai branch of Daiichi National Bank was stopped by opposition from Alexander Allan Shand, foreign advisor to Japan's Ministry of Finance (Ōkurasho) in October 1872, Ōkura Kihachirō and Shibusawa Eiichi alternatively established the bank's Pusan branch as a private business initiative.[5] Daiichi National Bank received ¥50,000 in government loans and ¥10,000 as a government subsidy, half the entire cost of opening the Pusan branch.[6] Although private, the Pusan branch had close ties to the Meiji government's foreign policy initiatives. The Korean branches of the Daiichi National Bank, including the Pusan branch, became important sources of revenue for supporting the main offices in Japan, even when the bank performed poorly.[7]

Beginning in 1884, Daiichi National Bank was entrusted with managing customs duties for three Korean ports: Incheon, Pusan, and Wonsan. This was important from two perspectives. First, if Daiichi National Bank loaned the Korean government money, customs duties could be used as security. Second, when the Western powers tried to offer loans to the Korean government with the aim of acquiring rights and interests, or when the Korean government tried to introduce loans from foreign countries independently, Daiichi National Bank could stop those attempts by its right to control customs duty management.[8] Despite early advantages, Japan's efforts to establish a central bank in Korea through which it could more thoroughly control Korean finances ended in failure because of political turmoil. In February 1896, King Gojong fled the royal palace with his supporters and took refuge in the Russian legation, fearing a coup d'état following the assassination of his wife, Queen Min, by Japanese agents under the direction of the Miura Gorō, Japan's resident minister in Korea. The event sparked Korean reform and independence movements, including the founding of the short-lived Independence Club in 1896. Korean reformists' considered the establishment of Western-style banks essential for Korean financial modernization under the Gabo Reforms of 1894–6.[9]

In 1888, Park Yeonghyo submitted an opinion paper on political reforms to King Gojong, strongly suggesting that Korea establish Western-style banks. Park had been a political refugee in Japan following the Gapsin Coup of 1884 and was well informed on the necessity and usefulness of a Western banking system and modern government financial institutions.[10] In 1894, institutional modifications were in preparation for the switch to tax payments in cash. The Joseon government needed to enforce the change in order to resolve issues related to the transportation and storage of metallic currency because Korea lacked paper currency.[11] During the Gabo Reform, the government established the Banking Bureau under the Department of Finance (*Takjiamun*), which was in charge of domestic currency conversion services.[12] The director of the Mint Bureau was also the director of the Banking Bureau, and the Banking Bureau was in charge of exchanging old coins for new coins. During the Eulmi Reform of 1896, the Department of Finance was renamed the Ministry of Finance (*Takjibu*), and the Banking Bureau was dissolved. Inspection and accounting departments were newly organized under the Account Bureau, with the Inspection Department overseeing banking businesses.

Korea's present-day treasury agency system was also created in 1895.[13] At the same time, the *Gumgogyuchik* (operating regulations of the *Gumgo* Department) under the Cashier's Department of the Ministry of Finance was published with several provisions that established the relationship between public and private finance. Article 1 stated, "A *gumgo* is an agent to keep or receive and disburse cash belonging to the exchequer." Provisions in Article 3 stated, "Branches of the Cashier's Department should be set up in convenient places in each prefecture, or banks and companies under the government's control will execute work for the branches."[14]

The founding of the Ministry of Finance and related institutions was designed to introduce a financial system and establish a modern bank with the aim of blocking Japan's financial penetration into Korea. It was also supposed to satisfy Korea's expanding financial needs and represents the transfer of the methods and processes of Western banking to the modernizing country. The Korean government, however, was too inexperienced to manage a modern banking system and, like Japan before it, consulted a foreign adviser, John McLeavy Brown, about Western banking in June 1896. At the time, Brown was serving as an advisor to the Treasury Department and the Chief Commission of Customs in Korea. King Gojong gave Brown total control over the Korean treasury prior to fleeing to the Russian legation. Before coming to Korea, Brown was secretary to the British Embassy in China between 1861 and 1872. His talent brought him to the attention of Robert Hart, inspector general of customs in China, who selected him as the first secretary to the Chinese customs bureau, where he worked for twenty years, and later recommended him for his post in Korea as manager of the Customs Department.[15]

The expansion of the commodity money economy in the late Joseon dynasty caused changes to the credit system. After the eighteenth century, promissory notes and bills of exchange, which were issued and circulated among Kaesong merchants, were widely used in commercial transactions. This lasted into the nineteenth century. Promissory notes and bills of exchange were also used for wage payments, travel expense payments, means of international trade, means of paying off deals for appointive offices (the spoils system), tax payments, and finance management. In short, the circulation of credit was widely prevalent. Although the *Yeogincheong*, comprised of the Six Licensed Stores or *Yukuijeon*, was not a bank,[16] it carried out banking functions such as bill clearing, bill discounting, security loans, etc. Hundreds of bill brokers (*geogan*) were engaged in bill discounting or bill clearing in Seoul. A commission agency (*gaekju*), which was engaged mainly in exchange services, appeared after opening the port of Ganghwa in 1876.[17] Waclaw Sieroszewski, a Polish-Russian writer who traveled the Korean Peninsula in 1903, noted that there were no banks in Korea, but that the alternative mechanism was working.[18] However, other foreigners held different views. *The Korea*, first published by the Russian Treasury in 1905, is representative. Regarding the financial situation from 1876 to 1899:

> It seems that the shortage of financial institutions is supplemented by many lenders' associations. A lender's association consists of a small number of members and they collect money to lend usuriously. Profits from lending money are distributed to members. However, this interest rate is absurdly high to Europeans. It is the custom to calculate interest every ten months, except in some cases. A person who has the best credit can borrow money at the interest rate of 20 percent every 10 months, which is the lowest rate available to him. [Interest rates of] 30 percent, 40 percent, even 50 percent are not rare cases. As a Catholic missionary mentioned, there are some cases to which the rate of 100 percent is applied.[19]

Commission agencies in open ports simultaneously managed accommodations, warehousing, and finance. At that time, the Daiichi Bank supply of money at a lower interest rate than Korean bill brokers or commission agencies had a strong influence on the traditional financial system. Daiichi Bank set up branches in Wonsan (1880) and Incheon (1883) and executed money exchange, documentary bills of exchange, and loans with advanced banking expertise.[20] The bank's expansion into Korea would benefit Korean merchants who traded with the Japanese in the open ports.

Despite the excessive weight of Korean coins and the difficulty that Koreans had in transferring money, there were no other means of remittance. Only certain people could use documentary drafts, and their range of use was limited to the main commercial areas, such as Seoul, Uiju, Pusan, and Daegu. Sometimes, if a store had branches or special agents in other commercial areas, people would pay them a 3 percent commission and buy a bill of exchange. Koreans also had to send the necessary sum in copper coins because silver coins or a kind of paper money were all used in open ports. Thus, Korean merchants were often forced to employ a porter or use beasts of burden to carry coins as if it were freight.[21]

Remittance remained difficult in the late nineteenth and early twentieth centuries. The 1894 requirement that tax payments be made in cash (rather than in-kind) exacerbated the problem. Once taxes were paid with coins in each prefecture, they needed to be transported to Seoul. Considering Korea's infrastructure at that time, we know that the transportation of heavy coins was expensive and untimely. Inflation and a lack of goods also took hold in Seoul, and monetary stringency was expected in each prefecture. There was an increase in merchants' arbitrage trading (*oehoek*), using the price differential between the center and the regions. *Oehoek* was used as a method to mobilize commercial financing for Korean merchants.[22] Despite the government's attempt to level the playing field between Korean and Japanese (and Chinese) merchants, the system proved to be inadequate. As a result, Korean merchants turned to the Daiichi Bank's port branches to secure much-needed capital.[23]

In March 1895, Takeuchi Tsuyoshi, Ozaki Saburō, Ōmiwa Chōbei, and others sought to establish a Korean central bank and acquire control of the Gyeongbu Railroad Company, which ran from Pusan to Seoul. This maneuver required prior consent from the Japanese prime minister, whose government only approved the banking plan. Japan's attempt to gain control of the Korean railroad failed because of the political changes surrounding the Eulmi Incident (*Eulmisabyeon*) and the Korean royal family seeking refuge at the Russian legation. Regardless, the Korean government and reformist bureaucrats saw Japan's bank initiative as a significant threat, and it became the stimulus for financial modernization.[24]

Top officials in the Korean government led in establishing commercial banks starting in June 1896. Minister of Finance Sim Sanghun, Vice-Minister of Finance Lee Jaejeong, Vice-Minister of Agriculture, Commerce, and Industry Yi Chaeyeon, Lord Chamberlain Kim Jonghan, a cabinet councilor An Gyeongsu, and *chamui* (a high-ranking official ranking under vice-minister) in the Ministry of Finance, Yi Geunbae, were determined to establish Korean national banks. Toward that end, the men attended John McLeavy Brown's lecture on banking, where they learned how to establish and manage a bank.

With government support, Kim Jonghan, An Gyeongsu, Yi Geunbae, and others began writing regulations and articles of association for banks starting on 17 June 1896.[25] Kim's group founded Hanseong Bank, An's group launched the old Joseon Bank, and Sim Sanhoon's group established Daehanchunil Bank with the assistance of some wealthy supporters. Daehanchunil Bank later became the Woori Bank and Hanseong Bank became the Shinhan Bank via a merger with the Choheung Bank.[26]

The old Joseon Bank was established on 2 February 1897. Its promoters gave it semi-governmental features so that they could utilize treasury funds in the same manner as the Bank of Japan. Brown, however, opposed this suggestion. In his opinion, they should wait for the proper time, until the old Joseon Bank would gain standing with ordinary people. Because of Brown's objections, Joseon Bank was established as a commercial bank, not a semi-governmental bank, much later than had been expected.[27] At first the old Joseon Bank's promoters planned to employ a foreign banking expert, but it is unknown if a foreign adviser was ever hired.[28]

Hanseong Bank acquired its license to operate on 8 January 1897, opening its doors on 19 February 1897. On the basis of the date of its license, the Hanseong Bank is Korea's first modern bank and its January 1897 articles of incorporation are the oldest in Korea. According to the articles, the bank had privileges beyond the scope of a typical commercial bank. Although a private bank, Hanseong Bank had the ability to issue convertible notes.[29]

Hanseong Bank's articles have important meaning in Korean financial history because they enable us to understand the state of bank management in the early twentieth century and they served as a model for later banks' articles of association. Because they were standardized, it is likely that Hanseong Bank's regulations were based on extant (foreign) banking regulations. Its authority to issue currency as described in the eighteenth article of association, for example, was most likely based on similar rights held by Daiichi National Bank (prior to May 1883).[30]

The Founding of Public Hanseong Bank and the Introduction of a Western Banking System

Public Hanseong Bank, which refers to the reorganization of Hanseong Bank as a joint-stock company in 1903, can be thought of as a by-product of the conflict between Russia and Japan over interests in Korea. There were two factors behind the bank's reorganization: a loan offer from Russia to acquire commercial concessions as well as railway and mining rights in Korea; and the slow pace at which Daiichi Bank circulated notes, despite the Korean peoples' objections. The Japanese government, the Japanese legation in Korea, and Daiichi Bank suggested that they had to establish a Korean bank with the support of Daiichi Bank, which was anticipated to settle these two problems. It was also the reason why Daiichi Bank urged the dissolution of Hanseong Bank when Russia abandoned its loan offer.[31]

Following the "Megata Reform," named for Megata Tanetarō, financial adviser to the Korean government dispatched by the Japanese Ministry of Finance, Korea experienced a cash crunch, which made necessary the establishment of modern financial institutions. Hanseong Bank survived this monetary crisis and transformed its ownership structure. Han Sangyong persuaded Lee Jaewan, president of Hanseong Bank, to change the bank's ownership structure from a joint-stock company to a publicly held corporation in September 1905. At this time, Hanseong Bank was completely dependent on Daiichi Bank for its operating funds.[32]

Following reorganization, Hanseong Bank officially settled its business accounts on 31 December 1905 and publicly reported its statement of accounts for the first half of the year in the newspaper *Hwangseong sinmun*.[33] This was the first corporate disclosure in Korean corporate history and illustrates the adoption of modern Japanese financial practices. Hanseong Bank expanded its domestic remittance service area to include the cities of Incheon, Pusan, Masan, Daegu, Gaeseong, Pyeongyang, Jinnampo, Wonsan, Hamheung, Seongjin, and Suwon throughout 1906.[34]

During this time and under the influence of Daiichi Bank, we see the transfer of Western banking technologies and business practices to Korea. It is commonly known that double-entry bookkeeping was invented in Venice during the fourteenth century. Korea relied on *songdosagechibu-bup*, a traditional bookkeeping method used by *songdo* (today's *gaesung*) merchants, since at least the twelfth century. Many sources show that *songdosagechibu-bup* continued to be used until the early 1900s.

As part of its technological transformation, Hanseong Bank adopted Western-style bookkeeping in 1903, approximately six years after its establishment. Prior to that it is likely that it used *songdosagechibu-bup* bookkeeping. Han Sangyong traveled to the Gyeongseong (present-day Seoul) branch of Daiichi Bank to learn Western-style bookkeeping and bank management techniques from the Japanese. Hanseong Bank also hired a Japanese advisor to instruct its Korean managers how to run a bank, including bookkeeping techniques, according to Western methods. However, the bank's president, Lee Jaewan, and vice president, Kim Jonghan, did not understand Western-style bookkeeping, so Han created a duplicate set of records written in Chinese characters for their approval.[35] Regardless, it is clear that technologies and methods of Western banking were transferred to Korea through Japan at the turn of the century.

The impetus for Hanseong Bank's technological transformation was the demand of Daiichi Bank that the Korean bank adopt Western-style bookkeeping techniques if it was to receive loans from the Japanese bank. Daiichi Bank dispatched a staff to monitor the issuance of loans and required the adoption of double-entry bookkeeping with horizontal writing and Arabic numerals.[36]

Daehanchunil Bank, established in 1899, also used *songdosagechibu-bup* bookkeeping until 1906. An economic recession and financial difficulties originating from Megata Tanetarō's compulsory monetary reforms forced Daehanchunil Bank to temporarily close in 1905. During this time it started a number of reforms, including a capital increase to 150,000 won, borrowing 200,000 won from the Korean government, revising its articles of association, and hiring a Japanese manager between 1905 and 1906. Daehanchunil Bank also decided to adopt Western-style bookkeeping techniques during its stockholders' general meeting on 11 October 1905.[37]

Given that Korea was under de facto Japanese control following the Russo-Japanese War of 1905, the abovementioned reforms were unavoidable.[38] The Japanese resident-general of Korea institutionalized the use of Western-style bookkeeping, and the Korean government under Japanese rule issued a banking act by imperial edict on 21 March 1906, stating that all banks in Korea had to submit a business report every six months to the Korean government and publish their balance sheets in the newspaper. The Banking Act of 1906 applied to other banks such as the Hanil Bank, the Agricultural and Industrial Bank, and local financial associations that were established between 1906 and 1907. Between 1907 and 1908, Western-style bookkeeping and financial reporting were standardized throughout Korea.[39] A textbook on Western-style bookkeeping was also published in 1908.[40]

Daiichi Bank's Operational Management Guidance to Hanseong Bank

Hanseong Bank became the Public Hanseong Bank on 7 December 1903, and Han Sangyong became its manager in charge of general affairs for banking services, e.g., deposits, withdrawals, money transfer, and commercial lending. Public Hanseong Bank was housed in a traditional Korean-style house in Anhyun (present site of Anguk Hospital) and employed four security guards because of the unstable political climate prior to the Russo-Japanese War.[41] Telephones were installed in the bank's head office on 8 September 1904,[42] a first for a private company.[43]

At that time, Public Hanseong Bank had to depend on Daiichi Bank for funds because it lacked working capital. Public Hanseong Bank received an unsecured loan of ¥35,000 from Daiichi Bank at an annual interest rate of 9.9 percent, which the Public Hanseong Bank lent at a rate of 21.9 percent (annually), allowing the bank to profit handsomely.[44] Despite a rate that today seems usurious,

Hanseong's loans were popular because their rates were lower than the generally accepted rates of 30 to 50 percent. A daily interest rate, which Public Hanseong Bank adopted, was advantageous to borrowers in comparison to Daehanchunil Bank, which adopted monthly interest rates.[45]

At that time, most loan collateral was in the form of land or houses. There were two steps to appraise real estate. First, a Public Hanseong Bank clerk evaluated the value of the loan collateral and decided the loan amount. Hanseong Bank then reported the conditions of the loan to the Gyeongseong branch of Daiichi Bank. Daiichi Bank sent its bank clerk to double-check the results of Hanseong Bank's appraisal and verified if there were any problems. If the re-evaluation was acceptable, Daiichi Bank lent money to Hanseong Bank, and Hanseong Bank in turn lent the money at a higher rate. This rather cumbersome process required a significant amount of time and occasionally put the bank in predicaments in its desire to secure collateral.[46] For a short time after the bank opened, there were no customers applying for loans, leaving management anxious over the state of the new bank. Then a merchant from Daegu applied for a loan to cover the costs of recent business purchases. Bank managers insisted on loan collateral, but all the merchant could provide in exchange was the donkey he had ridden to the bank office. After deliberations about using the donkey as collateral, the bank executed the loan. There was, however, one problem that the managers never considered. Until the Daegu merchant returned to Seoul to repay his loan, the bank had to ensure that the donkey did not die![47]

Daiichi Bank also undertook the proxy task of bill clearing for Public Hanseong Bank. Furthering the process by which modern banking technologies were transferred to Korea, the bank's manager, Han Sangyong, learned Western banking methods and management techniques at the head office of the Daiichi Bank when he was dispatched to Japan in 1906 as a member of a legation acknowledging the Japan-Korea Treaty of 1905.

Growth under Japanese Rule and Management Control by Joseon Industrial Bank

The stability of Hanseong Bank relied on securing ample funding – a difficult task in a country with scarce capital. Banks used three methods to raise funds for lending: acquire large numbers of deposits, borrow money from a central bank, or increase capital through public stock offerings. Han Sangyong attempted to attract depositors from among his relatives and friends because he believed that self-capitalization would free the bank from its dependency on the Japanese, i.e., the Daiichi Bank. But there was a scarcity of depositors and fair policy consideration from other banks, so Hanseong Bank had little choice other than to increase capital by issuing new stocks. The question was who would purchase the bank's stock and with what money. Daiichi Bank's 1876 experience provided Hanseong Bank with a good example.

In September 1910, Han was appointed executive director of Hanseong Bank. After taking office, Han tried to increase Hanseong Bank's capital tenfold – from ¥300,000 to ¥3 million. At that time, Han tried to use *eunsagongchae* (bonds that Joseon aristocrats received from Japan for their cooperation during Korea's annexation). Han received approval from the Japanese governor-general of Korea on 15 January 1911, following persistent negotiations. This process was similar to the one followed by the National Bank, which used *geumrokgongchae*, bonds for paying capital. Japan approved the establishment of the National Bank by covering 80 percent of the capital of the government loan, which was composed primarily of *geumrokgongchae* through revision of the August 1876 National Bank ordinance.

Following this precedent, Han increased Hanseong Bank's capital by a factor of ten. Because he used Joseon aristocrats' *eunsagongchae* bonds, Hanseong Bank was nicknamed the "aristocrats' bank," but this was an unavoidable strategy decision because of the scarcity of capital in Korea.[48]

In 1918, Hanseong Bank opened a branch office in Tokyo, the first instance of an overseas branch of a Korean bank. Japanese Prime Minister Terauchi Masatake persuaded Han to open the Tokyo branch, believing that the Tokyo branch of Hanseong Bank would show Koreans a model case of expansion to Japan from colonial Korea. To Hanseong Bank, business expansion in Japan was an important way to attract free (Japanese) capital. Japan's economy was unprecedentedly prosperous as a result of special procurement demands during the First World War. Shortly thereafter, in 1919, Han was again able to increase bank capital, this time by attracting financial support from Japanese investors.[49]

Subsequently, the Tokyo branch recorded a 27.2 to 36.1 percent increase in total deposits and a 14.7 to 19.5 percent increase in loans between 1918 and 1923. Excellent operating performance at the Tokyo branch convinced Hanseong Bank officers to open a second Japanese branch. In 1922, Han established the bank's Osaka branch.[50] Shibusawa Eiichi sent Han a congratulatory telegram on his latest efforts to further the expansion of Western banking techniques into Korea.[51]

When Han Sangyong decided in 1919 to increase Hanseong Bank's capital, he followed Shibusawa's advice and decided on ¥6 million, which was twice its previous capital holdings.[52] Han decided on two methods to increase the bank's capitalization, the most important of which was the abolition of the regulation that limited stockholders' eligibility in the bank to Koreans. Accordingly, when the Japanese governor-general of Korea abolished restrictions on stockholder qualifications for ethnic groups,[53] the portion of

Japanese stockholders increased steadily by 28.1 percent between late 1919 and the end of June 1923.[54]

In offering stock for public subscription, Shibusawa's influence was significant. As a Tokugawa family trustee, Shibusawa recommended that the family of the former shogun purchase stock in Hanseong Bank. The *Kunaisho* (Ministry of the Imperial Household) and many Japanese aristocrats also put their names on the bank's stockholder's list.

Strictly speaking, Hanseong Bank's capital development depended on Japanese capital. With the increase in Japanese stockholders, Han decided to appoint a board member and an auditor for Japanese nationals. Shibusawa recommended the appointment of Imanishi Rinzaburō, president of the Osaka Chamber of Commerce.[55] In October 1922, Mori Jusaku, a consultant from Daiichi Bank, left his position at Hanseong Bank. Mori's resignation signaled the Korean bank's financial independence from Daiichi Bank.[56] This also marked the full transfer of Western banking technologies and know-how to Korea via Japan.

In January 1923, Hanseong Bank's directorate held a general meeting of stockholders and appointed Han Sangyong as the bank's next president after Lee Yoonyong (bank president from 1909 to 1923) accepted responsibility for issuing bad checks and resigned. Because Han had been the de facto head of the bank since 1903, his inauguration was recognized as the natural result and climax of his business career. Despite ascension to his new post, 1923 also marks the beginning of Han's decline.[57]

In September 1923, the Great Kanto Earthquake rocked Tokyo, and Hanseong Bank's Tokyo branch was destroyed. The bank overcame the crisis with a loan from the Dongyang Colonization Company (DCC). The DCC assumed Hanseong Bank's real estate portfolio and issued mortgage bonds based on the properties. The bank realized these mortgage bonds in Tokyo securities markets, which the bank used in an attempt to cope with the crisis.[58] Regardless, the earthquake had a significant impact on the bank's overall performance despite the modernization of its practices over the previous decades.

In March 1928, Han resigned as president of Hanseong Bank, which he had managed for twenty-five years. He had to take responsibility for the bank's deteriorating management during the 1920s, a period of crises and prolonged economic recession. In addition to the earthquake disaster in 1923, a series of economic crises occurred in succession, including Japan's postwar depression and financial crisis (1927), and the "Showa Depression" (1930) – Japan's version of the Great Depression. Above all, rates of return decreased from 5.3 percent in 1920 to 0.6 percent in 1928, while the leverage rate increased by a factor of six (see figure 8.1).[59] Although Han tried to rebuild Hanseong Bank through financial assistance from the Japanese governor-general of Korea and with a

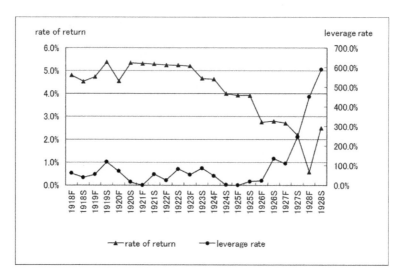

Figure 8.1. Hanseong Bank's Rate of Return and Leverage Rate

special loan from the Bank of Japan, the successive crises frustrated his plans and placed Hanseong Bank under the supervision of the Joseon Industrial Bank. Han blamed the bank's deteriorating management and finances on the establishment of the Japanese branches that he arranged in 1918 and 1922.[60]

Conclusion

The introduction and expansion of a modern banking system in Korea originated from external stimuli by the Western powers and Japan, coupled with the domestic necessity that accompanied an expanding financial monetary economy. The founding of the Pusan branch of Daiichi National Bank, entrusting customs duties management to foreign advisers, and Japan's attempt to establish a central bank, all carried out as part of Japanese imperialist expansion, drove Korea's need to modernize its financial sector. The penetration and expansion of Japanese financial institutions like the Daiichi Bank drove Koreans to modernize their traditional financial system under Japanese guidance. Regardless, foreign financial penetration provoked Korea's apprehension with the changing international order in East Asia and being incorporated into the capitalist world order.

Whereas traditional moneylenders tried to continue their practices in the face of foreign pressure, some individuals with the support of Japanese entrepreneurs such as Shibusawa Eiichi and Japanese officials realized that the key to Korea's financial stability and growth was through the adoption of Western-style banking techniques. While there were some influential Westerners such as John McLeavy Brown, whose lecture on the establishment and operation of banks was influential for high-ranking Korean officials, most banking technology flowed to Korea via Japan.

Several banks were established at this key juncture in Korean financial history, including the Joseon and Daehanchunil Banks, but the bank at the forefront of modernization was the Hanseong Bank. Influenced most directly by Shibusawa Eiichi's Daiichi National Bank, Hanseong Bank adopted and disseminated Western-style banking methods such as double-entry bookkeeping as a condition of its financial dealings with the Japanese bank. In its early days, Hanseong Bank relied on *songdosagaechibu-bup*, a traditional form of accounting. Following the Banking Act of 1906, Hanseong Bank adopted Western accounting methods, although its adoption may predate the Act by three years. Han Sangyong, who was responsible for most day-to-day operations at Hanseong Bank, learned Western bank bookkeeping at the Pusan branch and Tokyo head office of Daiichi Bank.

Ties between Hanseong Bank, Daiichi Bank, and the Japanese colonial authority continued throughout the early twentieth century, with the Korean bank eventually opening branch offices in Tokyo and Osaka at the recommendation of Terauchi Masatake, governor-general of Korea. This followed years of close relations between Daiichi Bank and Hanseong Bank and represents the apex of Korean penetration into Japanese markets and, importantly, the thorough transfer of Western banking technologies and techniques to Korean banking.

There were two paths through which Western-style banking systems were transferred to Korea: the development of a credit and monetary economy stimulated by tax reforms beginning in 1894, and the penetration of Japanese financial institutions such as the Daiichi Bank into Korea and their ties to colonial policy. Korea's credit and monetary economy started to spread nationwide during the late Joseon period, and Western-style financial systems necessarily started to be transferred into Korea through Japan at the same time. Full-scale introduction of Western bank management and banking techniques originated at the Public Hanseong Bank in 1903 and were systemized through its relationship with the Daiichi Bank. The growth of the Hanseong Bank during the colonial period, and the causes for its financial readjustment in 1928, were intimately linked to Japan's economy and to colonial policy in Korea.

NOTES

1 Kim Yeongho, "Hanmal seoyanggisului suyong" [Acceptance of Western technology at the end of the Korean Empire], *Journal of Asiatic Studies* 11, no. 3 (September 1968): 295–348; Sungshin University Humanities Research Institute, *Seogu gwahakgisul doibui*

sajeok gochal [Historical review of the introduction of Western science and technology] (Seoul: Ministry of Science-Technology, 1969); Seok Taemun and Lee Hocheol, "Gyeongbuk neunggumsaneobui baldalgwajeong: gisulsajeok gwajeong" [A study of the development process of the apple industry in Gyeongsangbuk-do] *Nongchonsahoe* 11, no. 1 (2001): 241–81; Jang Deoksam, "Seoyanguihagui doibgwa iyangpyeonui gyoyukjeok uimie gwanhan gochal" [A study of the introduction of Western medical science and the meaning of Iyangpyeon] *Gyoyugyeongu* 21 (2002): 1–12; Kim Yeonhee, "Gojongsidae seoyang gisul doip: cheoldowa jeonsin bunyareul jungsimeuro" [The introduction of railways and the telegraph during the reign of King Gojong], *Hanguk Gwahaksahakhoeji* 25, no. 1 (2003): 3–24.

2   "Gabo" corresponds to the year 1894. The Gabo Reform was a reform movement carried out by the Enlightenment Party between 1894 and 1896. The subsequent 1896 movement is referred to as the Eulmi Reform.

3   Kim Myungsoo, "Daehanjegukgi ilbonui geumyungjangak gidowa ilbon jeireunhaeng: 1903nyeon gongribhanseongeunhaengui seongribgwa gwarnyeonhayeo" [Japan's and Daiichi Bank's attempt to take control of Korean finances in the Korean Empire Period: Establishment of Hansung Bank as a Public Bank in 1903], *Japanese Cultural Studies* 47 (July 2013): 29–53.

4   The Yokohama Specie Bank (YSB) was in charge of financing trade within Japan and initiated its banking business in February 1880. The YSB's monopoly status was recognized by law as an international financial institution starting in 1887. See Kato Toshihiko, *Honpō ginkō shiron* [A history of Japan's banking industry] (Tokyo: Tokyo University Press, 1978), 68–9, 74–5.

5   Kimura Yuji, *Joseon ginkō zaininchu no kaiko* [Retrospective on the Bank of Joseon] (Gyeongseong: Joseon Ginkō Chosaka, 1940), 15–16.

6   Shimada Masakazu, *Shibusawa Eiichi no kigyō katsudō no kenkyū* [A study of Shibusawa Eiichi's entrepreneurial activities] (Tokyo: Nihon Keizai Hyōronsha, 2007), 322.

7   After Daiichi Bank acquired three special rights – the right to handle government money, the right to carry out currency reform, and the right to put Daiichi Bank bills in circulation – its profits in Korea increased significantly and formed 40 percent of the bank's total profits. See Shimada, *Shibusawa Eiichi no kigyō kakatsudō no kenkyū*, 320.

8   Shimada, *Shibusawa Eiichi no kigyō katsudō no kenkyū*, 324.

9   Han Baekheung, *Guhanmal minjogeunhaeng saeseongsa yeongu 1984–1910* [Study of the history of national banks during the late Joseon period, 1894–1910] (Seoul: Scenario Alta, 1996), 22–6.

10   Yoon Seokbum, Hong Sungchan, Woo Daehyung, and Kim Dongwook, *Hanguk geundae geumyungsa yeongu* [A study of modern Korean financial history] (Seoul: Segyungsa, 1996), 57.

11   Lee Haegyeong, "Joseon hugi segeum gammyeongwa hwapye yutonge gwanhan yeongu: jeonsereul jungsimeuro" [A study of the commutation of tax and money

circulation in the late Joseon], *Collected Papers of the Research Institute of Industry and Economy of Chonbuk National University* 22 (1992): 265–78.

12 Han Baekheung, *Guhanmal minjokeunhaeng saeseongsa yeongu*, 27–8.

13 Han Baekheung, *Guhanmal minjokeunhaeng saeseongsa yeongu*, 28–9.

14 *Official Gazette of the Late Yi Dynasty* 7 (8 April 1895).

15 Kim Hyeonsuk, "Hanmal gomungwan J. McLeavy Brown e daehan yeongu" [A study of the advisor J. McLeavy Brown in late Joseon Korea], *Journal of Korean History* 66 (September 1989): 104–9.

16 There were six licensed stores (*Sijeon*), which had exclusive rights to sell a particular item and special rights to prohibit unpermitted stores from selling that item. They were called *Yuguijeon* or *Yukjubijeon*. The six *Sijeon* had obligations for government procurement of particular goods: silk, cotton cloth, Korean paper, ramie cloth, and fish. See Ryu Kyoseong, "Seoul yukuijeon yeongu: Ijo dosisangupui ilgochal" [Seoul: The character of city commerce during the Yi dynasty], *Yoksa Hakbo* 8 (1955): 377–434.

17 The Japan-Korea Treaty of 1876, known as the Japan-Korea Treaty of Amity in Japan or Treaty of Ganghwa Island in Korea, was made between representatives of the Empire of Japan and the Joseon Kingdom in 1876. Negotiations were concluded on 26 February 1876.

18 Ko Donghwan, "Joseonhugi~hanmal sinyonggeoraeui baldal – eoeumgwa hwaneul jungsimeuro" [A study of the development of credit dealing in the late Joseon period and Korean Empire period – promissory notes and money orders], *Jibangsawa jibangmunhwa* 13, no. 2 (November 2010): 296–7.

19 Russian Treasury and Bureau of Forestry, Department of Agriculture and Commerce, eds., *The Korea*, trans. (Tokyo: Bureau of Forestry, Department of Agriculture and Commerce, 1905), 92.

20 Daiichi Bank, ed., *Kankoku ni okeru Daiichi ginkō* [The Daiichi Bank in Korea] (Tokyo: Daiichi Bank, 1908), 93.

21 Russian Treasury, *The Korea*, 93.

22 *Oehoek* was a system by which the central government attempted to provide capital to merchants through local tax receipts. See Yoon et al., *Hanguk geundae geumyungsa yeongu*, 58.

23 Joheung Bank, ed., *Joheungeunhaeng baenyeonsa* [The 100-year history of Joheung Bank] (Seoul: Joheung Bank, 1997), 32–3.

24 Han Baekheung, *Guhanmal minjokeunhaeng saeseongsa yeongu*, 35–6.

25 *Independent*, "Brief Notice," 18 June 1896, 3.

26 Yoon et al., *Hanguk geundae geumyungsa yeong*, 59.

27 Yoon et al., 61–2. When we examine the process that Daiichi Bank used to establish control over Korean finance to become the central bank of Korea, Brown's support and protection must not be ignored. Brown permitted the circulation of Daiichi Bank notes and thwarted the Joseon government's challenge to the compulsory circulation of Japanese notes and prohibition orders regarding Japan's

rights to control maritime customs. Japan's financial and monetary penetration into Korea subordinated Joseon's financial and monetary systems and contributed to the creation of Japan's colonial base. See Kim Hyeonsuk, "Hanmal gomungwan J. McLeavy Brown," 106–9, 131–5.

28   Han Baekheung, *Guhanmal minjokeunhaeng saeseongsa yeongu*, 44.

29   Joheung Bank, *Sajineuro boneun Joheung Euhaeng* [The 100-year history of Joheung Bank in pictures] (Seoul: Joheung Bank, 1998), 26–7.

30   Daiichi National Bank lost its authority to issue currency following a national banking regulation amendment in May 1883. See Hasei Chiyomatsu, ed., *Daiichi ginkō gojyunen shoshi* [Daiichi Bank: Fifty years, a concise history] (Tokyo: Daiichi Bank, 1926), 39.

31   Kim Myungsoo, "Daehanjegukgi ilbonui geumyungjangak gidowa ilbon jeireunhaeng," 33, 44–9.

32   Kim, "Daehanjegukgi ilbonui geumyungjangak gidowa ilbon jeireunhaeng," 33, 44–50.

33   *Hwangseong Sinmun*, advertisement, 28 February 1906, 3.

34   Joheung Bank, *Sajineuro boneun Joheung Eunhaeng*, 30–1.

35   Yun Geunho, *Hanguk heogyesa yeongu* [A history of accounting in Korea] (Seoul: Research Institute for Korean Studies, 1984), 300–1.

36   Afterward, Daiichi Bank dispatched Hayashi, a bank clerk (given name unknown) from the Gyeongseong branch and Mori Shigesaku. Han Ik-gyo, ed., *Kan Sōryū-kun o kataru* [A talk about Han Sangyong] (Gyeongseong: Seiun Shuppansha, 1941), 53.

37   Yun Geunho, "Gaeseongbugie gwanhan yeongu:daehan Cheonireunhaengui jangbureul jungsimeuro" [A study of Gaesong bookkeeping focused on the books of Korea Cheonil bank], *Dankuk daehaggyo nonmunjib* [Collected papers of Dankuk University] 3 (1969): 112.

38   Yun, *Hanguk heogyesa yeongu*, 301.

39   Han Baekheung, *Guhanmal minjogeunhaeng saeseongsa yeongu*, 121–2.

40   Im Gyeongjae, *Sinpyeon eunhaeng bugihak* [Bank bookkeeping: A new edition] (Gyeongseong: Huimungwan, 1908).

41   Joheung Bank, *Joheungeunhaeng baengyeonsa*, 45.

42   Joheung Bank, *Joheungeunhaeng baenyeonsa*, 54–5.

43   Han Ik-gyo, *Kan Sōryū-kun o kataru*, 54.

44   At that time, daily interest per 100 yen was adopted in the calculation of interest rates. It was called *Ilbo* in Korean and *hibu* in Japanese. If a person borrowed money at an interest rate of *Ilbo* 2 sen 7 rin per day per 100 yen, it meant an annual interest rate of approximately 9.9 percent, because 0.027 yen/day × 365 days = 9.855 yen per 100 yen.

45   Han Ik-gyo, *Kan Sōryū-kun o kataru*, 55.

46   Han Ik-gyo, *Kan Sōryū-kun o kataru*, 56.

47   Joheung Bank, *Joheungeunhaeng baenyeonsa*, 47–9.

48 Kim Myungsoo, "Kindai Nihon no Joseon sihai to Joseonjin kigyoka Joseon zaikai: Han Sangyong to Joseon jitsugyo kurabu wo chusinni" [Chosun's entrepreneurial and business world during modern Japan's rule over Korea: A study of Han Sangyong's business activities and the Chosun Business Club] (PhD diss., Keio University, 2010), 83–7.

49 Kim, "Kindai Nihon no Joseon sihai to Joseonjin kigyoka Joseon zaikai."

50 Kim Myungsoo, "1920nyeondae Hanseongeunhaengui jeongri wa Joseonin CEO Han Sangyong ui mollak" [The liquidation of the Hanseong Bank in the 1920s and the fall of Korean CEO Han Sangyong], *Yeogsamunjeueongu* [Critical studies on modern Korean history] 27 (2012): 182–6.

51 Han Ik-gyo, *Kan Sōryū-kun o kataru*, 180 and 211.

52 Han Ik-gyo, *Kan Sōryū-kun o kataru*, 192–3.

53 Han Ik-gyo, *Kan Sōryū-kun o kataru*, 198.

54 Kim Myungsoo, "1920nyeondae Hanseongeunhaeng ui jeongri," 190.

55 Han Ik-gyo, *Kan Sōryū-kun o kataru*, 215.

56 Kim Myungsoo, "Kindai Nihon no Joseon shihai to Joseonjin kigyoka Joseon zaikai," 71.

57 Kim Myungsoo, "1920nyeondae Hanseongeunhaeng ui jeongri," 189.

58 Kim Myungsoo, "1920nyeondae Hanseongeunhaeng ui jeongri," 190–2.

59 Kim Myungsoo, "1920nyeondae Hanseongeunhaeng ui jeongri," 193.

60 Kim Myungsoo, "1920nyeondae Hanseongeunhaeng ui jeongri," 198–201.

Bibliography

Abelhauser, Werner, Wolfgang von Hippel, Jeffrey Allan Johnson, and Raymond
  G. Stokes. *German Industry and the Global Enterprise – BASF: The History of a
  Company*. Cambridge: Cambridge University Press, 2004.
Adas, Michael. *Machines as the Measure of Men: Science, Technology, and Ideologies of
  Western Dominance*. Ithaca, NY: Cornell University Press, 1989.
Ahvenainen, Jorma. *The Far Eastern Telegraphs: The History of the Telegraphic
  Communications between the Far East, Europe, and American before the First
  World War*. Helsinki: Suomalainen Tiedeakatemia, 1981.
Akiha, Daisuke II. "Shinkoku Ei-ryō Honkon manyū kikō" [Travelogue of an excursion
  to the British Territory, Hong Kong]. "Collection of Documents relating to Akiha
  Shōten, 1902–3." Archives of the Edo-Tokyo Museum of History.
– "Tenjin Shanhai Honkon hanro kōchō shutchō nisshi" [A diary of an excursion to
  Tianjin, Shanghai, and Hong Kong seeking to expand sales [of rickshaws]].
Allwood, John. *The Great Exhibitions*. London: Cassell & Collier Macmillan, 1977.
Anderson, Benedict. *Imagined Communities*. Rev. ed. London: Verso, 1996.
Aso, Noriko. "New Illusions: The Emergence of a Discourse on Traditional Japanese
  Arts and Crafts, 1868–1945." PhD diss., University of Chicago, 1997.
– *Public Properties: Museums in Imperial Japan*. Durham, NC: Duke University Press,
  2014.
Auerbach, Jeffrey. *The Great Exhibition of 1851: A Nation on Display*. New Haven, CT:
  Yale University Press, 1999.
Bastid, Marianne. *Educational Reform in Early Twentieth-Century China*, translated by
  Paul J. Bailey. Ann Arbor: Center for Chinese Studies, University of Michigan, 1988.
Benedict, Burton. "International Exhibitions and National Identity." *Anthropology
  Today* 7, no. 3 (1991): 5–9.
Bennett, Tony. "The Exhibitionary Complex." *New Formations: A Journal of Culture,
  Theory, and Politics* 4 (Spring 1988): 73–102.
Blake, W.P., and Henry Pettit. *Reports on the Vienna Universal Exhibition, 1873 Made to
  the U.S. Centennial Commission*. Philadelphia: McLaughlin Brothers, 1873.

Brokaw, Cynthia J., and Kai-wing Chow, eds. *Printing and Book Culture in Late Imperial China*. Berkeley: University of California Press, 2005.

Bulliet, Richard. *The Wheel: Inventions and Reinventions*. New York: Columbia University Press, 2016.

Cao, Congpo, and Yang Tong, eds. *Zhang Jian quanji* [The Complete Works of Zhang Jian]. Nanjing: Jiangsu Guji Publication House, 1994.

Carlos, Ann M., and Stephen Nicholas. "'Giants of an Earlier Capitalism': The Chartered Trading Companies as Modern Multinationals." *Business History Review* 62, no. 3 (Autumn 1988): 398–419.

Chen, Zhengshu. "Yanjiang chengshi jiaotong jiegou jindaihua" [The modernization of the structure of transportation in cities along the Yangzi River]. In *Changjiang yuanjiang chengshi yu Zhongguo jindaihua* [Cities along the Yangtze River and Chinese modernization], edited by Zhang Zhongli, Xiong Yuezhi, and Shen Zuwei, 273–315. Shanghai: Shanghai Renmin Chubanshe, 2002.

Choi, Eugene K. "Another Path to Industrialisation: The Rattling Spindle, *Garabō*, in the Development of the Japanese Spinning Industry." Paper presented at the Asia-Pacific Economic and Business History Conference, Gakushuin University, Tokyo, 18–20 February 2009.

Choi, Jong-Tae. "Business Climate and Industrialization of the Korean Fiber Industry." In *The Textile Industry and Its Business Climate: Proceedings of the Fuji International Conference on Business History*, edited by Okochi Akio and Yonekawa Shin-ichi, 8:249–54. Tokyo: University of Tokyo Press, 1982.

Chow, Kai-wing. *Publishing, Culture, and Power in Early Modern China*. Stanford, CA: Stanford University Press, 2004.

Christ, Carol. "Japan's Seven Acres Politics and Aesthetics at the 1904 Louisiana Purchase Exposition." *Gateway Heritage* 17, no. 2 (1996): 2–15.

Chu, Samuel C. *Reformer in Modern China, Chang Chien, 1853–1926*. New York: Columbia University Press, 1965.

Clark, Gregory, and Robert C. Feenstra. "Technology in the Great Divergence." In *Globalization in Historical Perspective*, edited by Michael D. Bardo, Alan M. Taylor, and Jeffrey G. Williamson, 277–314. Chicago: University of Chicago Press, 2003.

Clark, W.A. Graham. *Cotton Goods in Japan and Their Competition on the Manchurian Market*. Washington, DC: Government Printing Office, 1914.

Coaldrake, William H. *Architecture and Authority in Japan*. London: Routledge, 1996.

Cohen, Paul A. *Discovering History in China: American Historical Writing on the Recent Chinese Past*. New York: Columbia University Press, 1984.

Conder, Josiah. "An Architect's Notes on the Great Earthquake of October 1891." *Seismological Journal of Japan* 2 (1893): 1–91.

Cowan, Ruth Schwartz. *A Social History of American Technology*. New York: Oxford University Press, 1997.

Cox, Howard. *The Global Cigarette: Origins and Evolution of British American Tobacco, 1880–1945*. Oxford: Oxford University Press, 2000.

Cox, Peter. *Moving People: Sustainable Transport Development*. London: Zed Books, 2010.

Daiichi Bank, ed. *Kankoku ni okeru Daiichi ginkō* [The Daiichi Bank in Korea]. Tokyo: Daiichi Bank, 1908.

Davenport-Hines, R.P.T., and Geoffrey Jones. "British Business in Japan since 1868." In *British Business in Asia since 1860*, edited by Davenport-Hines and Jones, 1–28. Cambridge: Cambridge University Press, 1989.

Dernberger, Robert F. "The Role of the Foreigner in China's Economic Development, 1840–1949." In *China's Modern Economy in Historical Perspective*, edited by Dwight H. Perkins, 19–47. Stanford, CA: Stanford University Press, 1975.

Dikötter, Frank. *Exotic Commodities, Modern Objects and Everyday Life in China*. New York: Columbia University Press, 2006.

Dreze, Gustave. *Le livre d'or de l'Exposition Universelle et Internationale de 1905. Histoire complète de l'exposition de Liège* [Golden Book of the Universal and International Exhibition of 1905. The Complete History of the Liège exhibition]. Liège: Impr. A. Benard, 1905.

Dyer, Henry. *Dai Nippon: The Britain of the East*. London: Blackie and Son, 1904.

Edo-Tokyo Museum of History Archives. *Catalogue: Jinrikishas & Accessories*. Daisuke Akiha, Tokyo, Japan, (*Jinrikisha katarogu*), 1911. "Collection of Documents Relating to Akiha Shōten."

Elman, Benjamin. *A Cultural History of Civil Examinations in Late Imperial China*. Berkeley: University of California Press, 2000.

Ennals, Peter. *Opening a Window to the West: The Foreign Concession at Kōbe, Japan, 1868–1899*. Toronto: University of Toronto Press, 2014.

Ericson, Steven J. *The Sound of the Whistle: Railroads and the State in Meiji Japan*. Cambridge, MA: Council on East Asian Studies, 1999.

Farnie, D.A. "Four Revolutions in the Textile Trade of Asia 1814–1994: The Impact of Bombay, Osaka, the Little Tigers and China." In *Asia Pacific Dynamism 1550–2000*, edited by A.J.H. Latham and Kawakatsu Heita, 49–69. London: Routledge, 2000.

Federico, Giovanni. *An Economic History of the Silk Industry, 1830–1930*. Cambridge: Cambridge University Press, 1997.

Feuerwerker, Albert. *The Foreign Establishment in China in the Early Twentieth Century*. Ann Arbor: University of Michigan Center for Chinese Studies, 1976.

Fujihara, Gingiro. *The Spirit of Japanese Industry*. Tokyo: Hokuseido, 1936.

Fukuzawa, Yukichi. "Datsu-A ron" [On leaving Asia]. *Jiji shinpō*, 16 March 1885.

– *Seiyō jijō* [On conditions in the West]. Tokyo: Shōkodō, 1866.

Galbraith, John Kenneth. *The New Industrial State*. Boston: Houghton Mifflin, 1967.

Gallegher, Rob. *The Rickshaws of Bangladesh*. Dhaka: University Press, 1992.

Gordon, Andrew. *A Modern History of Japan: From Tokugawa Times to the Present*. New York: Oxford University Press, 2003.

Grove, Linda, and Shinya Sugiyama. *Commercial Networks in Modern Asia*. London: Routledge, 2001.

Guo, Yuming, ed. *Zhongguo jindaishi jiaocheng* [A study of modern Chinese history].
    Shanghai: East China Normal University Press, 1997.

Haber, L.F. *The Chemical Industry, 1900–1930: International Growth and Technological
    Change.* Oxford: Clarendon, 1971.

Han, Baekheung. *Guhanmal minjogeunhaeng saengseongsa* yeongu 1894–1910 [Study
    of the history of national banks during the late Joseon period, 1894–1910]. Seoul:
    Scenario Alta, 1996.

Han, Ik-gyo, ed. *Kan Sōryū-kun o kataru* [Talking about Han Sangyong]. Keijō: Kan
    Sōryū-shi Kanreki Kinenkai, 1941.

Hanazato, Toshikazu, Tominaga Yoshiaki, Mikoshiba Tadashi, and Niitsu Yasushi.
    "Shaking Table Test of Full-Scale Model of Timber Framed Brick Masonry Walls
    for Structural Restoration of Tomioka Silk Mill, Registered as a Tentative World
    Cultural Heritage in Japan." In *Historical Earthquake-Resistant Timber Frames in
    the Mediterranean Area*, edited by Nicola Riggieri, Gennaro Tampone, and Raffaele
    Zinno, 83–93. Switzerland: Springer Publishing, 2015.

Harrington, W. Hague. *Science.* "The Japanese Earthquake." 18, no. 464 (15 December
    1891): 464.

Hasei, Chiyomatsu, ed. *Daiichi ginkō gojūnen shōshi* [Fifty-year history of the Daiichi
    Bank]. Tokyo: Daiichi Bank, 1926.

Hausman, William J., Peter Hertner, and Mira Wilkins. *Global Electrification:
    Multinational Enterprise and International Finance in the History of Light and Power,
    1878–2007.* New York: Cambridge University Press, 2008.

Hawks, Francis L. *Narrative of the Expedition of an American Squadron to the China
    Seas and Japan: Performed in the Years 1852, 1853, and 1854, under the Command of
    Commodore M.C. Perry, United States Navy.* New York: D. Appleton, 1856.

Hayami, Akira. *Japan's Industrious Revolution, Economic and Social Transformation in
    the Early Modern Period.* Tokyo: Springer Japan, 2015.

Heikkonen, Esko. *Reaping the Bounty: McCormick Harvesting Machine Company Turns
    Abroad, 1878–1902.* Helsinki: Finnish Historical Society, 1995.

Herschbach, Dennis R. "Technology as Knowledge: Implications for Instruction."
    Journal of Technology in Education 7, no. 1 (Fall 1995): 31–42.

Hirakawa, Hitoshi, and Shimizu Hiroshi. *Japan and Singapore in the World Economy:
    Japan's Economic Advance into Singapore, 1870–1965.* London: Routledge, 2002.

Hirschmeier, Johannes, and Tsunehiko Yui. *The Development of Japanese Business,
    1600–1973.* London: Routledge, 1975.

Hon, Tze-ki. *Revolution as Restoration:* Guocui xuebao *and China's Path to Modernity,
    1905–1911.* Leiden: Brill, 2013.

Hon, Tze-ki, and Robert J. Culp, eds. *The Politics of Historical Production in Late Qing
    and Republican China.* Leiden: Brill, 2007.

Hotta-Lister, Ayako. *The Japan-British Exhibition of 1910: Gateway to the Island Empire
    of the East.* Richmond, Surrey: Japan Library, 1999.

Hou, Chi-min. *Foreign Investment and Economic Development in China, 1840–1937.*
    Cambridge, MA: Harvard University Press, 1965.

Hughes, Thomas Parke. *Networks of Power: Electrification in Western Society, 1880–1930.* Baltimore, MD: Johns Hopkins University Press, 1983.

Hunter, Janet. "Regimes of Technology Transfer in Japan's Cotton Industry, 1860s to 1890s." Paper presented at Ninth Conference of the Global Economic History Network, Kaohsiung, Taiwan, 9–11 May 2006.

Igarashi, Akio. *Meiji isshin no shisō* [The Mental World of the Meiji Restoration]. Kanagawa: Seori Shōbō, 1996.

Im, Gyeongjae. *Sinpyeon eunhaeng bugihak* [Bank Bookkeeping: A New Edition]. Gyeongseong: Huimungwan, 1908.

Itō, Moemon. *Chiigai sanji yōroku* [Digest of domestic and foreign silkworms]. Tokyo: Itō Moemon, 1886.

Jang, Deoksam. "Seoyanguihagui doipgwa iyangpyeonui gyoyukjeok uimie gwanhan gochal" [A Study of the Introduction of Western Medical Science and the Meaning of Iyangpyeon.] *Gyoyugyeongu* 21 (2002): 1–12.

Jansen, Marius, ed. *The Emergence of Meiji Japan.* New York: Cambridge University Press, 1995.

Joheung Bank, ed. *Joheungeunhaeng baengnyeonsa.* [The 100 Year History of Joheung Bank]. Seoul: Joheung Bank, 1997.

– *Sajineuro boneun Johueung Eunhaeng* [The 100 Year History of Joheung Bank in Pictures]. Seoul: Joheung Bank, 1998.

Jones, Geoffrey. *Merchants to Multinationals: British Trading Companies in the Nineteenth and Twentieth Centuries.* Oxford: Oxford University Press, 2000.

– *Multinationals and Global Capitalism: From the Nineteenth to the Twenty-First Century.* Oxford: Oxford University Press, 2005.

– "Multinational Trading Companies in History and Theory." In *The Multinational Traders,* edited by Geoffrey Jones, 1–21. London: Routledge, 1998.

Judge, Joan. *Print and Culture: "Shibao" and the Culture of Reform in Late Qing China.* Stanford, CA: Stanford University Press, 1996.

Kashima, Shigeru. *Shibusawa Eiichi: volume I sorobanhen* [Shibusawa Eiichi, volume 1, business]. Tokyo: Bungei Shunjū, 2011.

Katō, Toshihiko. *Honpō ginkō shiron* [A history of banking in Japan]. Tokyo: Tokyo University Press, 1978.

Keene, Donald. *The Japanese Discovery of Europe, 1720–1830.* Stanford, CA: Stanford University Press, 1969.

Kikkawa, Takeo, and Patrick Fridenson, eds. *Ethical Capitalism: Shibusawa Eiichi's Business Leadership in Global Perspective.* Toronto: University of Toronto Press, 2017.

– eds. *Gurobaru shihonshugi no naka no Shibusawa Eiichi, gappon kapitalizumu to moraru* [Gappon capitalism: The economic and moral ideology of Shibusawa Eiichi in global perspective]. Tokyo: Tōyō Keizai Shimpōsha, 2014.

Kim, Hyeonsuk. "Hanmal gomungwan J. McLeavy Brown e daehan yeongu" [A Study of the Advisor J. McLeavy Brown in Late Joseon Korea]. *Journal of Korean History* 66 (September 1989): 103–156.

Kim, Myungsoo. "Daehanjegukgi ilbonui geumyungjangak gidowa ilbon jeireunhaeng: 1903nyeon gongriphanseongeunhaengui seongripgwa gwanryeonhayeo" [Japan and the Daiichi Bank's Attempt to Take Control of Korean Finances during the Korean Empire Period: Establishment of Hansung Bank into a Public Bank in 1903]. *Japanese Cultural Studies* 47 (July 2013): 29–53.

– "Kindai Nihon no Joseon shihai to Joseonjin kigyoka: Joseon zaikai-Han Sangyong to Joseon jitsugyo kurabu wo chushin ni" [Joseon's entrepreneur and business world during modern Japan's rule over Korea: A study on Sangyong Han's business activities and Joseon Business Club]. PhD diss., Keio University, 2010.

– "1920nyeondae Hanseongeunhaengui jeongriwa joseonin CEO Han Sangyong ui mollak" [The liquidation of the Hanseong Bank in the 1920s, and the fall of Korean CEO Han Sangyong]. *Critical Studies on Modern Korean History* 27 (2012): 175–218.

Kim, Yeongho. "Hanmal seoyanggisului suyong" [Acceptance of Western technology at the end of the Korean Empire]. *Journal of Asiatic Studies* 11, no. 3 (September 1968): 295–348.

Kim, Yeonhee. "Gojongsidae seoyang gisul doip: cheoldowa jeonsin bunyareul jungsimeuro" [The Introduction of the Western Technology during the Reign of King Gojong: Focusing on Railway and Telegraph]. Hanguk Gwahaksahakhoeji, *Journal of The Korean History of Science Society* 25, no. 1 (2003): 3–24.

Kimura, Yuji. *Chosen ginkō zaininchū no kaiko* [Retrospective of the Bank of Joseon]. Gyeongseong: Joseon Ginkō Chosaka, 1940.

Kiyokawa, Yukihiko. "Transplantation of the European Factory System and Adaptations in Japan: The Experience of the Tomioka Model Filature." *Hitotsubashi Journal of Economics* 28, no. 1 (1987): 27–39.

Ko, Donghwan. "Joseonhugi~hanmal sinyonggeoraeui baldal – eoeumgwa hwaneul jungsimeuro" [Study of the development of credit dealing in the late Joseon Period and the Korean Empire Period – focusing on promissory notes and money orders]. *Journal of Local History and Culture* 13, no. 2 (November 2010): 271–300.

Kobayashi, Yōkichi, comp. *A Guide to the Foreign Samples Building and Its Annexe of the Fifth National Industrial Exhibition at Osaka*. Osaka: Kobe Chronicle, 1903.

Kornicki, Peter. *Meiji Japan: Political, Economic, and Social History, 1868–1912*. 4 vols. London: Routledge, 1998.

– "Public Display and Changing Values: Early Meiji Exhibitions and Their Precursors." *Monumenta Nipponica* 49, no. 2 (1994): 167–96.

Kurosawa, Takafumi, and Hashino Tomoko. "From the Non-European Tradition to a Variation on the Japanese Competitiveness Model: The Modern Japanese Paper Industry since the 1870s." In *The Evolution of the Global Paper Industry 1800–2050: A Comparative Analysis*, edited by Juha-Antti Lamberg, Jari Ojala, Mirva peltoniemi, and Timo Särkkä, 135–66. Dordrecht: Springer, 2012.

Kusamitsu, Toshio. "Great Exhibitions before 1851." *History Workshop* 9 (1980): 70–89.

Kuwahara, Tetsuya. "The Business Strategy of Japanese Cotton Spinners: Overseas Operations 1890–1931." In *The Textile Industry and Its Business Climate: Proceedings of the Fuji International Conference*, edited by Akio Okochi and Shin-ichi Yonekawa, 8:139–66. Tokyo: University of Tokyo Press, 1982.

Law, John. "Technology and Heterogeneous Engineering: The Case of Portuguese Expansion." In *The Social Construction of Technological Systems: New Directions in the Sociology and History of Technology*, edited by Wiebe Bijker, Thomas Parke Hughes, and Trevor Pinch, 105–28. Cambridge, MA: MIT Press, 1987.

Lee, Haegyeong. *"Joseon hugi segeum gammyeongwa hwapye yutonge gwanhan yeongu: jeonsereul jungsimeuro"* [A Study of the Commutation of Tax and Money Circulation in the Late Joseon]. Collected Papers of Research Institute of Industry and Economy of Chonbuk National University 22 (1992): 265–78.

Lee, Leo Ou-fan. *Shanghai Modern: The Flowering of a New Urban Culture in China, 1930–1945*. Cambridge, MA: Harvard University Press, 1999.

Li, Jiaju. *Shangwu yinshuguan yu jindai zhishi wenhua de chuanbo* [The commercial press and the dissemination of modern knowledge and culture]. Beijing: Commercial Press, 2005.

Li, Renyuan. *Wan Qing de xinshi chuanbo meiti yu zhishi fenzi: Yi baokan chuban wei Zhongxin de taolun* [New media and Intellectuals in the late Qing Dynasty: A study of newspaper publishing]. Taipei: Daoxiang Chubanshe, 2005.

Li, Yu. *Wan Qing gongsi zhidu jianshe yanjiu* [A study of the corporate system in late Qing China]. Beijing: People's Publishing House, 2002.

Linder, Marc. *Projecting Capitalism: A History of the Internationalization of the Construction Industry*. Westport, CT: Greenwood, 1994.

Liu, Lydia H. *Translingual Practice: Literature, National Culture, and Translated Modernity – China 1900–1937*. Stanford, CA: Stanford University Press, 1995.

Lockyer, Angus. "Japan at the Exhibition, 1867–1970." PhD diss., Stanford University, 2000.

Lu, David John. *Japan: A Documentary History: The Late Tokugawa Period to the Present*. Armonk, NY: M.E. Sharpe, 1996.

Lu, Hanchao. *Beyond the Neon Lights: Everyday Shanghai in the Early Twentieth Century*. Berkeley: California University Press, 1999.

Ma, Min. *Shangren jingshen de shanbian: jindai Zhongguo shangren guannian yan jiu* [The evolution of merchant spirit: Research on the concept of "businessman" in modern China]. Wuhan: Huazhong Normal University Press, 2001.

Maeda, Kazutoshi. "Business Activities of General Trading Companies." In *General Trading Companies: A Comparative and Historical Study*, edited by Shin'ichi Yonekawa, 33–45. Tokyo: United Nations University Press, 1990.

Markwyn, Abigail. "Economic Partner and Exotic Other: China and Japan at San Francisco's Panama-Pacific International Exposition." *Western Historical Quarterly* 39, no. 4 (2008): 439–65.

Maybon, Charles B., and Jean Fredet. *Histoire de la concession française de Changhai* [History of the French Concession in Shanghai]. Paris: Librairie Plon, 1929.

McCallion, Stephen. "Silk Reeling in Japan: The Limits to Change." PhD diss., Ohio State University, 1983.

McCraw, Thomas K., ed. *America versus Japan*. Boston: Harvard Business School Press, 1986.

Minami, Ryōshin. "Mechanical Power in the Industrialization of Japan: A Case Study of the Spinning Industry." *Hitotsubashi Journal of Economics* 21, no. 1 (June 1986): 935–58.

Ming, Fung Chi. *Reluctant Heroes: Rickshaw Pullers in Hong Kong and Canton, 1874–1954*. Hong Kong: Hong Kong University Press, 2003.

Monclus, Javier. *International Exhibitions and Urbanism: The Zaragoza Expo 2008 Project*. Surrey, UK: Ashgate Publishing, 2009.

Morris-Suzuki, Tessa. *The Technological Transformation of Japan: From the Seventeenth Century to the Twenty-First Century*. Cambridge: Cambridge University Press, 1994.

Moser, Petra. "Determinants of Innovation: Evidence from 19th Century World Fairs." *Journal of Economic History* 64, no. 2 (2004): 548–52.

– "How Do Patent Laws Influence Innovation? Evidence from Nineteenth-Century World Fairs." *American Economic Review* 95, no. 4 (2005): 1214–36.

Nakamura, Tsutomu. *Nippon garabō shiwa* [History of the rattling spindle (*Garabō*) in Japan]. Tokyo: Keio Shuppankai, 1942.

National Diet Library. "Expositions: Where the Modern Technology of the Times Was Exhibited." http://www.ndl.go.jp/exposition/e/index.html.

Nihonshiseki kyōkai, ed. *Shibusawa Eiichi taifutsu nikki* [Shibusawa Eiichi's French Diary]. Tokyo: University of Tokyo Press, 1967.

Nozawa, Yutaka. *1903 nen no Osaka hakurankai to Chō Ken no rainichi* [The 1903 Osaka Exposition and Zhang Jian's visit to Japan]. Vol. 14. Tokyo: Chuo Daigaku Keiri Kenkyūjo, 1971.

The Official Guide-Book to Kyoto and the Allied Prefectures: Prepared Specially for the Eleven-Hundredth Anniversary of the Founding of Kyoto and the Fourth National Industrial Exhibition by the City Council of Kyoto with Three Maps and Sixty-Nine Engravings. Meishinsha. Kyoto, 1895.

Ogura, Ichio, ed. *Ōji Seishi no kiseki* [The history of Oji Paper Company]. Tokyo: Ōji Seishi Kabushiki Kaisha, 2004.

Ohno, Ken'ichi. *Globalization of Developing Countries: Is Autonomous Development Possible?* Tokyo: Tōyō Keizai Shimpōsha, 2000.

Omori, F. "Earthquake Measurement in a Brick Building." *Publications of the Earthquake Investigation Committee in Foreign Languages*. Vol. 4. 1900.

Ono, Akira. "Technical Progress in Silk Industry in Prewar Japan: The Types of Borrowed Technology." *Hitotsubashi Journal of Economics* 27, no. 1 (June 1986): 1–10.

Ōtsuka, Ryōtarō. *Sanshi*. 2 vols. Tokyo: Fusōen, 1900.

Parker, Calvin. *Jonathan Gobel of Japan: Marine, Missionary, Maverick*. Lanham, MD: University Press of America, 1990.

The Photographic Reproduction of the Fifth National Industrial Exhibition. Osaka, 1903.

Qin, Shao. *Culturing Modernity: The Nantong Model, 1890–1930.* Stanford, CA: Stanford University Press, 2004.

Reed, Christopher A. *Gutenberg in Shanghai: Chinese Print Capitalism, 1876–1934.* Honolulu: University of Hawaii Press, 2004.

Ren, Dai (Jean-Pierre Drege). *Shanghai Shangwu yin shuguan 1897–1949* [The Shanghai Commercial Press 1897–1949]. Beijing: Commercial Press, 2000.

Reynolds, Douglas R. *China, 1898–1912: The Xinzheng Revolution and Japan.* Cambridge, MA: Council on East Studies, Harvard University, 1993.

"Rickshaws of Bangladesh and Its History." http://weloveourbangladesh.blogspot.jp/2012/08/rickshaws-of-bangladesh-and-its-history_7522.html.

Rimmer, Peter James. *From Rikisha to Rapid Transit: Urban Public Transport Systems and Policy in Southeast Asia.* New York: Pergamon, 1986.

Rong, Shicheng. *Xunmi yueju shengying: Cong hongchuan dao shuiyindeng* [In search of the sound and shape of Cantonese opera: From red boat to movie camera]. Hong Kong: Oxford University Press, 2012.

Russian Treasury and Bureau of Forestry, Department of Agriculture and Commerce, ed. *The Korea.* Tokyo: Bureau of Forestry, Department of Agriculture and Commerce, 1905.

Rydell, Robert W. *All the World's a Fair: Visions of Empire at American International Expositions, 1876–1916.* Chicago: University of Chicago Press, 1984.

Ryu, Gyoseong. "Seoul Yuguijeon yeongu: ijodosi sangeobui gochal" [A Study on Seoul Yuguijeon]. *Yeoksa Hakbo* 8 (1955): 377–434.

Sasaki, Keiko. "Yokohama kyoryūchi no Seikokujin no yōsō to shakaiteki chii" [The character and social standing of the Chinese in the Yokohama foreign settlement]. *Kanagawa University Graduate School Studies* 10, no. 10 (2008): 213–37.

Satow, Ernest. *Records of a Diplomat.* Tokyo: Oxford University Press, 1968.

Saxonhouse, Gary. "A Tale of Japanese Technological Diffusion in the Meiji Period." *Journal of Economic History* 34, no. 1 (March 1974): 149–65.

Schatzberg, Eric. *Technology: Critical History of a Concept.* Chicago: University of Chicago Press, 2018.

Seok, Taemun and Lee Hocheol. "Gyeongbuk neunggeumsaneobui baldalgwajeong - gisulsajeok gwanjeom" [A study of the development process of the apple industry in Gyeongsangbuk-do: Through a technological perspective]. *Nongchonsahoe* 11, no. 1 (2001): 241–81.

Seth, Michael J. *A Concise History of Modern Korea: From the Late Nineteenth Century to the Present.* Lanham, MD: Rowman & Littlefield Publishers, 2010.

Shibusawa, Hanako. *Shibusawa Eiichi Pari Banpaku e* [Shibusawa Eiichi at the Paris Exposition]. Tokyo: Kokusho Kankōkai, 1995.

Shibusawa, Hideo. *Shibusawa Eiichi.* Tokyo: Shibusawa Seien Kinen Zaidan, 1988.

Shimada, Masakazu. *Shibusawa Eiichi no kigyōka katsudō no kenkyū: senzenki kigyō shisutemu no sōshutsu to shusshisha keieisha no yakuwari.* [Research on Shibusawa Eiichi's corporate activities: Creation of a postwar corporate system and the role of the entrepreneur]. Tokyo: Nihon Keizai Hyōronsha, 2007.

Shimatsu, Yoichi. "Japan's Silk Reelers Blazed an Asian Path of Economic Development." Chichibu. http://www.chichibu.com/CHICHIBUSILKHISTORY.html.

Shinoda, Shōsaku. *Shin-Nihon gōketsuden: jitsugyō risshin* [The lives of heroes of new Japan: Entrepreneurs who rose up in society]. Tokyo: Igyōkan, 1892.

Shinomiya, Toshiyuki. "Competition and Cooperation among Paper and Pulp Enterprises in Modern Japan Prior to World War II: The Rise to Prominence of a Powerful Triumvirate of Enterprises and Transitions in Cartel Activity." *Japan Yearbook on Business History* 14 (1997): 115–37.

The Souvenir Guide to Osaka and the Fifth National Industrial Exhibition Compiled by Osaka-fu. Osaka: Hakurankwai Kyosankwai, 1903.

Staudenmaier, John M. *Technology's Storytellers: Reweaving the Human Fabric.* Cambridge, MA: MIT Press, 1989.

Steele, M. William. *Alternate Narratives in Modern Japanese History.* London: Routledge, 2003.

– "Mobility on the Move: Rickshaws in Asia." *Transfers: Interdisciplinary Journal of Mobility Studies* 4, no. 3 (Winter 2014): 88–107.

– "The Speedy Feet of the Nation: Bicycles and Everyday Mobility in Modern Japan." *Journal of Transport History.* 3rd ser. 31, no. 2 (December 2010): 182–209.

Strand, David. *Rickshaw Beijing: City People and Politics in the 1920s.* Berkeley: University of California Press, 1989.

Sugiura Yuzuru Iinkai. *Sugiura Yuzuru zenshū* [The complete works of Sugiura Yuzuru]. Vol. 5. Tokyo: Sugiura Yuzuru Iinkai, 1979.

Sungshin University Humanities Research Institute. *Seogu gwahakgisul doibui sajeok gochal* [Historical review of the introduction of Western science and technology]. Seoul: Ministry of Science-Technology, 1969.

Tanaka, Kazuhiro. "Harmonization between Morality and Economy." In *Ethical Capitalism: Shibusawa Eiichi's Business Leadership in Global Perspective,* edited by Kikkawa Takeo and Patrick Fridenson, 35–58. Toronto: University of Toronto Press, 2017.

Tanimoto, Masayuki. "The Role of Tradition in Japan's Industrialization: Another Path to Industrialization." In *The Role of Tradition in Japan's Industrialization,* edited by Tanimoto Masayuki, 3–44. Oxford: Oxford University Press, 2006.

Tarumoto, Teruo. *Shoki shōmu inshokan kenkyū* [A study of the early commercial press]. Shiga-ken, Ōtsu-shi: Shimatsu Shōsetsu kenkyū, 2000.

Tipton, Elise K. *Modern Japan: A Social and Political History.* London: Routledge, 2008.

Tōkyōshi shikō [Tokyo city historical papers]. Vol. 51. Tokyo: Rinsen Shōten, 1996.

Tomioka Seishijōshi Hensan Iinkai, ed. *Tomioka seishijōshi* [A history of Tomioka silk filature]. Tomioka: Tomiokashi Kyōiku Iinkai, 1977.

Tomlinson, John. *The Culture of Speed.* Los Angeles: Sage Publications, 2007.

Saitō, Toshihiko. *Jinrikisha.* Tokyo: Sangyō Gijutsu Sentaa, 1979.

– *Kurumatachi no shakaishi* [A social history of wheels]. Tokyo: Chūō Kōronsha, 1997.

Transfers. "Special Section on Rickshaws." 3, no. 3 (Winter 2013): 56–130.

Sano, Tsunetami. *Ōkoku hakurankai hōkokusho: sangyōbu* [Report on the Austrian exposition: Industrial section]. 2 vols. Tokyo, 1875.

Twitchett, Denis, and John K. Fairbank. *The Cambridge History of China*. Vol. 11: *Late Ch'ing, 1800–1911, Part 2*. Cambridge University Press, 1980.

United States Monthly Consular and Trade Reports. 69, no. 260. Washington: Government Printing Office, 1902.

United States National Archives Microfilm Publications. Dispatches from U.S. Consuls in Osaka and Hiogo (Kobe), Japan, 1868–1906. M460. Roll number 6.

Vaporis, Constantine. *Breaking Barriers: Travel and the State in Early Modern Japan*. Cambridge, MA: Council on East Asian Studies, 1994.

Visscher, Sikko. "'Merchants, Empires and Emperors': Global and Local Factors in Elite Composition and Elite Representation of Chinese Businessmen in Colonial Singapore, 1819–1945." In *Entrepreneurs and Institutions in Europe and Asia, 1500–2000*, edited by Ferry de Goey and Jon Willem Veluwenkamp, 167–92. Amsterdam: Askant Academic Publishers, 2002.

von Tunzelmann, Nick. "Technology." In *The Oxford Encyclopedia of Economic History*, edited by Joel Mokyr, 5:84–90 Oxford: Oxford University Press, 2003.

Wang, Dunqin. *Chuantong yu qianzhan: Zhang Jian jingji sixiang yanjiu* [Tradition and foresight: Zhang Jian's economic thought]. Beijing: People's Publishing House, 2005.

Wang, Shengyun. "Zhang Jian yu Da Sheng shachang de xingshuai" [Zhang Jian and the rise and fall of the Da Sheng Cotton Mill]. *Journal of Wuhan Institute of Science and Technology* 14, no. 4 (2001): 54–9.

Warren, James Francis. *Rickshaw Coolie: A People's History of Singapore, 1880–1940*. Singapore: Singapore University Press, 2003.

Wei, Chunhui. *Zhang Jian pingzhuan* [A critical biography of Zhang Jian]. Nanjing: Nanjing University Press, 2001.

White, Trumbull, and W.M. Igleheart. *The World's Columbian Exposition, Chicago, 1893*. Chicago: J.S. Ziegler, 1893.

Wilkins, Mira. *The Emergence of Multinational Enterprise: American Business Abroad from the Colonial Era to 1914*. Cambridge, MA: Harvard University Press, 1970.

– "Multinational Enterprise to 1930: Discontinuities and Continuities." In *Leviathans: Multinational Corporations and the New Global History*, edited by Alfred D. Chandler Jr. and Bruce Lazlish, 45–79. Cambridge, MA: Harvard University Press, 2005.

– "The Role of Private Business in the International Diffusion of Technology." *Journal of Economic History* 34, no. 1 (March 1974): 166–88.

Wilson, Joseph M. *The Masterpieces of the Centennial International Exhibition, Illustrated*. Vol. 3: *History, Mechanics, and Science*. Philadelphia: Gebbie and Barrie, 1876.

Wittner, David G. *Technology and the Culture of Progress in Meiji Japan*. London: Routledge, 2008.

Wu, Chengming. "Zao qi Zhongguo jindai huaguo cheng zhong de waibu he neibu yinsu: jianlun Zhang Jian de shiye luxian" [The external and internal factors in the process of early Chinese modernization: Zhang Jian's industrial route]. In *Lun Zhang Jian: Zhang Jian guoji xueshu taolunhui wenji* [Collected essays of the international symposium on Zhang Jian], edited by Yan Xuexi and Ni Youchun, 157–8. Nanjing: Jiangsu Renmin Chubanshe, 1993.

Xu, Daling. *Qingdai juanna zhidu* [The system of taxes and levies in the Qing dynasty]. Beijing: Yenching University Press, 1950.

Xu, Jilin. *20 shiji Zhongguo zhishi fenzi shilun* [A study of the history of twentieth-century Chinese intellectuals]. Beijing: Xinxing Chubanshe, 2005.

Yamaguchi, Shinichi, ed. *Shokanshō yōtatsu shōnin meikan* [Who's who of merchants associated with government offices and ministries]. Vol. 1. Tokyo: Unyo Nippōsha, 1910.

Yonekawa, Shin'ichi. "General Trading Companies in a Comparative Context." In *General Trading Companies: A Comparative and Historical Study*, edited by Shin'ichi Yonekawa, 8–32. Tokyo: United Nations University Press, 1990.

Yoon, Seokbum, Hong Sungchan, Woo Daehyung, and Kim Dongwook. *Hanguk geundae geumyungsa yeongu* [A study of the modern financial history of Korea]. Seoul: Segyungsa, 1996.

Yoshida, Kenkō. *Shinshaku kanbun taikei* [A newly interpreted compendium of Chinese classics], vol. 1. "*Rongo*" ["The Analects"]. Tokyo: Meiji Shoin, 1985.

Yu, Chen. *Shibusawa Eiichi to "giri" shisō: kindai higashi Ajia no jitsugyō to kyōiku*. Tokyo: Perikansha, 2008.

Yun, Geunho. "Gaeseongbugie gwanhan yeongu: daehan Cheonireunhaengui jangbureul jungsimeuro" [A study of Gaesong bookkeeping focused on the books of the Korea Cheonil bank]. Collected Papers of Dankuk University 3 (1969): 111–167.

– *Hanguk heogyesa yeongu* [A study of Korean accounting history]. Seoul: Research Institute for Korean Studies, 1984.

Zhang Jizhi xiansheng shiye shi bianzhuan chu [Editorial office of Zhang Jian's business]. *Da Sheng fangzhi gongsi nianjian: 1895–1947* [The annals of Da Sheng cotton mill: 1895–1947]. Nanjing: Jiangsu People's Publishing House, 1998.

Zhang, Xiaoruo. *Nantong Zhang Jizhi xiansheng zhuanji* [Biography of Zhang Ji in Nantong]. Shanghai: Shanghai Bookstore Publishing House, 1989.

Zhang, Zhongli, Xiong Yuezhi, and Shen Zuwei, eds. *Changjiang yuanjiang chengshi yu Zhongguo jindaihua* [Cities along the Yangtze River and Chinese modernization]. Shanghai: Shanghai Renmin Chubanshe, 2002.

Contributors

Jeffer Daykin, MA, Portland State University, MAT, Lewis and Clark College, is instructor of history and international studies at Portland Community College. His publications include "International Ambitions of an Exhibition at the Margin: Japan's 1903 Osaka Exposition," in *Cultures of International Exhibitions, 1840–1940: Great Exhibitions in the Margins*, ed. Marta Filipová (Ashgate, 2015).

Tze-ki Hon, PhD, University of Chicago, is professor at the Research Centre for History and Culture, Beijing Normal University (Zhuhai campus). He is the author of *The Allure of the Nation* (Brill, 2015); *Teaching the Book of Changes* (Oxford University Press, 2014), with Geoffrey Redmond; *Revolution as Restoration* (Brill, 2013); and *The Yijing and Chinese Politics* (SUNY Press, 2005); and co-editor of several books. He is researching Cold War Hong Kong and the reception of the *Book of Changes* in Europe and the United States.

Kimura Masato, PhD, Keio University, and PhD, Kansai University, is visiting professor of cultural interaction at Kansai University. He has published numerous monographs and articles on US–Japanese relations, including *Shibusawa Eiichi: The Economic Giant Who Built Japan's Infrastructure (Shibusawa Eiichi: Nihon no infura o tsukutta minkan keizai no kyojin)* (Chikuma Shobō, 2020) and *Tumultuous Decade: Empire, Society, and Diplomacy in 1930s Japan*, co-edited with Tosh Minohara (University of Toronto Press, 2013).

Kim Myungsoo, PhD, Keio University, is professor of Japanese studies at Keimyung University, Daegu, Korea. He has published numerous monographs and articles on Korean and Japanese economic history, including "The Attempt to Take Control of Korean Finance by Japan and Daiichi Bank during the Korean Empire Period: Hansung Bank's Reorganization in 1903," *Japanese Cultural Studies* 47 (Daegu: Association of Japanology in East Asia, 2013); and "The

Trend of Chosun Society and Chosun Business Club during Wartime Period (1937–1945)," in *The Fall of the Japanese Empire: Interregional Population Movement and Change of Regional Community*, co-edited with Yanagisawa Asobu and Kurasawa Aiko (Keio University Press, 2017).

David B. Sicilia, PhD, Brandeis University, is Henry Kaufman Chair in Financial History and associate professor at the University of Maryland, College Park. He has published many monographs and articles on U.S. and global business history, economic history, and technology history, including *Constructing Corporate America: History, Politics, Culture*, co-edited with Kenneth Lipartito (Oxford University Press, 2004), and *The Greenspan Effect*, co-authored with Jeffrey Cruikshank (McGraw-Hill, 2000), which was published in ten foreign-language editions.

M. William Steele, PhD, Harvard University, is professor emeritus at the International Christian University in Tokyo, Japan. He specializes in the social and cultural history of Japan in the late nineteenth century. His major publication is *Alternative Narratives in Modern Japanese History* (Routledge, 2003). His recent publications focus on mobility and environmental issues, including the history of rickshaws, bicycles, and automobiles in modernizing Japan.

David G. Wittner, PhD, Ohio State University, is distinguished professor of East Asian history and director of the Center for Historical Research at Utica College in Utica, New York. He is the author of several monographs and articles, including *Science, Technology, and Medicine in the Modern Japan Empire*, co-edited with Philip C. Brown, (Routledge, 2016), and *Technology and the Culture of Progress in Meiji Japan* (Routledge, 2008, 2009).

Yu Chen, PhD, University of Tokyo, is associate professor of international strategy organization, Yokohama National University. He has published many monographs and articles in Japanese, including *Shibusawa and His Ideas on the Relationship between Righteousness and Benefits: The Industry and Education of Modern East Asia* (Perikansha, 2008) and "Research on Confucianism in Modern China by Comparing with Shibusawa Eiichi's *The Analects of Confucius and Abacus*," in *How Shibusawa Eiichi Interacted with Sinology*, edited by Machi Senjuro (Minerva Shobo, 2017).

Index

Daiichi National Bank, 11, 139, 145,
148–51, 156, 160, 166–7, 170
Date Munenari, 149
Dollar, Robert, 130
Dongyang Colonization Company, 165
double-entry bookkeeping: Japan,
141–2, 150–1; Korea, 161–2, 167

Edo period (or era). *See* Tokugawa era
Educational Association, 127
Eulmi Incident, 159
Eulmi Reforms, 157, 168
Eunsagongchae (Colonial Korean
bonds), 164
exhibitionary complex, 77
Exposition Universelle, Paris, 1867, 15,
79, 80, 84, 140
Exposition Universelle, Paris, 1878, 82,
88, 90
Exposition Universelle, Paris, 1900, 89

Fifth Domestic Industrial Exhibition,
1903. *See* Fifth National Exposition,
Osaka, 1903
Fifth National Exposition, Osaka, 1903,
11, 76, 89, 90, 94, 108, 126
Fifth National Industrial Exposition,
1903. *See* Fifth National Exposition,
Osaka, 1903
Finance Ministry (Japan). *See* Ministry
of Finance (Japan)
First National Industrial Exposition,
Ueno, Tokyo, 1877, 61, 86, 90, 104
First Opium War. *See* Opium War
First World War, 20–1, 24, 29–30, 76,
132, 140, 164
foreign advisers, 6–7, 26, 28–9, 35, 48–9,
52–3, 59, 66–8, 97, 122, 127, 156–8,
160, 166
Fourth National (Domestic) Exposition,
Kyoto, 1895, 88–9
Fu Sheng Sericulture Company, 127

fukoku kyōhei (rich nation, strong army),
67, 145–6
Fukuzawa Yukichi, 86, 97–8
fully-differentiated exhibition format,
84–6, 89–92

Gabo Reforms, 155, 157, 168
Gapsin Coup, 157
garabō, 61–2
General Electric Corporation, 26
geumrokgongchae (Korean bonds), 164
Godai Tomoatsu, 140
Great Kanto Earthquake, 111, 165
Guang Sheng Oil Company, 132
Gumgogyuchik (operating regulations),
157
Guoxue baocunhui yinshua suo. See
Association for the Preservation of
National Learning
Gyeongbu Railroad Company, 159

Han Lin Academy, 124
Han Sangyong, 161–5, 167
Hanil Bank, 162
Hanseong Bank, 155–62
Hart, Robert, 158
Hayami Kensō, 49, 50, 52–3, 56
Hècht, Lilienthal and Company, 48, 53
Honda Toshiaki, 100
Hongkong and Shanghai Banking
Corporation, 25
hybrid technology, 3, 13–4, 49, 51–3,
56–7, 65, 100, 112–13

Imanishi Rinzaburō, 165
Imperial Tobacco Company, 23
industrialization, 6, 9, 10–11, 14, 20, 55,
57, 62, 66–8, 89, 113–14, 122–3, 127,
140, 147, 151
Inoue Kaoru, 58, 145–6
International Exhibition, Vienna, 1873,
12, 79, 81, 85–8, 90–2, 94

Osaka Cotton Spinning Mill, 48, 60–8, 414, 151

Osaka Exhibition, 1903. *See* Fifth National Industrial Exposition, Osaka, 1903

Overseas Development Society, 6

Ozaki Saburō, 159

Paris Exposition, 1867. See *Exposition Universelle*, 1867

Paris Exposition, 1878. See *Exposition Universelle*, 1878

Park Yeonghyo, 157

Philadelphia Exposition, 1876, 12, 79, 81–2, 87–8, 90

planography, 35–6

Platt Brothers, 60–2

Press for the Society of National Glory, 41

print capitalism, 9, 11, 33–43

Public Hanseong Bank, 11, 14, 160, 162–7

Queen Min, 8, 157

Russo-Japanese War, 4, 22, 27, 129, 141, 155, 162

ryōgaeshō (money exchangers, Japan), 141, 147

Saiga Fujisaburō, 102

Sakai Cotton Mill, 60

Sanjūshi Bank, 127

Sano Tsunetami, 86

SCOT (Social Construction of Technology), 4–5

Second National Exhibition, Tokyo, 1881, 88, 92

Second World War, 6, 31, 112

Self-Strengthening Movement (China), 17, 27, 122, 124

semi-differentiated exhibition format, 12, 78, 81–2, 86–93

Shand, Allan Alexander, 151, 156

Shanghai Cotton Spinning Company, 26

Shanghai Steam Navigation Company, 21

Shantung Railroad, 24

Shibaura Engineering Works, 26

Shibusawa Eiichi: and banking, 11, 15, 139–42, 144–53, 156, 164–7; and *gappon* capitalism, 11, 15, 139, 142–9; and international exhibitions, 55, 86, 140; and Japanese industry, 9, 15, 48, 52, 56–60, 62–3, 68–9, 73, 141; and Japanese modernization, 12–15, 54–5, 64–8, 141 (*see also* modernization, Japan); pre-business years, 9, 15, 55, 69, 86, 141, 148

Shimada Glassworks, 127

Shimada *zaibatsu*, 58

Shimomura Cotton Mill, 66

Shinhan Bank, 160

shōhō kaisho (combined bank and trading company, Japan), 148

shokusan kōgyō ("encouragement of new industry"), 87, 140

Shōshi Kaisha, 9, 47, 58–9, 62, 68, 151

Showa Depression, 165

Sim Sanghun, 159

Sino-Japanese War, 1894–1895, 4, 7, 10, 21, 27, 88–9, 121, 124

Six Licensed Stores (*Yukuijeon*), 158

Songdosagechibu-bup (traditional Korean bookkeeping), 161–2

songdo (traditional Korean merchants), 161

South Manchuria Railway, 23

Suzuki Tokujirō, 100, 102

Taiping Rebellion, 128

Takahashi Korekiyo, 149

Takamine Jokichi, 141

Takayama Kōsuke, 100

Takeuchi Tsuyoshi, 159

Takjiamun (Department of Finance, Korea), 157

Takjibu (Ministry of Finance, Korea), 157

Takuzenkai ("Choose Virtue Society"), 151, 153

Japan and Global Society

Milton Keynes UK
Ingram Content Group UK Ltd.
UKHW041347291223
435175UK00019B/149/J